The Admiral Gift

Volume I

The Admiral Gift

Today's First-Century Apostle

BERTRIL A. BAIRD

Volume I

RESOURCE *Publications* • Eugene, Oregon

THE ADMIRAL GIFT: VOLUME I
Today's First-Century Apostle

Copyright © 2010 JKK. All rights reserved. Except for brief quotations in critical publications or reviews, no part of this book may be reproduced in any manner without prior written permission from the publisher. Write: Permissions, Wipf and Stock Publishers, 199 W. 8th Ave., Suite 3, Eugene, OR 97401.

Resource Publications
An Imprint of Wipf and Stock Publishers
199 W. 8th Ave., Suite 3
Eugene, OR 97401
www.wipfandstock.com

ISBN 13: 978-1-60899-958-3

Manufactured in the U.S.A.

To the darling wife of my youth
  Who has served the Lord and me with the utmost
     commitment, dedication, and loyalty for over 42 years
         —Jacqueline Millicent Baird

Contents

Author's Preface / ix

Overview of the Book / xi

BOOK I Overview of In Search of the Authentic Apostle / 1

1. Analyzing the Admiral Gift / 3
2. Old Testament's Apostolic Archetype / 15
3. The Ultimate Apostle and a Secular Counterpart / 22
4. The Pharisee Who Became an Apostle / 35
5. Is this Gift for Today? Capital "A" or Lower-Case / 45

BOOK II The Apostle's Mindset / 61

Introduction and Overview / 61

1. Makings of a Mindset / 64
2. God's Perfect Plan: The Kingdom of God / 72
3. Wrapping Our Brain Around This Kingdom Mindset / 97

BOOK III Essential Outcomes of Apostolic Ministry / 110

Introduction and Overview / 110

1. Fear of the Lord as an Outcome / 113
2. Outcome: Divine Favor / 131
3. Shalom as an Outcome / 142

BOOK IV The Apostolic Toolbox:
    Tools Essential to the Apostolic Ministry / 157

   Introduction and Overview / 157

1 Fasting & Prayer: Tools Used in Tandem / 164

2 Deliverance / 173

3 Healing: Part of the Deliverance Toolkit / 181

4 Exorcism: Part of the Deliverance Toolkit / 194

5 Repentance as a Tool / 206

6 Kingdom Preaching as a Tool:
   Communicating Truth to a Contrary Culture / 218

   Entry Notes / 233

Author's Preface

Today's First-Century Breakthrough Apostle

As the song says, "...*everything old is new again.*" Entrenched in post-modern thinking, the world is once again nearly where it was in the Upper Room.

Although better trained than his first-century colleagues, today's apostle oversees a multifaceted ministry. However, like his first century peers, he builds on a foundation laid by this *breakthrough* gift.

"Breakthrough"—the word conjures images of walls being breached; boulders the size of a Volkswagen being inched out of the way; or ground as hard as cement crumbling into soil that looks and smells like a seed would be welcome.

What an apt description of the apostolic role: smashing barriers, removing obstacles, and breaking up fallow ground.

Why does he, armed only with a kingdom mindset, an anointing to heal, and exorcize, does he dare to challenge worldviews antagonistic to the Gospel?

As at Pentecost, the Apostle remains God's Breakthrough person. He pioneers a nation's transformation.

As the Steelpan enriches any Island lyric, the Admiral Gift blesses society like a westerly cooling a tropical evening.

Bertril Baird,
2010

Overview of the Book

Mapping Our Overal Learning Journey

APOSTLES! DIDN'T THEY ALL die out at the end of the first century? Didn't I just encounter a person using that title while channel browsing?

Confusion swirls about this exotic word, "Apostle"! Some consider it as a title rendering them sort of a General Officer in God's Army. These use it to enhance their brand, garner prestige, and wield power over constituents. Others, like the magician, Simon Magnus, think the gifts of the Holy Spirit are for building an entrepreneurial enterprise.

Others see it as a way of viewing the call to be a pioneering type of missionary service. While they rightly refer to such missionary statesmen as William Carey and Hudson Taylor as apostolic in scope and achievement (laying foundations), they insist that a narrow interpretation of that biblical passage that says that an apostle saw the risen Savior with a 'naked eye'.

In truth, the legitimate apostle possesses a unique spiritual gift that equips him to partner with Christ as He establishes His kingdom on this earth, and lays a foundation in a new territory upon which subsequent people—pastors, teachers, and evangelists—can build the church.

Recently, a movement within the church, supported by a blizzard of publications, insists that because we are in the final years before the return of Christ, this gift, dormant for nineteen centuries, has been divinely revived, and is now integral to a full-orbed ministry.

Who is right? In due course, we will attempt an answer. To that end, this book explains this gift; the Kingdom mindset it requires to function; the tools it employs; and the outcomes it seeks to facilitate.

As just mentioned, the church is currently embroiled in a discussion over the nature of the church. At the heart of this discussion, guess what topic looms as large as an elephant in the room—the nature, purpose, and relevance of the apostolic gift's usage now.

This circumstance is fortuitous. It provides us a wide audience to this gift and its relevance, and a showcase to testify to His bestowal of our gift. After all, we have exercised it for the past four decades, traveling millions of miles throughout the Caribbean region, the USA, Latin America, and Africa to fulfill His calling. In the process, a strategy to transform and restore a nation emerged, along with a clear idea of the principles necessary to its effective implementation.

After countless seminars and mass meetings, people constantly urge us to leave them a detailed discussion of this strategy. After all, it is the substance of our speaking ministry. About a year and a half ago, the Lord presented an opportunity to produce this book.

Initially, our goal was to present only the Laws of Transformation and the Principles required implementing them. However, as we began, we realized that their understanding required a context. Its construction required us to ask this prior set of questions: what does the Bible say regarding the nature of this gift? What is the unique mindset necessary to execute it? What are the tools necessary to execute it? What are the principles and laws we seek to inculcate? What are the personal outcomes we trust the Holy Spirit to produce in those who respond to our message.

We no sooner plunged into the task of researching these answers than it dawned on us that we had stumbled into the center of that heated theological debate triggered by this question: is this gift's original capacity available today? Our goal in adding all of this "set-up" information was to provide you with a thorough understanding of this gift from a biblical perspective.

When this material was added to that originally planned, the resulting book had ballooned to a size that would scare off most non-fiction readers. Our publisher agreed; statistics leave no doubt that today's reader of Christian books prefers them not to exceed a hundred pages by much.

To resolve this dilemma, we discovered that the content divided logically into three major themes. Voila, three books were born. The following presents a map of each volume. Each volume is similarly structured. Its presentation is segregated into two primary sections, which we call BOOKS. Each of these is divided into Chapters. While the number varies per BOOK, each chapter is subdivided into major supporting sub-topics we call Parts.

VOLUME ONE

The first volume contains the following four major divisions. In BOOK ONE, you gain a clear understanding of the meaning of this word, and insights into those who modeled it in the pages of the Bible. We conclude this major section by tackling the question of its relevance today. In BOOK TWO, we detail the kingdom mindset and how it differs from a church mindset. In BOOK THREE, we pinpoint the most important personal outcomes that we depend on the Holy Spirit to achieve through our exercise of the apostolic gift. In BOOK FOUR, we lay out the Tools necessary to fulfill our apostolic calling. Incidentally, a similarly detailed outline for each BOOK'S learning journey introduces it.

VOLUME TWO

This volume details the Seven Laws we use to transform and restore a nation to wholeness (BOOK FIVE); the Principles necessary for their implementation (BOOK SIX), and three strategies we employ (BOOK SEVEN).

THREE AUDIENCES

We have written this book to serve three types of readers. The first is for that person who, after attending our seminar, desires to explore the subjects introduced in detail.

The second type of reader occupies a strategic position in your nation. Your copy was a gift from one representing our ministry. Read it to understand our intention, motives, and strategies to bless and support your efforts. Consider it as an ambassador and mentor.

The third reader is ensconced in the swirling debate regarding the nature and relevance of the apostolic gift in this century. As the title of this book implies, we embrace the relevance of first-century apostleship today. However, our goal is not to persuade but to instruct, i.e., shedding light not increasing the BTUs surrounding this heated discussion.

Incidentally, Pastors, Students, and Teachers will find the bibliography worth the price of the three-volume set.

In conclusion, when you realize the energy surrounding this current discussion of apostleship, it is humbling and heart-warming to realize that the Spirit of God has nudged us into a project He considers strategic. For this, we have another reason to praise and thank Him for having called us to this unique office, apostleship.

Our prayer is that the Holy Spirit will take this content and do for it in your mind as He did with that Galilean boy's five loaves and two fishes.

Bertril Baird
May 2010

Book I

Overview of In Search of the Authentic Apostle

BOOK ONE EXPLORES THE nature and purpose of this gift that now figures into the current controversy over the relevance of the spiritual gifts.

Chapter 1: We pinpoint the meaning of this word

Chapter 2: We then explore the Old Testament Apostolic Archetype

Chapter 3: We then examine the Ultimate Apostle: Jesus

Chapter 4: We then investigate the Pharisee who became an Apostle

Chapter 5: The answer: Is this gift, as modeled by first-century apostles, relevant today?

Chapter 1

Analyzing the Admiral Gift

If you appreciate the passion for detail, excellence, and ingenuity of Japanese technology, not to mention the elegance of its art, food, and fashion, you have an Admiral of the U.S. Navy to thank.

When Commodore Perry's fleet first appeared in the harbor of Tokyo, a rural seaside community, its citizens, like all Japanese, were called "*Sakoku*". The word means "locked in chains". Perry encountered a people in abject bondage by the Shogunate leaders. Since their reality considered all ships to be sailing vessels, they perceived the steam-powered USS Powhatan to be a smoke-breathing dragon.

It took Perry a year, wrestling with the highest powers, to negotiate a trade agreement. Yet it changed their perception of reality. As a result, many "chains" fell off, and the nation began to transform.

Since many other naval expeditions, motivated by imperialism, produced tragic consequences; why bring up Admiral Perry? First, the words apostle and admiral share a common etymological ancestry, therefore, what happened in Tokyo Bay to Admiral Perry illustrates our ministry.

Second, although, over forty years ago, God called us to preach the Gospel, a few decades into that career, God anointed, gifted, and confirmed our call to an apostolic ministry. Out of this experience, the Holy Spirit helped us fashion a strategy to bring restoration to a nation. Since only a mind guided by this gift could have conceived this plan, to understand it, you must first become acquainted with this gift. Consider this chapter as the key to understanding the Laws and Principles you will shortly be shown.

Third, at every hand, people have queried us to explain the nature, function, and purpose of this unique gift. Consider this chapter as our in-depth answer.

Perhaps this map of how we will supply this answer is helpful: First, we will analyze the meaning of the word; then probe Biblical passages for insights from Moses, Jesus, the Twelve, and Paul; and finally compare the careers of a foremost ancient military apostle with that of the premier ministry example. In the process, we will wrestle with these questions: how does this gift relate to the others in Ephesians 4; and is this gift viable today.

From all the data we harvest, you will not find it difficult to construct your own composite picture of what an apostle is and does.

PART 1: INSIGHT FROM WORD-MEANING ANALYSIS

A Chinese proverb puts it well: "The beginning of wisdom is calling things by their right name". Words are the fundamental carriers of any concept. Unfortunately, incessant usage and bad theology have obscured the true meaning of "apostle". In addition, its definition as described in lexicons ("a sent one") is woefully inadequate to define fully its rich meaning.

Our need for an adequate definition is crucial to the understanding of the restoration strategy we will present. Fortunately, there is a way to overcome this problem: examine the word in the languages that first used it.

This exercise will help us recapture the nuance of the original meaning of our word that was lost in the English translation. Since the word is used in both Testaments, studying its meaning in Hebrew and Greek will yield much insight into the nature and function of an apostle.

Tracing the Word's Old Testament Roots

As children resemble their parents, the Hebrew word, *Shaliah*, sheds much insight that the seventy Jewish scholars were able to capitalize on, when they translated the Torah into Greek. What can we learn about 'apostle', by examining this Hebrew word?

Hebrew was developed before dictionaries were invented. Therefore, the Hebrews devised a way to use the letters, as pictograms, to tell the story of its meaning. It enabled a word to be defined; the arrangement of the letters spelling the word served as a built-in dictionary.

Deciphering the meaning of the word from the pictographic letters was not unlike reading a modern bumper sticker. Each word was designed using three core consonants.

Consonants as Bumper Stickers

Three decades ago, a bumper sticker message became widely popular throughout the USA. Its message promoted tourism in New York City, and the medium chosen so it could be read at a glance. It contained only three simply pictorial symbols: a picture of an eye, followed by a picture of a valentine, followed by the logo for the New York Yankee baseball team. Motorists could read it in, well…, er, a New York minute: "I love New York".

Here is how that system works. Begin with a meaning you wish to convey. Then select three consonant/pictograms whose combined meaning served as a composite picture of the meaning you intended the word to convey.

Think of our Hebrew word for 'apostle' as a "bumper sticker". It is comprised of three Hebrew consonants:
- *Shem* (the source of its first-syllable's "sha" sound);
- *Lamed* (the source its second syllable's "li' sound).
- *He* (the source of the third syllable, and the "hay-eh"

Pronounce the word, "sha-li-hia".

To determine its originally intended meaning, we only need to reconstruct the pictographic meaning of each consonant:
- *Shem's* pictogram: two front teeth. Attached meaning:" cutting action", achieved by severing (such as when one severs a bite-sized piece from a carrot stock.
- *Lamed's* pictogram: shepherd's staff. Attached meaning: "to lead".
- "*He*" portrayed a stick-figure of a man with his arms raised upward. Attached meaning: to honor one with praise and allegiance.

Now to construct the original meaning for *Shalia* from these three consonant:

> A person is separated in order to provide leadership…for one esteemed…

Later, when the Hebrew Lexicon _was_ invented, the meaning gained additional nuance:

> a person sent away by another in order to fulfill an assigned responsibility for which he assumes full accountability to the one who sent him.

Notice that in the expansion, everything that originally expressed by its ancient pictograms is retained.

Notice, also, in this expanded definition of apostle these implications: all connections are severed between sender and the one sent; the one sent assumes full responsibility to accomplish a mission authorized and resourced by the sender; and the motivation for accepting accountability is allegiance and respect for the sender.

In addition, as scholars, in time, added nuance to its meaning, they never altered the meaning originally captured in the pictograms.

As such, it remained defined as one person, sent completely away by another (therefore completely independent), in order to fulfill an assigned responsibility for which he assumes full accountability on behalf of the one who sent him, to whom he owes his allegiance.

Now do you see why this word was used in a military context? It fits perfectly fits the job description of an Admiral, or General. This will become apparent as we now discover how this meaning of the word serves to characterize some of Israel's outstanding leaders, especially its prophets, and even a few of its kings.

Prophet-Apostles

God gifted prophets with the twin spiritual gifts of apostle and prophet. We have already mentioned Isaiah, but there were others, including Jeremiah. This giftedness served the nation. After all, apostles are revolutionaries, among the first to spot the need for reform, and then ardently lead it.

Like Isaiah, Jeremiah received a dual appointment. He was sent to confront the apostate mindset pervading Israel (more on him later). Likewise, Isaiah was also commissioned to "...turn a stubborn backslidden people back to God (Isa. 6:4).

Judge-Apostles

We could add Gideon (Judges 6:14) to that list. He was commissioned as a *Shelliah*; notice the similarity with the above Hebrew word. He was given a valid apostolic commission, accompanied by sufficient powers to fulfill it.

King-Apostles

Since we have examined this word in the context of Admirals, why not look at a king of Israel who so modeled the word that he could have posed as a poster child—Uzziah.

Therefore, in the sketch of his exploits, we gain an insight into how the gift functions.

Ascending the throne as a sixteen year old, Uzziah ruled Israel for five decades. Except for a blunder at the end of his life, he was the third most successful monarch after David (after Solomon and Jehoshaphat). His success earned him the reputation as a very capable ruler. Early in his life, he enjoyed the mentoring of the prophet, Zechariah whose influence helped him to "...do that which was right in the sight of the Lord" (2 Chronicles 26:4).

Zechariah, a man known to understand in the visions of God influenced Uzziah to make it a priority to seek the LORD. Putting Him first released divine authority and favor. As a result, God prospered his efforts (2 Chronicles 26:5). Ask the Philistines and Arabians.

Uzziah led his army to smash the Philistine city walls of Gath, Jabneh, and Ashdod, and then demolished similar Arabian towns. He then built Jewish settlements among all of them (2 Chronicles 26:6-7).

In studying the things that marked his career, three things stand out: Divine Favor (help from God), Constant Opposition (a wall at every turn that required smashing), and Sustained Victory (enemies subdued). I bear testimony that these have marked my own apostolic ministry.

First, Uzziah went defeated Israel's old enemy, the Philistines. Apostles must confront a culture; Uzziah's experience confirms—the victory is the Lord's; it is appropriated by stepping out in faith.

In addition, Uzziah broke down the wall of Gath. As mentioned, the apostolic ministry must tear down, before it can restore.

Third, Uzziah built cities around Ashdod and among the Philistines. Likewise, the apostolic gift subdues evil and dominates demonic strongholds as the apostle advances the Kingdom in the midst of such negative influence.

Also, Uzziah built and fortified towers throughout Jerusalem's walls and gates. The apostolic ministry is one that positions itself to safeguard against incoming attacks.

Fifth, he dug and many wells to support his expanding cattle herds. Likewise, the apostolic gift must generate resources to supply an ever-expanding need as his ministry grows.

Finally, he built an effective team; 2,600 officers, competent to lead approximately 3500 well-trained warriors, skilled at using the military technology he had designed and manufactured. Apostolic ministries draw spiritual warriors, who engage spiritual enemies, in opposing cultures, to subdue enemies, tear down, and restore to wholeness by setting up the kingdom of God

Now that we have examined the Hebrew heritage of the word, we find in the New Testament, it is time that we turn to the Greek word itself.

New Testament Descendant: apostolos

Since the Greek language has 1000% more vocabulary, and the parts of speech number 496 compared to 59 parts for Hebrew verbs, one would expect that the language greatly expanded the meaning of this word. In this, the language does not disappoint.

First, notice how the structure of the Greek word mirrors that of the Hebrew equivalent. It was constructed by combining two words: "from" ("*apo*") and "loose" ("*lupo*"). Notice how these combined syllables resemble the first two consonants of the Hebrew word. The meaning: Something/someone has been deliberately separated from something/someone, to fulfill a specific, important purpose.

Since so much of the Hebrew root word was transported to its Greek descendant, you will be better informed if we focus on the things that the subsequent language added. I will highlight three.

Technical Aspect

First, the term took on a technical flavor; it became the term used for national leaders to send messengers. The primary emphasis was on the sender and the purpose for sending the surrogate. In the New Testament, men were sent out by Jesus Christ, and some commissioned by the church. In the case of Paul and Barnabas, we have people commissioned as apostles by both (Acts 13:2).

Aspect of Authority

Second, the word gained another characteristic—sense of supreme, self-contained, unquestionable authority. To explain, permit me to use the word that best captures this characteristic, the Greek word *exousia* (pronounced "ek-oo-see-uh"). Think of a scene from an old-time Western movie. After learning that six mean outlaws have created havoc at the local Saloon, he must go in, confront, disarm, and arrest them.

He addresses them with a mild, respectful tone: "In the name of the Law, you fellahs will need to unbuckle your gun-belts, and come with me to the jail. You're under arrest for murder and destroying property, among other charges." They laugh, exposing about a dozen teeth between them.

The biggest and ugliest person speaks. "You think you can take all six of us, Sheriff?" Without further talk, he reaches for his gun. In a flash, a deafening sound, he slumps to the floor with no pulse. Instantly, two others make their move, and follow him into eternity. The remaining three get up to follow the Sheriff, but one feels lucky enough to draw on him. Now, the two live outlaws march out the door and into jail cells.

What can we learn from this Wild West fantasy that will help us better understand this component of the meaning of *apostolos*? Permit me to point out several things:

- The sheriff had complete authorization to do what he did, by law, or public approval from anyone to do what he did. His authority was absolute.
- His confidence derives from having been duly elected to his assignment.
- He possessed the inner strength to execute his mission.

Those people who had gathered in that Nazareth synagogue observed this authority in the eyes of Jesus as He stood up at the outset of His ministry read from Isaiah 53. Recall that these verses described what the Messiah would do that confirmed the legitimacy of His ministry. When Jesus finished reading this passage, he then sat down. Then, after a moment to capture everybody's attention, He said with the finality of that sheriff in our previous illustration, "This day, these words are fulfilled in front of your eyes".

This aspect marked the New Testament Apostle. In the presence of the Savior, the Twelve healed no one or gave no sermon; they were learners as meek as a child can be.

However, when sent forth, they moved into a crowd with the intestinal fortitude of that same Sheriff. Their confidence lay in this: the power of the One who had sent them would flow through their hands so that no diseased body or demonized soul could escape from God's sovereign power executing His will that people should be well (body); be whole (mind); or be gone (Satan).

No need or circumstance on this mortal earth could resist the onslaught produced by their use of these words, "In Jesus' Name!" The power bestowed on them by the One who sent them was universal, all-powerful, and available to any need they felt compelled to direct it. It was a power to speak a word; and the power to execute what the word described.

Also, they lacked no resource that Jesus possessed. Everything flowed from Him through them to the needs they touched. How else could Peter address the crippled man with these words, "in the name of Jesus of Nazareth, Get up!"

The Apostles also conveyed another aspect of this word's meaning—the courage produced by such a commission. This important aspect of *apostolos* is also one of the first and striking things you notice about the Apostles after the Holy Spirit has arrived on the Day of Pentecost.

Immediately we observe the boldness of Peter and John in public ministry. Hauled before those that had crucified Jesus, they were threatened with a life-threatening whipping if they did not stop witnessing and preaching that Jesus was the Son of God and alive from the dead and very much at work in Jerusalem. Their reply,

> "Whether it is right in the sight of God to listen to you rather than to God, you must judge, for we cannot but speak of what we have seen and heard."(Acts 4:20)

These men reacted to such frightening words as though they had heard a *caged* lion roar!

This sense of regal authority; and all the force of heaven and earth at one's disposal to ensure that your will become reality—this is the second characteristic of the Greek offspring of the Hebrew word for apostolos.

Integration of Sender with the One Sent

For the third nuance of meaning, we look to the word meaning's proximity to another Greek word, *pempein* (pronounced "pem-pain") and transliterated as "pempein", meaning, "to send". If *Shaliah* is the father, and *apostolos*, enjoys the relationship to much like a son to a father, then what is its relationship to pempein? Think of it as a first cousin.

Because this is the common, everyday word for "*to send*" the Biblical writers opted to avoid it, and for reasons already discussed. They felt it properly conveyed the level of seriousness that commissioning a royal viceroy warranted. Paul, for the same reason, refused to use this word in his epistles.

Not so, the apostle John. He used both extensively, but always in the same contextual setting. When Jesus wants to ground His authority in that of the Father as the One who is responsible for His words and works, and who guarantees their correctness, truthfulness, appropriateness, and "rightness", He uses *apostolos*.

Secular Application of *apostolos*

When we probe the secular literature and business documents of Hellenistic Greek, we discover that the word was widely used in three ways:

1. In a business context: Party of the First Part sent Party of the Second Part to perform services on his behalf, with full power of attorney. In this manner, Eliezer, acting on behalf of Abraham, secured a wife for his son, Isaac.
2. In a marital context: Under Jewish law, a husband had the right to end his marriage, completely severing her from access to his possessions or affection. Jesus condemned this right among Jewish men.
3. In a military sense: A military officer would be sent on a mission, e.g., the Centurion serving Caesar, or Moses, commissioned by YHWH to deliver Israel from Egypt to the Promised Land.

Notice how the qualities we have mined by analyzing the meaning of this word for apostles from the beginning of literature until the generation of the Twelve can be found in these three practical uses for the word.

PART 2: SKETCHING THIS GIFT'S CHARACTERISTICS

As no two snowflakes are alike, no two apostles fit a single mold. Some apostles were better at one facet of ministry than others. For instance, James, as the biblical record shows, was known (and chosen) to lead meetings where doctrinally important issues were discussed.

Likewise, the apostle, John developed the exceptional ability to bring harmony to situations recovering from the chaos caused by members divided over serious doctrinal issues.

Peter could step in front of a crowd of religious Jews, boldly confront them about their culpability regarding Jesus' murder, and then use the Bible to lift Him up in a way that turned many to saving faith. However, enough similarities exist to help us sketch a profile.

To that end, permit me to draw your attention to Paul's description of the gifts in Ephesians chapter five. The passage is valuable, because, by listing them side by side, we learn about this apostolic gift by comparing it with the other four.

In a word, the apostle governs. That being the case, what single word captures the essence of the four areas of giftedness? After we do this, we shall amplify what this idea means.

The Evangelist gives life. The evangelistic gift serves as the king's herald, i.e., mandated to confront unsaved people with the salvation message. Only about ten percent of the Body possesses this gift that is uniquely capable of making the complex truth of the Gospel of grace sensible to people with no prior knowledge or ability to perceive spiritual truth. The

The Pastor primarily guards the flock. He shepherds the congregation, teaching, draining, mentoring, and persuading them to embrace the truth he presents in order to move toward spiritual maturity and ministry.

The Teacher primarily grounds the believers. He provides the truth, and its understanding that equips the true believer with the doctrinal skills to prevent false teaching from creeping in, and to provide an ever-increasing understanding of the nature and purpose of our Lord, as well as how to enjoy and serve Him.

The Prophet guides. The prophetic gift is equipped with spiritual radar. These people are able to spot potential problems, give direction, identify people gifted for ministry, and alert the Body to issues with a potential to created spiritual warfare.

Analyzing the Admiral Gift 13

As promised, in light of these task analyses, let us consider in greater depth where does the apostle fit into the broad strategy Paul outlines regarding these five gift-sets. Specifically, permit me to glean from his writings sufficient insights into the apostolic ministry to construct a composite profile of six of the major features of this gift in action.

These characteristics generally mark the ministry of a first century apostle, including Paul. First, they viewed their ministry as foundation-laying master builders. Paul said as much in his letter to the Corinthian believers:

> "By the grace God has given me, I laid a foundation as a wise master builder, and someone else is building on it. But each one should be careful how he builds. For no one can lay any foundation other than the one already laid, which is Jesus Christ" (1 Corinthians 3:10,11).

In addition, they sovereignly targeted specific people-groups. In this case, it was Hellenized Gentiles.

The Savior also chose this high-ranking, nobly classed Jewish man with two earned degrees (PhD equivalency) to penetrate a world far removed from his thinking, culture, and roots. (Rom. 15:20).

One other priority needs to be spotlighted. They all made a big thing out of disciple-making, especially training and empowering a cadre of leaders about them. Think of the men whom we know because their names appear in the New Testament: Barnabas, Timothy, Titus, Mark, Luke, and Silas, to name a few of the more prominently reported. In addition, they appointed Elders and served as consultants to them in problem-solving situations.

A fourth important facet of their ministry: they tackled problems to resolve them. They swept nothing under the rug, including doctrinal issues as well as interpersonal strife.

Another (fifth) characteristic: when the need required, they had no hesitation in using their divinely given authority. The record shows, they prevailed.

Add to the picture this sixth characteristic: they often used the gifts of healing and exorcism with which the Holy Spirit had gifted them. The New Testament is replete with examples of them miraculously healing the sick and casting out demons. One purpose for this was to demonstrate ministries that mirrored that of Jesus (therefore confirming theirs and

His were from the same source. The other purpose was to validate their apostolic credentials.

Finally, the biblical record shows that an apostle's authority was limited to the place and situation God sent him to serve. The calling was not universal; it was relationally connected. The reason is simple: the headship belonged to the Lord Jesus; and He never intended an apostleship to become a calling to become the chief officer, existing at the top of a sort of chain of command.

As you can see from this brief analysis, by piecing together these seven characteristics you end up with a good idea of what the nineteen men mentioned in the New Testament did as apostles. The apostle primarily governs.

That said, the discussion now turns to this question: what sets the apostolic gift apart from other godly, anointed ministry callings? While one must not overly generalize, it remains clear that the apostolic gift is distinct in the four following ways.

First, their Calling was unique. Luke reports that from all His disciples, Jesus chose twelve as apostles. In this, He qualified them to sit on thrones to rule the Kingdom when it is fully restored in the New Heaven and earth. Reading of Paul's unique calling to Gentiles, we can see that the divine calling of the Twelve was to the 'lost sheep of the Household of Israel—the Jew.

Second, their Calling involved preaching that was confirmed by supernatural signs. The apostle had special divine authority to remit sins, or bind/loose. In essence, God called apostle to represent Him on earth in a special way, i.e., remitting sins, and binding/loosing evil forces.

Also, this gift was associated with special Qualifications: The qualifications of the apostles are given in Acts 1:21-22. They were with Jesus during His earthly ministry (v.21), been baptized by John the Baptist (v.22), and been eyewitnesses of the resurrected Christ (v.22).

To that special qualification, add this one: Paul explained that what he considered that validating the legitimacy of his apostleship (versus that of a false prophet) was this: "Truly the signs of an apostle were wrought among you in all patience, in signs, and wonders, and mighty deeds." (II Corinthians 12:12)

These characteristics will be useful to you as we now begin to observe the ministries of men who modeled this gift including Moses.

Chapter 2

Old Testament's Apostolic Archetype

THE BIBLE IS NOT the only record of the extraordinary leadership skills of Moses. Thanks to Josephus, secular history confirms the facts recorded in the Scripture.

Incidentally, Josephus records Pharaoh's daughter's name: *"Thermuthis.* His description mirrors that of the Exodus record: as she waded along the edge of the Nile. Spying a floating basket, she called to her attendants to retrieve it. Being barren, she became overjoyed at the sight of the beautiful infant inside. Realizing he was Hebrew, she kept him, giving him the name Moses, which in Egyptian means saved from the water" . . . Incidentally, his name is remarkably close to his Egyptian sibling, Thutmosis.

Josephus describes an event that demonstrates Moses' leadership ability as a young adult, about which the Bible is silent. According to Josephus, Egypt went to war with their Ethiopian neighbors. As defeat loomed, the Egypt priests urged Pharaoh to appoint Moses to command the army. He then led them in a surprise attack that won the war. The value of that incident is that it corroborates his extraordinary leadership skills.

However, we seek to demonstrate why God bestowed an apostleship upon him. Permit me to present evidence supporting his appointment, because, as surely as God made little green apples, Moses was every inch as much of an apostle as Peter, John, or Paul.

Both Yahweh's words spoken from that burning bush "*I will send you* (Ex. 3:10), and Hebrews 3:1-6, comparing Moses' apostolic ministry to that of Jesus, confirms this fact. Those apostolic characteristics discussed in the previous chapter fit him like a glove.

From birth, Moses experienced a long season of sustained divine favor. It prepared him to resist losing hope in those bad times he would inevitably face. Without it, the trials and temptation ahead might overwhelm.

Moses' ministry may have begun with a special divine encounter at the Burning Bush, but his pre-calling preparation was long and arduous.

It began with his self-exile in Midian desert. The name (Midian) means "quarrelsome contentiousness". Add to that his apparent loneliness (he named his son, Gershon (which means "stranger"). Mix with these factors his subordination to his father-in-law as a full-time shepherd. Next, combine all of these the fact that he endured prolonged periods of isolation, and you have a recipe that uniquely equipped him for such a ministry. It enabled him to deal with bickering and loneliness. It infused him with the competence to masterly shepherd six million people through a vast wilderness as a servant leader.

No wonder he emerged with a true and in-depth understanding of himself and his purpose in life; and a good understanding of human nature. This unique preparation of the Lord enabled him to possess one of the best apostolic skill-sets of any apostles in the Bible.

I have observed that his training is not unlike that which the modern apostles experiences.

God seems to divinely prepare individuals chosen for an apostolic ministry by moving them through times of self-searching, exile, testing, setbacks, and personal discovery.

Nevertheless, the day dawned when YHWH summoned Moses to leave his training behind and enter the gateway into ministry. It occurred during an encounter with the Lord at the burning bush when he turned aside to stare at the flames engulfing a dry desert bush, but not consuming it to ashes. It was a metaphor for what was about to happen to him: he would become a man driven by a raging supernatural loving force, yet not burning out.

After learning what God was commissioning him to do, although reluctance chilled his fervor, he proceeded by faith to fulfill the ministry to which he had been called. As a result, he discovered that the Lord used the skills and experiences he had gained during his 'Midian' preparation to transform him into a leader. God was enduing him with the ability to persuade, confront, exert influence, exercise divine authority, wield supernatural power, and bring about true change.

Thanks to his long training period, marked by an early season of divine favor, subordination, isolation, hard choices, practical skills training, and a dramatic spiritual encounter with God, Moses walked into Pharaoh's court every bit an apostle as was Paul, standing before Caesar. Both confronted the world's most powerful rulers. Both used an array of signs and wonders to defeat Satan and launch spiritual revolutions. Both leveraged a close personal friendship with God to move His kingdom forward. Both significantly increased the world's written knowledge regarding God, man, the origin and conclusion of life, as well as His purpose and plan for redeeming humankind.

PART 1: NEW TESTAMENT CONTEXT TO VIEW MOSAIC ARCHETYPE

God designed the Old Testament to present truth in types and shadows that the New Testament states clearly and boldly. For example, the Passover Lamb described in Exodus 12 (i.e., slain to save the household from the Angel of Death) connects perfectly with Jesus, especially as John the Baptist introduced Him: *"Behold the Lamb of God that takes away the sin of the world"*. Therefore, it is helpful to put the events and people integral to Moses' life in a New Testament context—once we have established Old Testament precedence.

Joseph a Picture of Blessing

Although the types of Israel and Pharaoh are pivotal to our purpose, we must not forget the man who started it all—Joseph.

His brothers sold the favorite son of Jacob, Joseph, into slavery; the owners then hauled him to Egypt. Yet, in hindsight, we realize that God was using these experiences to raise him up to bless Egypt in order to bless His covenant people and prepare them for Moses to lead to the Promised Land. He no sooner solved the problem of famine, and restored Egypt to prosperity, when God used him to bring Israel (at this time only a large extended family) to Egypt to save them from starvation. His career models that of an apostolic ministry.

Israel, a Picture of the Church?

To an extent, Israel foreshadows the church. That is not the same as saying that the church is spiritual Israel. My point: there are enough comparative elements to see that the nation traversing the Sinai to the Promised Land (Canaan) bare a strong resemblance to the body of Christ traversing life as redeemed people enroute to their Promised Land (heaven). Both were a people called by God, redeemed by His shed blood, therefore His chosen people. Therefore, the necessity for such a ministry as the apostolic gift provides makes sense in both contexts.

Egypt a Picture of the World

Egypt is a type of the *kosmos* (world system) under the control of the Evil One. It claims to satisfy man's deepest longings, but the hope it offers leads to slavery; its blessings are generally pleasure-centered and prosperity-driven. It promises hope and promotes prosperity for all, but in the end, the promises turned out to be as worthless as fool's gold.

The parallels are striking: God builds His church by reaching into the world system to save us by redemption, just as He did Israel, redeeming her out of Egypt's bondage. Also, notice that in both instances, He used men anointed with the apostolic gift.

Pharaoh: Type of Satan

From whom did the Israelites need to be redeemed? It was the despotic world leader whose dictatorial thumb they lived under—Pharaoh. Each day they went to work building his empire, constantly controlled by his desires and pressure. Sounds a lot like my life before the Lord Jesus saved me.

As you can see, when you view the world in which Moses ministered to that of the New Testament apostles, the parallels leave no doubt: his ministry was as apostolic as the Twelve's.

Permit me to spend the rest of this discussion pointing out ways in which Moses' life was an ideal model of what our last chapter defined as true apostoling.

PART 2: FACETS OF MOSES' APOSTOLIC BEARING

As we prepare to conclude this conversation regarding Moses as an apostle, I will 'paint with a broad brush' some features of this gift that the Bible notes regarding him.

Architect and Builder

Foremost, the apostle's central purpose is to provide leadership intentionally to build a spiritual community. Certainly, Moses did this. The extended family of Jacob that first showed up at Joseph's door, left the nation four centuries later six million strong. He molded this "family" into a nation that remains intact to this day. Under his apostleship, the family of Jacob became the nation of Israel.

Notice, in this regard, that Paul explains that he approached his ministry with the same purpose, i.e., to unite them in heart, balance and vision. As he said, *"My purpose is that they may be encouraged in heart and united in love..."* (Col. 2:2). This is a community agenda. With all of the ministries demonstrating specialized aspects of Christ's own character, the apostle represents the Lord's heart to keep them balanced, working together to build spiritual communities.

The apostle is an architect. He organizes and executes a plan to lay a foundation upon which to build a vibrant community. Like today's construction manager, he must concern himself with all aspects of its design, function, and form.

Pioneer

He is the first one on the scene. Moses walked back into the palace of Pharaoh forty years after vanishing in the night. Starting from dead zero, he proceeded through one confrontation after the other until he stood peering across the Jordan river four decades later to deliver his final message before his death. Did Joshua, then a series of Judges, not to mention David, Solomon and the prophets build on his ministry? Of course—but, his task was to launch the extended family of Abraham into a full-blown nation.

Therefore, think of him as a trailblazer, not unlike the modern apostle who takes a stand in the midst of a nation to minister to it, and, in successive steps, influences its soul, moves it toward spiritual wholeness, and leaves behind a clear path for others to build upon.

Father-Servant

Bill Schiedler (*Apostles, the Fathering Servants*) insists that apostoling is a lot like parenting. Moses served as the father of this vast tribe proceeding across the Sahara. Paul would agree; he wrote, *"For you know that* we dealt with each of you as a father deals with his own children...." "(by) encouraging, comforting and urging..." (1 Thess. 2:11-12). To sum up this characteristic in a word, think "*relational*" ministry. The apostle, in this instance focuses on gaining the respect of others in order to exercise legitimate authority as a servant leader.

Visionary

The apostle has a solid idea of what the result will resemble before he ever picks up a tool.

People-developer

The apostle is trolling for people whom he can train and mold into leadership. To use a sports metaphor, he is ever 'trolling' for talent in order to develop a strong 'bench' of team leaders. From the outset, Moses had Joshua, whom he so effectively discipled that when Moses died, Joshua was ready to step into his shoes and lead Israel into the Promised Land.

CONCLUSION

Those living in Israel at the time of Jesus' appearing had been living in expectation for a messiah whom they were convinced was "one like unto Moses" (Deut. 18:15-19).

As I reflect on this, two parallel scenes come to mind. Exodus 19:16-19 describes the first. The Lord had just descended upon Mount Sinai with such a display of force that the mountains shook and thunder and lightning put on a show, and shrouded everything in thick black darkness or infused with fire. This sight understandably terrified the people whom Moses led. They ran as if the Second Coming was descending upon them. Yet in the midst of it, their Advocate and mediator with God, the man who preceded them out of Egypt, Moses was present.

Then, in my mind's eye, I fast-forward to the Mount of Transfiguration. Suddenly, blinding light bathes this lanky, tallish man just entering middle age. It creates stark terror in the hearts of the three apostles witnessing it. Yet, again, who is comfortable in its presence? Moses walked and talked with this Person in Pure Light. There is good reason for this: the man fellowshipping with our Savior, whose true nature is fully revealed, had predicted the Messiah's appearing in his farewell sermon millennia earlier.

Even his death turned out to be an extraordinary event. While only Enoch and Elijah escaped physical death, his burial by God alone is nearly as dramatic, as Irish hymn writer, Cecil Francis Alexander (The Burial of Moses) captures so poignantly:

> By Nebo's lonely mountain, on this side Jordan's wave, in a vale
> in the land of Moab, there lies a lonely grave. And no man knows
> that sepulcher, and no man saw it e'er/
> For the angels of God upturned the sod, and laid the dead man
> there.

The apostles performed wonderful miracles, but none was on the scale as those God accomplished through Moses. Likewise, even though the ministries of Peter and Paul were extraordinary, they do not quite measure up to his accomplishments.

Moses as God's minister, towers above all New Testament examples. This titan, a colossus, wielded the power of the Holy Spirit, virtually alone, over and again, in such a manner and on such a scale as to preserve the people of God from extinction.

Excepting the Lord Christ himself, and perhaps John the Baptist, whom the Lord says may have been his equal, it is hard to think that a bigger apostle has ever walked in this world.

Chapter 3

The Ultimate Apostle and a Secular Counterpart

A MAN CONFRONTED A pastor after a service: "I think that rather than emphasizing Jesus' death, it would be more profitable to focus on Him as the ultimate teacher and example".

The pastor then asked, "Would you be inclined to follow Him, in that case?" The man affirmed that he would. "Okay, then let's take this to the next step: He did not sin. Could you follow that?" The man shrank, "Oh no, I confess that I sin" "Then you need a Savior not an example." That preacher was right! However, concerning this next discussion, we will observe Jesus as an example.

The Bible confirms that our Savior, Lord, and King of Kings was, because of His nature, the ultimate Bible:

"I must preach the kingdom of God: for therefore I was sent (*apostello*). (Luke 4:44)."

"He shall send (*apostello*) Jesus Christ (Acts 3:20)"

"The father sent (*apostello*) the Son to be the Savior of the world." (I John 4:9, 14)

Without doubt, this aspect of His ministry was crucial; chosen by the Father, His was an apostolic mission. The Gospels show that every word from His mouth, every action of every waking moment was directed toward the mission of disarming the Evil One's stranglehold, and bringing people into His Father's Kingdom.

We begin our investigation where we left off (last chapter) by comparing Jesus' apostleship to that of Moses (as the writer to the Book of Hebrews did in Heb. 3:1-3).

Similarities of Jesus and Moses' Apostleship

I am convinced that the point of the Hebrews passage was to make the apostleship of Moses an archetype of Jesus'. The similarities are striking:

- Both were born under miraculous circumstances: in infancy, they were spared death by the leaders they would later destroy (Pharaoh and Herod).
- At the outset of their ministries, both had divine favor.
- Both spent years preparing in isolation.
- God commissioned both by verbal acknowledgement.
- Both received their authority from heaven that they exercised supernaturally.
- Both received divine plans and blueprints for God's Tabernacle, both the physical building, and the spiritual habitation (God's people with Him indwelling them).
- God commissioned both to shepherd His people from bondage to the Promised Land.

As you can see, the evidence that Moses was the archetype Old Testament apostle is most compelling.

Wayne Gruden (*The Gift of Prophesy in the New Testament and Today*) argues that when considering which of the four ministering gifts mentioned in the list recorded in Ephesians chapter four, that the Old Testament prophet most closely resembled, one should consider it to be more akin to an apostle's than a prophet's.

With this comparison in mind, let us assess the Master's unique role as an apostle.

PART 1: JESUS THE ULTIMATE APOSTLE

Why did the Son of God, the second Person of the Trinity, the One who spoke the worlds into existence choose to conduct His earthly ministry as an apostle? The answer lies in an inviolable principle of leadership: to exercise authority, you must be under authority. This law is so universal that even the Members of the Godhead adhere to it. Therefore, in this instance, for Jesus to appoint the Twelve and other disciples as apostles, He must also function as an apostle, i.e., become one sent by the Father to carry out His divine will and purpose.

Since the evidence is overwhelming, I will only summarize the more important areas.

First, He was chosen and sent by God, as His personal representative, to this world on a Divine mission (John 3:16). In the first chapter of his Gospel, Mark points this out. After a night of healing people, a huge crowd gathered early the next morning. Peter searches for the missing Jesus; finds Him praying; urges Him to return, and use the occasion to enhance and expand His ministry. Jesus flatly turned him down, saying, He had no choice in the matter of building His ministry—the Father who was in charge of had sent him, and executing a plan for everything He did. The apostleship is not a franchise; one operates under divine guidance.

Second, He approached ministry with a unique mindset: a kingdom vs. church focus. In addition, he functions in an environment in which other views are tolerated and respected. (Unlike a church focus which ministers to true believers ("wheat") he ministers to "wheat and tares".

Third, he used unique tools: a different type of preaching, use of supernatural power of healing and deliverance. While we will deal with these in detail in a later chapter, suffice it now to point out four characteristics of apostolic preaching: i) it is kingdom focused; ii) it speaks to a culture; iii) demonstrations of supernatural power accompany it; and iv) it is principle-based. By this, we mean that it presents laws and principles, that when embraced by the mind, begin to change the life of that individual, and then, through his influence, those about him (i.e. leaven impacts flour to make bread).

Example: Jesus heals a demon-possessed Gadarene, and then urges him to use his changed life to impact his hometown with the Good News that they (and their society) could be transformed by that same Jesus.

In this regard, notice that Jesus' ministry was not only directed to saving and improving lives, but also it was also directed to their culture and society. This is why He constantly told those healed to remain and share with the people about them the power of God to change the entire community.

Demonstrations of supernatural power always accompanied His ministry. This was for two reasons. First, His message introduced them to a new reality (Kingdom of Heaven existing in parallel to the physical universe). His miracles confirmed the existence of this reality. Second, as the miracles disarmed the spiritual forces controlling the people, people's worldviews became recalibrated, enabling spiritual liberation, and forming a nucleus that would launch His apostolic mission of kingdom building.

Fourth, his goal was to tear down and restore. Restoration in this context includes bring "shalom" (spiritual wholeness) and "*esheri*" (Hebrew word for "divine favor"). His ministry is not only directed to improving lives, but also transforming culture by bringing the power of God to bear on its most pressing issues.

Fifth, his ministry was always team-based. He realized that an apostolic ministry has no chance of success without the concerted efforts of supporting teams, such as the Twelve, and later, after the Ascension, the ministering teams they chose. Also, writing the Gospels and the Acts of the Apostles involved team efforts. Likewise, where would the expansion into the Gentile world have been without Paul and his close support team?

Sixth, Christ's ministry was nation-focused. He was able to unlock ears and hearts to receive His message. Apostles know how to be dependent upon God for this direction.

Final Snapshot of Jesus' Apostleship (Mark chapters 5 – 8)

Mark spends three chapters describing the apostolic ministry of Jesus. In chapter four, the Savior teaches that He is the Bread of Life, and then to introduce them to this new realm of reality, He feeds the five thousand, creating hundreds of pounds of edible bread from a few ounces.

Then, in chapter 5, Jesus travels across the Sea of Galilee in search of a culture/urban center controlled by evil. He then confronts this demonic empire, by focusing on a demonic. In the process, Jesus transforms the economic base of the culture—no more swine ranching. This is why, to repeat an earlier point, Jesus urges the fully restored man to introduce the community of his origin to the One who had healed him.

In these chapters, we find a glimpse of the apostolic ministry, then and now. As we have learned much by examining the Savior's ministry for clues as to the nature, purpose and function of this apostolic gift, what might we glean from the Twelve?

PART 2: ANALYZING THE TWELVE'S CALLING

Since the ministry of Jesus was integrally connected to that of the Twelve, we need to examine their ministry for insights into the nature and purpose of this spiritual gift.

First, let the Bible set this discussion by its description of their calling:

> These twelve Jesus sent out after instructing them. And when he had called unto [him] his twelve disciples, he gave them power [against] unclean spirits, to cast them out, and to heal all manner of sickness and all manner of disease. Heal the sick, cleanse the lepers, and raise the dead, cast out devils: freely ye have received freely give. But go not into the way of the Gentiles and into [any] city of the Samaritans enter ye not. And as ye go, preach, saying, the kingdom of heaven is at hand. And ye shall be brought before governors and kings for my sake, for a testimony against them and the Gentiles (excerpted from New Testament passages).

These verses provide us many insights into the nature of a true apostle.

First, their ministries developed in this order: people were instructed, then commissioned, and finally sent with specific instructions. Second, these were His goals for them: introduce a new reality (parallel Kingdom), subdue opposition, rescue lives, and appropriate God's rule at each location. Next, the primary tools provided to them for their ministry included delivering, with authority, the message given to them to those He specified; and accompanying this with exorcisms, and healing. Third, those they served were to supply their needs. Fourth, they were to introduce a kingdom-focus; i.e., approach people as a culture; make no effort to be exclusive; i.e., separating false believers (tares) from true (wheat), and confront national, political, religious, and cultural leaders

This pattern emerged for a strategic apostolic approach to ministry: i) they proclaimed the presence of the Kingdom as good news, and how to connect with it via faith and repentance; and, ii) they then confronted its ruling spiritual powers, not only to subdue all opposition, but also demonstrate its reality. The upshot of this strategy: they disrupted and changed every city in which they introduced apostolic preaching.

Because of this strategy, they all left behind people reconciled to God and able to live before Him in righteousness, peace, and joy. These people, previously owned by the powers of darkness had through apostolic ministry, become whole, and taking dominion. Also, the process resembled that of leaven or a mustard seed: it began with individuals, and eventually, controlled entire areas.

What a price these dear chosen vessels paid for responding to the call to become apostles:

- Matthew suffered martyrdom by being slain with a sword at a distant city of Ethiopia.
- Mark expired at Alexandria; authorities cruelly dragged them through its streets.
- Luke was hanged upon an olive tree in the classic land of Greece.
- Authorities crucified Peter at Rome with his head downward.
- Authorities beheaded James the Greater at Jerusalem.
- James the Less was thrown from the Temple's roof, and then clubbed to death.
- Bartholomew was flayed alive.
- Andrew was bound to a cross, from where he preached to his persecutors.
- Thomas was run through the body with a lance in the East Indies.
- They shot Jude to death with arrows.
- It seems that only John died of natural causes at the ripe age.

Upon reflection, an ingenious factor emerges. Almost every conceivable variety of Christian is represented in the apostolic band. The doubter finds himself in Thomas; the opinionated, impulsive man finds himself in Peter; Andrew was the cautious businessperson; John was sympathetic and understanding; Judas was the fickle, insincere, hypocrite. And so on with all the apostles.

That group typifies all of us called to this ministry. Surely, there was an all-wise purpose in Jesus' selection of men with such varying characteristics.

Think about it: if such an unlikely group, using His power, could turn the world upside down, what could a ministry such as ours accomplish?

Now that we have established that Jesus was the ultimate apostle, compared his ministry with the Old Testament archetype, Moses, one final comparison serves our purpose—the comparison of His ministry to that of Alexander the Great.

PART 3: SECULAR MODEL OF AN APOSTLE

As He announced the Twelve Jesus used the word "apostle" for the first time. In the minds of those hearing Him, a model for the role sprang to mind—Alexander the Great. Rome, in urging leaders to emulate him, used his exemplary qualities as their epitome of a military apostle. For this reason, they attached "Great" to his name, and urged people to worship him.

To help you understand their adulation, permit me to share these clues to his greatness:

1. His character. In his send-off address to his troops, his nobility of purpose shines through: "Our mandate will not be to conquer nations, or acquire wealth. It will be to unite all people by bringing to them Greek justice and peace".
2. His use of power from achievement. Those he conquered testified that he was tolerant, improved their economy, respected their traditions, and assigned leaders from their ranks to govern.
3. He rid cities of oligarchs, dictators, thugs, and crooks. He built libraries, theatres, schools, and roads. He collected and preserved so much literature he sparked the Renaissance. As he advanced, a path of restored order, justice, and hope trailed. Alexander the Great altered the nature of Asia, Northern Africa, the Middle East, and Europe.

Therefore, thanks to Romans making this military "apostle" into a household word, those who heard Jesus use this word for the first time, would have had no trouble understanding His using it in a ministry context.

When I compared the characteristics that defined Alexander as a military apostle to those in Bible describing a ministering apostle, three conclusions leaped out. First, the qualities that marked his life fit the Biblical profile of an apostle. Martis is right; Alexander was a military apostle.

Second, the traits that the Great One exhibited as a *military* apostle mirror those demonstrated by Jesus, the ultimate *ministering* apostle.

Third, using these shared characteristics, I was able to construct a clear, composite picture of what an apostle does. Permit me to list them, and then discuss them in detail:

- Both were similarly appointed

- Both appointments were prophetic
- Both were uniquely and perfectly prepared
- Both were similarly commissioned
- Both were required to constantly confront and subdue evil opposition
- Both were sent to overthrow existing Governments
- Both were sent to Tear Down, then Restore to Wholeness
- Both Were Respected by Opposing Leaders
- Both Exhibited a Single-mindedness that Proved Fatal
- Both left a legacy that continues today

Now, permit me to discuss them in detail.

Both were Similarly Appointed

When an assassin murdered Philip, king of Macedonia, his son ascended to the throne. At his commissioning ceremony, Alexander outlined life and its purpose: he would, by military conquest, impose on the world a value-based democratic way of life, literature, language, culture, and provide it access to Greek protection, and free enterprise. He then explained his purpose: to honor the father who gave them to him. Thereafter, the son approached every challenge as if acting as his father's emissary, and credited him with every achievement.

Likewise, Jesus was appointed by His Father, who twice (Baptism and Transfiguration) confirmed aloud his pleasure with His Son's life and ministry. Once when his Disciples urged him to go to a certain place, He vetoed their request, saying that the Father who had sent Him directed His every move (Mark 1:38). Jesus so considered Himself His father's apostle, that to receive Him was to receive the One who sent Him (Matt.10:40)

Both appointments were Prophetic

As a boy, Alexander was so fascinated by Achilles, the hero of Homer's Iliad that he vowed to model himself after the mythical hero. To help, his mother lied that the gods had personally confirmed that her son was descended from Achilles. For the rest of his life, Alexander daily read it, and slept with a copy under his pillow. Later, he learned that the true God had predicted his success. As he prepared to invade Jerusalem, its leaders showed him the passage from Daniel's prophecy that, centuries before, predicted him as a conqueror of the world. Alexander was so impressed that he not only spared the city from complete destruction, but granted special dispensation and benefits.

The Old Testament records hundreds of prophecies regarding the coming Messiah. He, too, knew them to be about Himself. Therefore, when He preached from Isaiah 61:1 at the outset of His ministry, He declared that He was its fulfillment before their eyes.

Both Uniquely and Perfectly Prepared

Alexander had a father's model, and the tutelage of Aristotle. No expense was spared to equip him with an extraordinary grasp of God, nature, human nature, government, leadership, tactical military strategy, as well as the ideas that elevated man to his God-given value.

While the Gospels are silent about His training, it provides two glimpses of its thoroughness: the fear of religious leaders to challenge His theology the shock of that audience listening to His first sermon at His deep knowledge and clear explanations.

Both were Similarly Commissioned

At his death, Philip said to him, "My son, look thee out a kingdom equal to and worthy of thyself, for Macedonia is too little for thee." Alexander considered these memorable words to be his commissioning.

Think of the scene described in Mark: Jesus stands in the Jordan before John the Baptist, who, against his will, has just baptized the Messiah. Suddenly, the heavens open and a voice was heard, "This is my beloved son in whom I am well pleased".

Both viewed themselves as Servants

At the outset of his military career, Alexander took a vow of poverty. As a result, he gave away all of his money, belongings and property, and refused every offer of wealth from those he conquered. At his death, he owned nothing.

Likewise, Jesus laid aside every access to wealth and privilege. By His admission, the foxes and birds lived better.

The Ultimate Apostle and a Secular Counterpart. 31

Both Callings Necessitated Confronting and Subduing Evil Opposition

As soon as the teenage Alexander inherited the kingdom from his father, many Greek City-states tried to overthrow him. Unfortunately, they discovered they were no match for this fearless warrior who loved leading his troops into combat.

Likewise, Jesus took no thought of the consequences of saying and doing whatever was required to fulfill his ministry. Even in the Garden of Gethsemane, and before Pilate.

Both Were Called to Overthrow

In his initial military campaign, Alexander burned the rebellious city-state, Thebes to the ground, and put to death or enslaved every resident. Once other city-states and kingdoms from Persia to Asia "got wind" of his viciousness, they quickly pledged their allegiance. After each bloody conquest, he would infuse its culture with his values, subdue all opposition, and install a government friendly to his purpose.

Likewise, this strategy mirrored that of Jesus. Demons trembled before Him; mortals feared opposing Him; theologians lost their nerve in the face of His logic.

Both Called to Tear Down

As we have shown, the pattern of Alexander's conquest of Thebes, and Tyre were repeated throughout his career. He figured that the best was to rebuild was by first tearing down the bad elements.

Jesus, in His apostolic ministry functioned much like Jeremiah, one "sent" to the adulterous House of Israel. The LORD described his mission: "to pluck up and to pull down, to destroy and to overthrow, to build and to plant." It proved to be a very difficult ministry, ending in the populace's rejection of His message. Likewise, in Jesus' first sermon, people spoke well, then began to murmur, "How could this son of Joseph be the Messiah?"

During the last week of His ministry, Jesus entered His "tearing down" mode. He ousted the moneylenders. Next, He cursed a fig tree. His point: since the old religious system is incapable of bearing fruit (its intended purpose), then it would be destroyed and replaced. Then, when, as a Disciples remarked about what an extraordinary edifice the Temple was, Jesus replied that, shortly, it would be destroyed; He would be the cause (the Stone of Daniel's prophecy smashing the empire ruling the earth); and the new ("virtual") Temple, designed with Him as its chief corner stone, would become the seat of true worship.

Both Were Called to Restore

Alexander, after tearing down and overthrowing, moved to that which he enjoyed doing most—restoring. Therefore, throughout his eleven-year campaign to conquer the world, Alexander battled his way across 22,000 miles, founding seventy cities, and restoring many existent ones.

His pattern was always the same. First, he would oust all political leaders who did not advocate values-based democracy. In addition, he was hardest on those thugs, dictators, and bureaucrats known to use their power to steal, exploit, or brutalize others. Likewise, he would then build schools, roads, libraries, and theaters. As a result, when he moved on, he left a city dramatically improved.

Jesus provides us a fascinating glimpse into His restoring ministry in His gracious response to the disciples of John the Baptist, sent to inquire if He was the true Messiah. His advice: report to this great man that the prophecy stated in Isaiah 61:1 is being fulfilled. Luke 4:18, 19 provides us an important glimpse into Jesus' restoration ministry:

1. "To preach good news to the poor;
2. "To proclaim freedom for the prisoners";
3. "To proclaim recovery of sight to the blind";
4. "To release the oppressed"; and,
5. "To proclaim the year of the Lord's favor".

These five statements reveal many insights, including these. First, cultures controlled by evil forces hold people hostage. Second, the Gospel can transform both individual hearts as well as the soul of a city. Third, the power of the Gospel extends to every realm of reality, including nature, health, and demonic oppression. Four, Jesus not only delivers us from evil, but, via the indwelling Holy Spirit, He exerts power to oversee our needs in ways to superior to any that once may have dominated us.

Elsewhere, Jesus beautifully summed up His restoration ministry: "I am come that they might have life, and have it more abundantly."

The Ultimate Apostle and a Secular Counterpart. 33

Both Were Respected by Opposition

Because his leadership was grounded in wisdom, values, and sincere desire to do the right thing, there are many acts of kindness; the record of the conquered who came to revere him is a long one.

Alexander captured the entire family of Darius, including his pregnant wife and mother. When the wife died giving birth to a son, Alexander buried her with full royal honor. Alexander eventually married a daughter. The mother lived a long time. Alexander treated her so well that she proclaimed him "a son". After Alexander's premature death, she fasted for five days, and then committed suicide.

A wife of one of the ruler's captured menservants managed to escape. She then reported to Darius, the Persian king, "You have been conquered by an enemy whose character is far superior of any other human…This enemy is virtuous and brave".

Later, when Darius was informed of all the kindnesses extended to his family in captivity he said, "If I return a conqueror I want to be able to return Alexander's kindness during my family's misfortune, and if we cease ruling may the gods intervene so that none other than Alexander should occupy the throne of Persia".

This was also true of Jesus. With so much opposition, constant combat with the political, religious, and supernatural powers, you would think that Jesus was either loved (disciples), or hated (enemies). However, the Gospels record that many people, upon hearing His message, observing His acts of kindness, and mercy, developed respect for Him. Two examples come to mind.

Nicodemus, after hearing Him, said, "You almost persuade me". Later in the mock trial of his fellow Pharisees, he refused to participate. Joseph of Arimathea, after hearing Him, became a disciple; this prompted this leader among the Pharisees to provide the grave in which the body of Jesus lay in repose while His spirit confronted conquered and destroyed physical and spiritual death; humankind would never again have inevitably to face them.

Both Exhibited Single-mindedness that Proved Fatal

Alexander considered the day he embarked on his career of military conquests to be a walking dead man. Daily, he flirted with death, leading wave after wave of soldiers into hand-to-hand combat. Death was inevitable.

Likewise, Jesus began His ministry, with the Cross dead in His sights. Paul explains his mindset in Philippians chapter two: "(Jesus) who… for the joy before Him, despising the shame, endured the cross."

Now you have a better idea of why we used Commodore Perry, as an example of the apostolic ministry.

Is it not amazing how Jesus chose this military term to model the kind of leadership that He desired collaborating with Him in building His kingdom? At the outset, the selection of such a rag-tag group of thoroughly common people seemed so strange. Yet from the outset, Jesus knew this gift, and those who exercised it were destined for success. He reminds me of Eiffel.

To highlight its impending opening, a major international exposition commissioned an artist to erect a structure to commemorate the occasion. In 1889, its construction was no sooner completed than a public outcry demanded it be torn down.

However, from the moment he conceived it, and sketched it on paper, he knew in his heart that it was destined for worldwide renown. Today, Alexandre Gustave Eiffel's tower is considered one of the world's greatest pieces of architecture; it now defines the city that commissioned it.

When I pondered Eiffel's loyalty to his structure, my mind turned to reflect on the structure, the Kingdom of God, and those integral to its success, i.e., the apostles He chose to establish its foundation came to mind.

Even today, to those who view it as outsiders, they (and we) must seem like incapable blunderers. But Jesus, the architect of the kingdom of God, knew that He was launching a structure destined for immortal greatness; one in which the gift of apostleship was to play a central role.

It is now our privilege to examine one stellar example of a New Testament apostle, the man from Tarsus with two earned doctorates. His ministry shaped the early church. Then we will be ready to tackle the knotty matter of whether or not this gift is relevant in the 21st century.

Chapter 4

The Pharisee Who Became an Apostle

WOULD YOU HIRE THIS man?
A certain church found itself suddenly without a pastor, therefore formed a search committee. In due course, it received a letter from a man applying for the vacant position. The committee chairperson read:

"I am considered to be a good preacher, and I have been a leader in most of the places I have served. I have also done some writing on the side.

"I am over 50 years old, and while my health is not the best, I still manage to get enough work done to please any parish.

"As for references, I am somewhat handicapped. I have never preached anywhere for more than three years. Moreover, most of the churches I have preached in have been small, even though they were located in rather large cities. I had to leave some places because my ministry caused riots and disturbances. Even where I stayed, I did not get along too well with other religious leaders, which may influence the kind of references these places will supply. I have also been threatened and physically attacked. I have even gone to jail several times for my preaching.

"I am not particularly good at keeping records. I have to admit I do not even remember all those whom I have baptized. However, if you can use me, I should be pleased to be considered. I feel sure I can bring vitality to your church."

When the chairperson finished reading the letter, the committee members were aghast. How could anyone think that a church like theirs would consider a man who was nothing but a troublemaking, absent-minded, ex-jailbird? What was his name? "Well," said the chairman, "the letter is signed, Paul."

Why is it that this strongest New Testament example of an apostle has had to endure so much more that the others? I think it stems from his unique call to ministry, and the nature of the people God sent him to serve—the Gentiles.

Paul did not become an apostle in the same manner, as did the rest of the apostles. Our first glimpse of him is at the stoning of Stephen in Acts 7. Acts 8:3 says, "But Saul began ravaging the church, entering house after house; and dragging off men and women, he would put them in prison."

In addition, when compared to the conversions of the original apostles, his conversion was unique and much more dramatic. First, being confronted by the resurrected Savior, whose non-existence had been his pretense to incarcerate and execute Christians, was stunning.

Even in the first words of ministry he received from Ananias were dramatic:

> "The God of our fathers has appointed you to know His will, and to see the Righteous One, and to hear an utterance from His mouth. For you will be a witness for Him to all men of what you have seen and heard. (You are) a chosen instrument of Mine, to bear My name before the Gentiles and kings and the sons of Israel." (Acts 9:15 ff).

The launch of his public ministry was dramatic: After obeying the command to "be baptized, washing away your sins immediately he began to proclaim Jesus in the synagogues, saying, "He is the Son of God"" (Acts 9:20).

Yet the church leaders were reluctant to embrace him, since they feared the possibility that his conversion was a ruse to get at them to wreck havoc on true believers. Given his past, their concerns are not unfounded

It seems that throughout his most productive career, Paul constantly had to defend the legitimacy of his apostleship.

It happened as he ministered to the Corinthians, where several argued that he was not a true apostle (10:2, 7, 8, and 10).

PAUL DEFENDS HIS APOSTLESHIP

Concerning the claims of these Corinthian detractors, Paul argued that their existence as true believers and as a genuine congregation was proof of his apostleship (10:14-15), (see Acts 18:1ff; 1 Corinthians 2:1ff; 4:15)

He also offered these reasons to confirm the legitimacy of his apostleship. First, he imposed no financial burden on them. Secondly, he endured much suffering for Christ.

Third, he boasted of his weakness, which he asserted was the mark of a true apostle 4:7-15; 5:11-12; 6:4-10; also 1 Corinthians 4:9-13; even going so far as to assert that his vision was a display of weakness in that he gained nothing he could express (12:4).

Further, he asserts that the "thorn in the flesh" divinely imposed upon him to ensure his humility as a true servant of the Lord in 12:11 confirmed his apostleship.

Next, he states that the signs, wonders, and miracles of a true apostle were performed among them to accompany his proclamation of the Word confirmed the legitimacy of his apostleship.

Finally, Paul affirmed that the purpose of his apostolic ministry (unlike that of the false apostles) i.e., to build them up, not tear them down; proving his sincere love for them and desire to give of himself for their benefit served as confirmation of his apostleship being genuine (12:15).

Despite his blatant defense given to the church in Corinth, Paul was actually very humble about his former way life and subsequent conversion and apostleship. In 1 Corinthians 15:9, he wrote, "For I am the least of the apostles, who is not fit to be called an apostle, because I persecuted the church of God." He went on to express his thankfulness in v10: "For by the grace of God I am what I am, and His grace toward me did not prove vain; but I labored even more than all of them, yet not I, but the grace of God with me." He further exhibits his humility in 2 Corinthians 3:5: "Not that we are adequate in ourselves to consider anything as coming from ourselves, but our adequacy is from God."

However, it is impressive that the Lord sent the leader of the original band of apostles to speak up for him, and affirm the legitimacy of his apostleship—Peter.

PETER DEFENDS PAUL'S APOSTLESHIP

Probably the greatest proof of Paul's apostleship and authority is found in 2 Peter 3:15-16. There Peter refers to Paul as "our beloved brother." He states that Paul wrote "according to the wisdom given him." Finally, Peter refers to (apparently) a collection of Paul's letters and calls them "Scripture."

It is true that, in the early church, the term "Scripture" was generally used to refer to that of the Old Testament. However, notice that Peter categorized the writings of Paul in the same class as "the rest of the Scriptures," thus giving a clear indication that Paul's writings are indeed truthful and authoritative.

Jesus said, "But when He, the Spirit of truth, comes, He will guide you into all truth" (John 16:13). The Holy Spirit in their teaching and writing would thus divinely guide the apostles. The apostle John was inspired when he recorded those words of Jesus. Luke was inspired when he wrote the account of Paul being called to be an apostle. Peter was inspired when he wrote that Paul's writings were Scripture. Thus if Paul is not to be accepted as a true apostle and his writings as genuinely inspired, then several other inspired writers must also be shunned.

In my research, I discovered the following things in this regard:
- Only Jesus Christ and the Father could bestow this gift, not man. (Gal. 1:1).
- Once divinely bestowed, the gift could only be revoked by apostasy (I Cor1:1).
- Its purpose was to fulfill the Messianic Mission (establishing global Kingdom)
- Its bestowal was not intended either as a reward or for self-aggrandizement.
- Possession of the gift was verified by the ability to perform signs and wonders specific to the mission (2 Cor. 12:12; Rom. 15:19).
- The gift was accompanied by specialized suffering (I Cor. 4:9-11).
- The gift gave the apostle special insight into the mystery (I Cor. 4:1).
- Possession of gift did not elevate one as superior to other spiritual gifts.

As you can see, our study of Pauline passages produced much insight into what an apostle is and does. However, it raises this question: *How does the apostolic ministry relates to the other gifts described in Ephesians chapter four?*

HOW PAUL RELATES TO THE APOSTOLIC GIFT TO THE OTHER FOUR

The apostolic gift differs with the other ministering gifts listed along with it in the fourth chapter of Ephesians in several ways:

> "…it was He who gave some, apostles; and some prophets; and some evangelists; and some pastors; and some teachers until we all come in the unity of the faith, and of the knowledge of the Son of God, unto a perfect man, unto the measure of the stature of the fullness of Christ " Eph. 4:11-13 (KJV).

The Central Difference

The apostolic differs from the other four gifts in that it is kingdom focused. It seeks to transform the soul of a culture, confront and subdue supernatural opposition so kingdom building can occur. In contrast, the other four ministering gifts, prophesy, evangelism, pastoral ministry, and teaching are church-focused: they deal with individual souls, from salvation to maturity. This is because the church is not equivalent to the Kingdom of God; it began with John the Baptist and continues forever. On the other hand, the church began at Pentecost and ends when its members share the throne of the King of Kings, ruling this Kingdom.

How the Gifts Complement Each Other

Having pointed out how they differ in function, we are ready to understand how they complement each other. Before I point these out, you need to understand the context for this listing.

Context for Gift Discussion

To appreciate Paul's discussion of the five ministering gifts, an understanding of the context will be helpful. This brief synopsis of what precedes this chapter in Ephesians will serve this purpose.

Synopsis of the Preceding Ephesians Chapters

Synopsis of Chapters One: Paul reveals salvation from God's perspective: Before creation, for His own purpose, He designed a plan to create a race of people to share His nature, and Presence forever. The chapter explains how God, in the three Persons of the Trinity accomplished this.

Synopsis of Chapter Two: Paul reveals this process from man's perspective. We learn that the man was chosen for salvation when spiritually dead, therefore, capable of making no input in the matter of his salvation. It was accomplished by grace, bestowed as man exercised saving faith, after having expressed true repentance.

Synopsis of Chapter Three: Paul reveals that each redeemed individual was placed into a community so organic integrated and unified that it is analogous to the ten systems within the human body, except in the case of the church, Jesus is its head. The nature and purpose of the church was so unique that had the Holy Spirit not revealed it, it would have remained a mystery throughout heaven, and all of history.

Synopsis of Chapter Four: Based on this revelation, and with the analogy explaining its complex nature, Paul reveals the Divine plan to maintain its operation—through the exercise of these five ministering gifts. As we examine them, we discover the nature and function of each gift. We also learn of a common purpose the share: to bring every member of the true church to spiritual maturity.

Fortunately, Paul discusses them in related passages. As a result, we can piece together a composite picture of their function:

- Birth an authentic government that reflects heaven's strategy
- Oversee the spiritual life in the church
- Develop church order and structure that allowed the life in the Spirit to flow
- Bring accountability to the members and its appointed leaders
- Teach doctrine that produce fruit-bearing disciples moving toward maturity.
- Develop and qualify leaders for full-time ministry
- Overthrow the government of Darkness
- Assert kingdom dominion and influence.
- Lay a strong foundation for future spiritual generations.

Together, these five ministering offices are God's gift to the church for its growth, edification, blessing, and accomplishment of its divine mission. To explain how, permit me to briefly refer to something previously mentioned, but will help you grasp the function of each gift.

In a word, *the Apostle governs*. Before we delve into this, let us consider this. Can we capture the essence of the other four areas of giftedness in a single word?

The Prophet grounds: The prophet, like a watchman on the wall maintains constant vigilance for incoming satanic attacks that threaten to steal the hearts and minds of a true believer. The prophetic gift has this primary goal: use discernment to detect and safeguard the minds of true believers from incoming false doctrine and apostate ideas.

The Evangelist gathers: He directs his message at unsaved hearts. His gift equips him with a special ability: he is able to communicate spiritual truth to people with no capacity to receive it; nevertheless, they receive his message, turn from sin, receive eternal life, and begin to walk in obedience to the One who saved them. The Evangelist gives life. The evangelistic gift serves as the king's herald, i.e., mandated to confront unsaved people with the salvation message. Only about ten percent of the Body possesses this gift that is uniquely capable of making the complex truth of the Gospel of grace sensible to people with no prior knowledge or ability to perceive spiritual truth. The

The Pastor guards: He shepherds the congregation, teaching, draining, mentoring, and persuading them to embrace the truth he presents in order to move toward spiritual maturity and ministry. The pastoral gift functions like spiritual radar spotting potential problems, giving direction, identifying people gifted for ministry, and alerting the Body to issues capable of creating spiritual warfare.

The Teacher guides: He provides the truth, and its understanding that equips the true believer with the doctrinal skills to prevent false teaching from creeping in, and to provide an ever-increasing understanding of the nature and purpose of our Lord, as well as how to enjoy and serve Him.

These two gifts function so close together that many theologians consider them as a single gift (Pastor-Teacher). They take up where the Evangelist leaves off. They draw into a spiritual community those new believers the Evangelist's message created. They shepherd these true believers through failure, crises, and pain. They lead them in worship, and oversee the ministering processes that bring them to maturity, by instructing them in the Biblical principles. Their goal is to move the true believer to spiritual maturity.

As promised, in light of these task analyses, let us consider in greater depth where does the apostle fit into the broad strategy Paul outlines regarding these five gift-sets. Specifically, permit me to glean from his writings sufficient insights into the apostolic ministry to construct a composite profile of six of the major features of this gift in action.

These characteristics generally mark the ministry of a first century apostle, including Paul. First, they viewed their ministry as foundation-laying master builders. Paul said as much in his letter to the Corinthian believers:

> "By the grace God has given me, I laid a foundation as a wise master builder, and someone else is building on it. But each one should be careful how he builds. For no one can lay any foundation other than the one already laid, which is Jesus Christ" (1 Corinthians 3:10,11).

Also, they sovereignly targeted specific people-groups. In his case, it was Hellenized Gentiles. The Savior chose this high ranking, noble classed Jewish man with two earned degrees (PhD equivalency) to penetrate a world far removed from his thinking, culture, and roots. (Rom.15:20).

Compare that with the way the apostle views this congregation. He sees it as a place where the life and power of the kingdom is in manifested. Nevertheless, he operates outside it. His focus is to continually confront the culture with the reality of Christ, and opposing evil that constantly raises its head, and ever ready to tear down and restore at this wider sphere.

THE APOSTLE GOVERNS

In the Divine Plan of the Godhead, the Kingdom precedes the church. Therefore, the apostolic ministry serves as the first wave of penetration into a culture or nation. It pioneers contact in virgin territory. Its goal is to establish the Kingdom, a new reality where God's Spirit rules over evil ones; and the people are free to enjoy the blessings outline in chapter one, peace, authenticity and divine favor. To this end, the apostle confronts the culture, challenging its core values. He introduces them to a new reality by confronting demons, and healing sickness, and bringing true restoration to the individuals and the culture as a whole. He oversees the ongoing expansion of the Kingdom; and that requires him to exert influence on the work of the other four gifts, as they establish and grow churches within this Kingdom environment.

Apostleship is frontline ministry, rather than 'managerial ministry'. His spiritual gift enables him to perceive when things are out of order. The reason: his governing mindset equips him with a special concern for the proper design, form, and function of spiritual communities.

Therefore, as the other ministering gifts guard (prophet), gather (evangelist), and guide (pastor), the apostle governs. His approach to ministry is foundational. Like a builder and architect, he designs strategies to tear down and lay a good foundation, establish his authority to speak for God, build teams of people, and then motivate them to form cohesive, vibrant, balanced community able to resolve key problems and issues.

Like the prophet and teacher, he speaks to the issues confront the culture he stands before in such a way as to enlighten them with the laws and principles needed to bring about wholeness. Like the Evangelist, the apostle presents the salvation message to individuals. Like the Pastor, he seeks to guide the true believers toward establishing a community, guided by biblical values that can help them fulfill the demands of the Kingdom of God.

Incidentally, as we learned from studying our Old Testament models, when he joins forces with the prophetic gift, the combination is most effective against the powers of darkness.

As the other four gifts create a Body, with Christ as the Head, the apostle lays a foundation for a spiritual Temple, with Jesus as its Cornerstone. The difference between the works of New Testament apostles from their Old Testament counterparts is this. The Temple they jointly construct is spiritual, and not physical, whereas that which Moses designed, and Nehemiah rebuilt from was physical. Also, the materials used are different. The stones of this virtual edifice are made of each true believer, perfectly positioned by his spiritual gift to transform it into a virtual place that in an edifice as superior in its magnificence, as the *Taj Mahal* is to a chicken coop.

CONCLUSION

What we have learned about Paul's apostleship helps us make sense of the culture-transforming strategy we will shortly present.

While our Savior founded the Christian faith, without exaggeration, Paul doctrinally defined it. His ability to interpret the mission of Jesus, define the way in which a person becomes a true believer, as well as to describe the process of his sanctification, and provide a glimpse of what life will be after death makes his contribution incalculable.

It is not surprising that many of the first-century churches surviving into the second became known as the "Pauline" churches. This group maintained a doctrinal integrity that became their hallmark since it stood in contrast to the doctrine espoused by the catholic hierarchy. Ironically, this biblical orthodoxy continued until the Reformation Movement embraced and universally promoted it.

Certainly, the longevity of his apostolic ministry speaks volumes for its quality.

In the next chapter, we shall use this model of first century apostoling to investigate this question: Is the claim of Bertril Baird to possess this gift valid in this century?

Petrarch did not have Paul in mind; nevertheless, they are as true of him as anyone: *Where you are is of no moment, but only what you are doing there. It is not the place that ennobles you, but you the place; and this only by doing what is great and noble.*

CONCLUSION

Throughout my ministry, like Paul, I have had to defend and justify my calling as an authentic apostle. Permit me to share the two areas of truth that provide me the confidence to proceed as a first-century apostle.

This is why I am delighted to take up this question: do the attributes of today's apostolic gift mirror that of the first-century? The answer matters because if we cannot satisfactorily demonstrate that it does, then every apostolic ministry from the second to the 21st is nullified.

Therefore, I put the question to you,

…is Bertril Baird a true apostle?

Chapter 5

Is This Gift for Today?

Capital "A" or Lower-Case

Every healthy congregation has many who pastor others. Some shepherd toddlers; others care for people with specialized needs. In certain aspects, what they do resembles that of the one called to be the spiritual shepherd of their congregation. Like their Pastor, those who "pastor" also care, lead, etc., and nurture. However, two things distinguish their ministries from the one who leads them.

First, his calling has been confirmed by an anointed ability to use certain gifts vital to minister the Word from the pulpit that produce demonstrable results: people getting saved; people maturing in the Lord; palpable momentum; articulated vision; and, a compelling aura of fellowship.

Second, when we refer to their gift of pastoring we think of it as "doing" (i.e., a verb) and spell it with a small "p". In contrast, when we speak of the person called to this spiritual office, we see his pastoral ministry of both what he does and who he is, and therefore personify his giftedness and calling by spelling it with a capital "P".

BOOK ONE is nearly complete: we have thoroughly informed you about the nature and purpose of the gift of Apostleship. Yet one final question demands an answer—maybe the most vital in this day. Because of its strategic importance to this discussion, we must properly frame it by making sure you understand what the question does not entail. The issue is not whether the gift exists today; all agree that it does. We must resolve this question: *Does it exist today as the New Testament apostles modeled it?*

The Kingdom is blessed by the army of missionaries sent by congregations to pioneer new ministries in remote places speaking different languages and viewing the world through different 'lenses. The apostle's calling is distinct from that of a missionary in the way God authorizes him to use certain supernatural gifts as first-century counterparts did. Also, he operates with a different mindset (kingdom-centric). Further, he pursues different outcomes (impact the soul of a nation). None of these attributes renders him spiritually superior to the ministry of missionaries, any more than he ranks above pastors or teachers. But like the pastoral example above, his ministry is different from those dear believers who wake up each morning to lead, govern, and pioneer new ministry related ventures. These also use the apostolic gift, but do so in a way that warrants spelling it with a small "a". In contrast, his calling is all consuming. It defines who he is as well as what he does. Therefore, he deserves to be called Apostle with a capital "A".

As the title for this chapter suggests, the final question regarding the nature of this gift today comes down to whether you use a capital or lower-case "a" to spell the word that mirrors that demonstrated in the Book of Acts. "Caps" (those who capitalize the word) define this office as mirroring the power demonstrated in by those present in the Upper Room. "Lower-casers" (those spelling the word using the lower-case) reject placing modern apostles on such a par with their first-century counterparts, (especially the use of such supernatural gifts as healing, and exorcism). The only time they spell the word apostle with a capital "A" is when it starts a sentence.

While good and godly people disagree, the goal of this chapter is to make a compelling case why the word defining my ministry warrants being capitalized. To begin, let us trace the roots of this church-splitting controversy. Then we will make our argument, first by attempting to refute those arguments opposing the relevance of first-century apostleship today.

PART 1: TRACING THE ROOTS OF CONTROVERSY

How did something so integral to the roots of the church become ignite such a raging battle that splits churches and fragments seminaries? True, the insertion of those supernatural gifts heats this discussion. In our research, we were able to trace six factors heating this issue into a controversy.

1. The Reformation's influence: it produced an aversion to any type of clerical hierarchy, and its leaders declared that the last apostle died 1500 years earlier.
2. The entrepreneurial nature of today's local church makes it reluctant to embrace a ministry that has a kingdom (vs. "church") mindset.
3. Denominations: some Leaders view this gift's itinerant nature as potentially undermining, or a threat to losing control.
4. The exposure of people abusing the apostolic gift by the Press has fired waves of detractors.
5. Those opposing the Pentecostal movement are quick to "nix" this gift. because of the supernatural gifts associated with its ministry.
6. The growing prominence of the 'Fivefold Ministry" movement is a catalyst. By insisting that the Holy Spirit resurrected the apostolic gift to function on a par with that described in the New Testament, it has elevated this discussion to 'center stage'.

While the first five are self-explanatory, this last factor warrants a closer investigation.

Fivefold Ministry Movement

A decade ago, Peter Wagner, through his writing and speaking, helped launch the "Five-fold Ministry" movement. This former Dean of the School of World Mission at Fuller Seminary started one of the influential organizations continuing to provide leadership for this movement, the International Coalition of Apostles.

This term relates to the five spiritual gifts highlighted **in Ephesians 4:11:**

> "It was he who gave some to be (1) apostles, some to be (2) prophets, some to be (3) evangelists, and some to be (4) pastors and (5) teachers." Further, it correctly reasons that since these gifts were given "to prepare God's people for works of service, so that the body of Christ may be built up until we all reach unity in the faith and in the knowledge of the Son of God and become mature, attaining to the whole measure of the fullness of Christ."

Most concede that for nineteen centuries, the Body of Christ was built up using those gifts above numbering two through five. However, this Movement argues that in these last days, with so many signs pointing to the soon return of Jesus, the Holy Spirit re-activated gift #1, making this last phase of building Christ's church a "Fivefold" ministry. As a result, they claim, many people are now divinely anointed with an apostolic gift that functions on a par almost as it did by the Upper Room generation.

However, Wagner and the other leaders insist that this movement really began 200 years ago. While its appeal to church history is not compelling, its defining tenets do have merit:

- The purpose Paul states for giving these gifts has not yet been attained.
- The Biblical signs confirmed by newsprint do point to the immanency Christ's return.
- The use of four of these gifts has not produced results comparable to those achieved when all five were operational.

Therefore, this movement contends, the apostolic gift Ephesians lists must be re-activated to operate as in the first century. This conviction that the Holy Spirit now authorizes all five gifts defines this movement, "the Fivefold Ministry".

Since we agree with their definition of the apostolic gift, people often ask our opinion regarding the fivefold ministry. Let me summarize our initial response: i) our experience confirms this view's interpretation of the gift; ii) from what I know of their leadership, they embrace biblically oriented views regarding Christ and salvation; and, iii) those proponents that I am familiar with seem prompted by a genuine desire to lift up Jesus by the use of the supernatural gifts.

Permit me to share five reasons why I choose to remain independent of this movement, then I shall proceed to present to you my reasons for be a "Cap", you will learn why I believe this gift, as fully demonstrated in the New Testament, explains my career of vocational ministry as an Apostle.

Five Reasons for Our Independence

First, the argument for this movement's origin some two centuries ago lacks sufficient historical evidence to warrant my "buy-in". In the third century of the church, a man rose to prominence by claiming he was the final true New Testament Apostle. Mani of Persia, in the third century announced that he was the last and final apostle to exist on this earth, and promoted himself as "The Apostle of Light".

Second, my call to the apostolic ministry began in a rural village in a remote island in the southern end of the Caribbean region by the Holy Spirit. My calling, nearly fifty years ago to this Apostleship was not prompted by an invitation from such an organization; perhaps I was too far from the mainstream to catch anyone's notice. Yet, to His praise, God provided outstanding ministers to encourage and counsel me. Since, I was pursuing a career in Medicine my appointment to this type of ministry had to be through leading that was demonstratively divine.

My first clue that the Holy Spirit was appointing me to this office came during a ministering situation; He manifested the supernatural gifts associated (as you will learn) with the work of apostoling. We invited people to step forward for healing or seek deliverance from demonic bondage. As we prayed, many were made whole or set free. Now, approaching my fifth decade of ministry, I no longer feel any compunction to join this or any movement.

This is why the exercise of the supernatural gifts of healing and exorcism, and kingdom preaching remain the center-pole of my ministry. In this, I share the gifts, empowerment, and endument that the Twelve enjoyed (after all the same Holy Spirit that indwelt Jesus and the Twelve inhabits my regenerated spirit). I say this with this caveat: among these Twelve, certain ones penned the Gospels, Letters, and Epistles comprising the New Testament. None of this aspect of apostolic ministry is available to anyone after them (including today). Certainly, this caveat applies to my ministry; the blessed Book is a closed Canon.

Therefore, my apostolic ministry is more like the eight apostles whose names are mentioned in the New Testament along with the Eleven and Paul. Still, I rejoice in knowing that through the exercise of my healing, exorcism, and kingdom preaching gifts, I have functioned like my New Testament counterparts.

Third, my fear is that those who minister as apostles from the context of such a movement must function differently. The analogy that comes to mind is that of a lion in the jungle vs. one living in a zoo. Captivity renders him incapable of functioning in the wild, i.e., to protect himself from other predators or provide for his own needs. Likewise, I fear (rightly or wrongly I am not completely sure) that such an association might render me unable to fully and freely exercise the supernatural gifts as my first century counterparts wielded.

Fourth, the appearance of this "fifth" gift two centuries ago flies in the face of two factors observable throughout church history. From the Upper Room until today, church history contains widespread evidence of apostolic ministries impacting their generation; no hiatus existed for the first 1800 years.

To support my point, consider the amount of apostolic ministry that church history records as flourishing in two eras. First, the Reformation era: It was a period when the true church rediscovered the infallibility of the Scriptures, and that the key to eternal salvation was by grace through faith.

How could that have happened without the pioneering, breakthrough apostoling that took place by the Holy Spirit's anointing and calling?

Next, mentally fast-forward two centuries to the great missionary era. These pages of church history are dominated by godly men and women trekking off to places as far away as the other side of the moon to transform entire nations, and in the process sacrificing themselves on the altar of missionary service.

Think of those who opened up dangerous, inaccessible places, buried wives and precious children, and entered the ground before a ripe old age because they had been called to the apostolic ministry. How could they have hoped to bear fruit without the demonstration of the supernatural gifts?

Looking more broadly, throughout the history of the church, people whom we will never hear about went about exercising this gift in its fullness. I cannot conceive that what the Holy Spirit began with such power on the heels of the Ascension, He suddenly pulled back from exercising as He had through the ministries of Paul and the Eleven until two hundred years ago.

Fifth, throughout its twenty centuries of existence the church had access to the Word of God, the catalyst to accomplishing the goals stated in the above Ephesians passage. I find it fascinating that a group of true believers congregating about the Word, surrendered to the Holy Spirit, can manifest any or all of these five gifts even without any outside assistance.

Therefore, I am happy to support the ideas that this movement advocates which I know to be true from my own ministering experience. One more caveat: one should not conclude by my reluctance to join this movement a tacit rejection of its contentions. I do "amen" many of the things its leaders teach concerning this gift and its exercise without climbing aboard. Further, I warmly regard many excellent pastors, teachers, and true believers who hold to the view that both this "movement" and I embrace.

So, then, if I choose not to embrace the moment's reason for my Apostleship, what are my reasons for insisting that my giftedness conforms to the New Testament model? Again, this is not the same as opposing these excellent folk.

Reasons for Capitalizing the Word

First, permit me to repeat two important caveats. First, some aspect of the Twelve's level of giftedness can never be duplicated. All of them defined the doctrine we know as Christianity, and some put it on paper, without error. Not all of the twenty apostles listed in the New Testament had the use of this unique area of supernatural giftedness. Likewise, today, this aspect is not available at al. To prove this, we only need to examine the last verse of the New Testament. It warns that anyone attempting to add to the revelation that begins in the first verse of Genesis and concludes with the last one will be divinely cursed. True; we may receive insights (Greek word, "*rhema*"), but we never receive a new revelation worthy of being added to the New Testament. Second, people whose souls belong to the Savior and who are precious in His sight do hold views opposing these I shall now present.

That said, in what areas does our use of the gift mirror that of the Upper Room generation? While the reasons occupy the remainder of this book, permit me to summarize the tenets of my argument.

PART 2: REFUTING PROPONENTS WHO SPELL APOSTLE WITH A SMALL "A"

The arguments proposing that our Apostleship, as commissioned by Christ, and exercising the gifts demonstrated in the New Testament is no longer relevant in this 21st century need to be answered.

Permit me to summarize each, and provide refutation.

1. Apostles saw risen Christ. We know of eight apostles in addition to the Eleven' many make no claim to having seen the resurrected Savior.
2. The Twelve were given a special calling to lay the lay the church's foundation. This point we agree with. We have been engaged in such work for many decades.

   Peter expresses their authority: "Beloved, I now write to you this second epistle...that you may be mindful of the words which were spoken before by the holy prophets, and of the commandment of us, the apostles of the Lord and Savior" (2 Pet. 3:1-2).

   Yet, when meeting in a church council or Presbytery, the apostles did not exercise a separate autocratic authority. "When the question of the observance of the Mosaic ritual by Gentile Christians arose at Antioch and was referred to Jerusalem, it was 'the apostles and elders' who met to discuss it (Acts 15:2, 6, 22), and the letter returned to Antioch was written in the name of 'apostles and the elders, brethren' (verse. 23)."
3. In arguing against succession, the critics are correct. The Roman Catholic Church promotes the idea that Peter became the fixed and settled apostle in Rome (who as the head of the apostles was the first pope); that he transmitted to successors the same power and authority he possessed; and each successor is authorized to pass it on unto this day. This is patently incorrect.

   What we argue is that from the command from Christ to the Twelve given just before His Ascension, became a function of the Holy Spirit to bestow on individual in each succeeding generation (i.e., the bestowal of the gift of evangelism) was passed on from one regenerate spiritual leader to the next until now. The fact that it exists without a political structure makes it remarkable.

   The only ecclesiastical linkages seems to be that one congregation of regenerate members ordained and laid hands on individuals who went forth to serve as a Sent One (apostle).
4. Claim that upon a true apostle, the Savior bestowed gifts of healing and exorcism is true. Again, our own track record confirms this. We bear witness that God has used us to heal and deliver many, without fanfare, or manipulative appeals, or secret agenda

to use these gifts to generate revenue or build personal prestige. As Paul declared:

"And through the hands of the apostles many signs and wonders were done among the people" (5:12; cf. 3:6-11; 5:15-16; etc.). The verb tense (imperfect) indicates that miracles "continued taking place." When Paul and Barnabas preached, the Lord "was bearing witness to the word of His, granting signs and wonders to be done by their hands" (Ac. 14:3).

The apostles had the ability to perform authenticating sign miracles. Note, the apostle Paul tells the Corinthians that the miracles he performed proved his apostolic authority. "Truly the signs of an apostle were accomplished among you with all perseverance, in signs and wonders and mighty deeds" (2 Cor. 12:12).

This revelation is significant because it shows that if such signs and wonders were common in Paul's day, this statement would have made no impact, since it proved nothing.

Therefore, rather than disproving modern day apostles, the credible evidence of their existence proves that the Apostle's ministry continues in this century.

5. Purpose for All Gifts Not Yet Fulfilled. The purposes for which God bestowed these gifts, as expressed in Ephesians 4:11-16, are not concluded. Therefore, the gift in its fullness remains as relevant as it was in the first century. To appreciate this position, consider this question: For what purpose did Christ give these five gifts to the church?

These gifts are given at the discretion of Jesus, working through the Holy Spirit (1 Corinthians 12:11) for the equipping of the saints for the work of ministry that the body of Christ would be built up (expanded and strengthened). For what purpose? Paul answers this question: "*Until we all come to the unity of the faith and the knowledge of the Son of God to a perfect man in order that we should no longer be...tossed about....*" Notice how this statement jibes with both the ultimate purpose of God (Ephesians 1:10) and the mystery of God revealed through Paul (Ephesians 3:6).

The goal of the exercise of these gifts is to bring true believers and congregations to maturity. These gifts are to produce stability in individual lives as well as the local church.

As mentioned, since these goals are not complete then the office of apostleship, life its four counterparts, remains viable to this day. Further, since these four gifts operate as they did in the Book of Acts, then there is no logical explanation for assuming that the apostolic gift would operate differently.

PART 3: PERSONAL CONFIRMATION OF A BIG 'A' PROPONENT

As we conclude this chapter, permit me to share evidence for my "Big 'A' Apostleship. It will also serve to provide you with a sense of the way the remainder of this Volume One shall take.

1. *Our Mindset is Kingdom-centric*

Without a mindset, insanity ensues. With so life throwing so much information at your brain, you have no choice to develop ways to filter out the extraneous. Further, when you engage in an important mission, you must stay focus. As a result, you develop a sophisticated set of protocol questions; they function like an algorithm. Every one of the other four gift categories has their own algorithm to simplify the decision-making process they face in accomplishing their calling.

The Apostle's mindset is kingdom-centric. Contrast this with that of the Pastor who has a church-centered mindset. In the next section, BOOK TWO, you will learn about this in great detail. However, suffice it now for me to show you that the Apostle's kingdom-centered mindset uniquely identifies him. It enables him to see his mission as to a culture or nation, and to influence its worldviews and establish a foundation upon which the other gifts can build.

Permit me to briefly sketch why this mindset is so necessary for the apostolic ministry. First, among his important responsibilities include governing, leading, and vision casting—all of which require him to prioritize his tasks and functions. Second, since he is sent, he must develop filters to ensure he can always deal with the cultural implications, enemy threats, and opportunities to advance his agenda of outcomes as he ministers "on site". Trust me, without this kingdom mindset; the Apostle's ministry has no chance for success.

What is fascinating is that the development of such a mindset comes naturally to one gifted with an apostleship, whereas, the pastor naturally thinks with a church-centered mindset. The presence of this kingdom-centric mindset marks my calling as genuinely apostolic.

2. Our Ministry Outcomes match those of First-century Apostles

We straddle two aspects of the kingdom: we want to facilitate individuals finding salvation, but we do so in the context of ministering to the nation/culture as a whole. We are foundation-layers. That which we construct will form the basis for all the church planting, training, and outreach that follows on our heels.

Therefore, our ministry has three outcomes not necessarily uppermost in the minds of those with the other gifts mentioned in Ephesians 5:11, 12. After I explain them to you, the difference will be most evident. They are to inculcate within the culture, the following three qualities: i) the fear-of-the-Lord; ii) Divine favor; and, iii) stable, tranquil wholeness. Permit me to amplify how the apostolic gift-set works to bring about these outcomes. I will describe them only minimally since we devote BOOK FOUR to a complete discussion regarding them.

Outcome: Fear-of-the-Lord

The seminar aspect of our ministry emphasizes this attitude, so unique that only the Holy Spirit can bestow it upon a redeemed heart. Nevertheless, as the true believers model this 'grace', the officials in the government, and the leaders of its major institutions begin to appreciate that when people, in their attitudes, begin to embrace this value, then the need for prisons diminishes, for the simple reason that with this attitude, the people police themselves.

This attitude can also trigger vision casting, self-assessment, and humility. This attitude is also the key to unity, since people begin to be willing to subordinate the meeting of their own needs to meet those of others. This attitude also fires up individuals to take responsibility for improving their own life situations.

Outcome: Divine Favor

Many years ago a High School, the Boiler that creates the steam to heat a three-story edifice blew up, destroying the school. Fortunately, no students were present. The Principal, while shaving, had pondered if the previous night's snowfall was sufficient to warrant canceling classes, decided to do just that. It turned out that no other Principal had cancelled classes. So, when the bell announcing the first Period's classes rang, no students took their seats. As a result, when the rubble buried ever seat and locker, not one life was lost. Newspaper headlines barked, "God Saves Eddystone High!" The Principal gave the Lord the credit. As you can imagine, many attended their church's worship services the following Sunday. Certainly, many more were suddenly freshly aware of the closeness and accessibility of the Lord to hear and answer the prayers they would ask.

We use the supernatural gifts of the Spirit to demonstrate His Presence, His Sufficiency to deal with sickness, and release troubled souls from demonic slavery, and His willingness to work on behalf of anyone and everyone without discrimination. For people to move toward Him, they must first believe that He is, and that He is rewards those who seek His help.

For this purpose, foundation building requires that we fulfill this outcome: to create the sense of, and longing for His divine favor. This evidence is so compelling because all can see that neither they nor we did anything to produce it—God did it. Suddenly, they experience the uplifting thought: the God of the Bible is alive and well and is now working in our midst. You can imagine how this strengthens their sense of significance, and nudges them toward community-building.

Outcome: "Shalom"

When we arrive in the country to which God sends us, we inevitably find daily headlines of crime, exploitation, and turmoil pervades the society's life. Then the Spirit begins to transform lives, set spirits free, renew hearts, and create palpable change. From the pulpit, we begin to explain that their nation was meant for the same kind of stability that individuals enjoy in Christ. We make the case that to embrace biblical values; the nation will reduce its budget outlay for prisons, police, and execution chambers. The reason is that by His transformation, people experience the reality of His love, see firsthand His power, and when they are able for the first time to view life through the eyes of a mind made whole, they begin to approach life with true hope.

We speak to the culture in order to free its people so they can pursue the best for themselves and those they love. As a result of the peace Jesus provides, they can now proactively seek His will and believe in the possibilities of all things thanks to His anointing power, instead of always having to live on the defense .i.e., always having to act with the inevitable possibility that bad things and people are in pursuit of them.

These are the key qualities that move a nation toward sustainability; that free its people to vision-cast; that elevate the quality of life at the cultural as well as individual levels. For these reasons, and many you will learn about later, the apostle's mission seeks to fulfill these unique outcomes.

Incidentally, in BOOK THREE we discuss at length the outcomes we seek to accomplish in our apostolic ministry.

3. We use the Tools of First-century Apostles

After nearly five decades of ministry, we could no more venture across the oceans to fulfill apostolic missions without implementing it than we would board a plane without with a credit card. This will become clear as we now describe the other gifts we use that are associated with the apostolic skill set. Permit me to segregate their treatment according to their area of usefulness: generating spiritual resources; deliverance, and pulpit ministry.

Fasting and Prayer: Tools used in Tandem

In our apostolic ministry, we use two tools in tandem—prayer and fasting. They accomplish their divinely designed joint-purpose with the finesse of a couple figure skating.

We could no more operate with them than the carpenter could build without a hammer and saw, or an artist could paint without brushes and canvass. They are so vital to our spiritual progress that their loss would render our ministry powerless.

Therefore, we will help you to first understand the nature of biblical fasting, and, and then show you how to connect it to intercessory prayer. As a result, you will understand why such faith is so crucial to the apostolic ministry (i.e., it defines it). Transforming a nation requires faith capable of moving mountains and casting out demons; and for that to happen consistently, we must employ these two apostolic tools in tandem.

As a result, you will know how to preparing for spiritual warfare, smashing strongholds, facilitating breakthroughs, and making important decisions.

Deliverance Toolkit

Christian deliverance means God rescuing someone from bondage, oppression, hardship, or domination by evil. This truth is at the heart of the Lord's Prayer, "Deliver us from the evil one," (Mat 6:12-13). When people received deliverance from works of Satan, it is called exorcism. Freeing them from infirmity, disease, etc., involves healing. Besides the obvious benefit of these gifts to satanically trapped individuals, the use of these tools also demonstrates the reality, viability, and relevance of the kingdom of God, thereby aiding its expansion. Could any motive more clearly prove that the use of these gifts serves the purpose for which Jehovah-Rophi calls apostles?

Healing Gift as a Deliverance Tool

In our meetings, we encounter problems that are scary to behold. Nevertheless, people turn to the Savior for healing, and after decades, we bear witness that He is so faithful and merciful, not only removing the consequences of evil, but also restoring the individual to wholeness. The purpose of healing is to destroy the harmful effects inflicted by the Evil One. Therefore we devote a chapter to presenting the purpose, and process of healing. You will also meet a man who influenced my thinking in this area. Finally, we will share with you our efforts in research and dealing with some of the top causes of death. We consider these 'immune-deficiency' problems, chronic and infectious diseases as preventable and curable. You will see how through the gift of healing, the laying on of hands and the spoken Word, God has left the church a way to destroy the works of Satan.

Gift of Exorcism as a Deliverance Tool

As the healing gift offers the promise of freedom from disease and disability, so this gift promises escape from malevolent invisible spiritual forces seeking to impose sinister wills. Exorcism was integral to Jesus' earthly ministry. Therefore, we devote a chapter to discussing the origin of demons, how they use sexual enticement, fear-casting, why they inhabit human bodies, and why cultures that Jesus sends Apostles to confront are overwhelmed with the influence of the Evil One and his minions. Also, you will learn about the territories of influence that demons inhabit and over which we have control.

Repentance as a Tool

No aspect of our apostolic ministry is more important than preaching the Gospel and conducting the seminars to transform a nation. What moves hearts to embrace our individual message of salvation as well as act on the principles and Laws of our transforming message? Nothing occurs at the deepest spiritual level until the Holy Spirit acts in power; and only one thing prompts Him to action—repentance. It sets in motion a divine process that enables the repentant sinner to replace all God-dishonoring, Christ-belittling perceptions and dispositions and purposes with those that treasure God, and exalt Jesus, i.e., be born again. Therefore, we devote a chapter to understanding it completely.

Kingdom Preaching as a Tool

Preaching is as vital our apostolic ministry as a paddle is to a canoe caught in rapids. We have no choice since the One who commissioned me to apostolic ministry made it the centerpiece of His ministry strategy. Therefore, we devote a chapter to analyzing all aspects of this form of pulpit ministry.

In BOOK FOUR we shall discuss at length all of the tools we use in our apostolic ministry. There you will also discover evidence confirming our own level of supernatural giftedness.

4. Our Calling was not by Human Appointment

I started out to become a physician. The call to the ministry was a surprise, albeit, a welcome one. Nevertheless, He chose me. As I responded, the gifts bestowed on me became increasingly evident. Therefore, I did nothing to gain this calling, I felt no need to justify or explain it. All any critic then and now would need to do would be to follow our ministry, observe the exercise of gifts, and examine the fruit produced by our seminars transform people's worldviews. They would also see that the need for this gift remains as critical today as it was in the Upper Room generation.

In truth, one viewing our ministry over these past five decades of ministry would find solid reason to see a spiritual gift-set consistent with those described in the new Testament (except canonical revelation).

SUMMARY OF CHAPTER

Why does this restoration matter? Because only this gift, miraculously validated, is capable of spearheading such a missionary like task; no other spiritual gift need apply.

Unless we restore "apostle" to the role it enjoyed in the New Testament, I fear that the resultant concept, although labeled 'church', will not be worthy of the word of which Christ is its cornerstone.

As surely as the success of the first-century church born in the Upper Room was due to the leadership and gifts of the Apostles, so the final century will owe its effectiveness to that major category of giftedness, and its employment of those same supernatural gifts.

...Now that we understand the nature, purpose, and relevance of this gift, we are ready to explore its special mindset.

Book II

The Apostle's Mindset

Chapter 1   Makings of a Mindset

Chapter 2   God's Perfect Plan: The Kingdom of God

Chapter 3   Wrapping Our Brain Around the Kingdom Mindset

Introduction and Overview

IN RETROSPECT, THEY MUST have thought this axiom to apply, "no good deed goes unpunished". What had begun as an introspective church-group discussion was suddenly an international *phenom* with its own jewelry line. For a public moment, "WWJD" was almost as ubiquitous as the Nike 'Swoosh'.

Why was it easier to stiff-arm a Tsunami than to keep "What Would Jesus Do" from becoming the alpha-topic of every talk-show, and sermon? The answer matters, because it also provides a breath-taking insight into what makes the apostolic mind "tick", and his important thinking tool—the Kingdom Mindset.

Why is a mindset so helpful? First, life throws more information than any brain is capable of processing; to preserve sanity, we must develop a way of systematically filtering out the relevant stuff from the extraneous. Second, God created humans with four core needs: hope, belonging, significance, and meaning/purpose. Since gratifying those eats up about 23 or every 24 hours, we need to sift through an on-going incoming stream of data for that which will help us with these top needs.

Enter the mindset; this device enables us to filter all incoming data, using an elaborate set of protocols. Functioning like algorithms, they simplify one's decision-making process. It provides an early-alert system to spot approaching problems, and tag innocuous-appearing information for possible future review.

You can see how this serves the apostle. A highly sensitive kingdom mindset enables him to stay on mission until he has accomplished that for which the Holy Spirit has called him to do in a specific place. It is such a valuable "tool", and for these reasons. First, his primary role is that of governing. This requires him to prioritize.

Second, being "sent", he therefore needs to maintain a finely tuned sensitivity to all incoming data so that he is able to deal with cultural implications, and not commit some *faux pas* with the potential to derail his mission.

Third, his mission has a clearly defined ultimate outcome

> "Then I saw a new heaven and a new earth, for the first heaven and the first earth had passed away, and the sea was no more. And I saw the holy city, New Jerusalem, coming down out of heaven from God, prepared as a bride adorned for her husband. And I heard a loud voice from the throne saying, "Behold, the dwelling place of God is with man. He will dwell with them, and they will be his people, and God himself will be with them as their God. He will wipe away every tear from their eyes, and death shall be no more, neither shall there be mourning, nor crying, nor pain anymore, for the former things have passed away." (Rev 21:1-4 ESV)

Therefore, this kingdom mindset enables him to focus vigilantly on incoming data for early signs of people, and ideas relevant to his mission, as well as threatening opposing forces.

Regarding enemy threats, he has no choice. He must fulfill his mission in the midst of a destiny-defining war raging between Jesus God and Satan to control every square inch of creation, and minute of time. This mindset keeps him "on his toes".

With the Ascension, the Twelve, in partnership with the risen Son of God, operating through the governance of the indwelling Holy Spirit, the fulfillment of the Kingdom took a decided turn toward the final stage of fulfillment. Since the apostle becomes directly engaged in this ongoing process, he requires a kingdom mindset in order to have a prayer of successfully doing his part.

Book Two focuses on this subject to provide you a clear understanding of this mindset so integral to the apostle, we shall answer three questions, organized into three chapters: *What is a mindset? What does the Bible mean by the term, Kingdom of God?* And, *what is a kingdom mindset?* The third chapter, we will construct it from information provided in the first two chapters.

With a mindset, the apostolic mind becomes like that of the Irish Wolf Hound. This gigantic dog (150 lbs) is built for speed; his over-sized chest cavity, and enormously long legs serve this purpose, beautifully. He resembles a Greyhound. Good thing; he survives by capturing his favorite entree—wolf. To catch and kill one, he locates it, and then chases it, sometimes for nearly 20 hours. Finally, the exhausted wolf collapses; no strength remains to defend itself. Supper occurs in short-order.

The kingdom mindset, as you are about to discover, is one of the Apostle's most valuable tools. Like the Irish Wolf Hound, the kingdom mindset enables him remain single-minded, on-task, and vigilant for the ever-present dangers that inhabit the vicious hostile spiritual environment in which he must operate.

As you will learn, the Kingdom mindset is as essential to the apostle's mission as his calling, authority, and gift-set.

Chapter 1

Makings of a Mindset

People have no choice; they must make sense out of the world they interact in.

Unfortunately, the amount, complexity and ambiguity of incoming data exceed the human brain's capacity to absorb or process. To solve this problem, we all establish a filtration process—a mindset—to help us select what to choose as well as ignore.

The mindset is universal; everybody has one. Think of it as a fixed group of foundational assumptions to help you make decisions. Drastic change can influence it, but, generally, once it is set, altering it is akin to removing the odor of skunk-spray.

Your mindset is not only invaluable for providing guidance and solving problems; it also helps satisfy one of your essential human need—to belong. Planting yourself within a community of people who operate on the same mental "wavelength" is a sure way to maximize your pleasure and peace of mind, as well as minimize your need for guard- dogs, and legal fees. This is also the same mental process used to join up with a leader, whose views sufficiently mirror yours that you view the benefits of joining his cause to outweigh the risks.

Some mindsets are easy to pinpoint. Thanks to Paul, we know the mindset of Jesus:

> ...who, though he was in the form of God, did not count equality with God a thing to be grasped, but made himself nothing, taking the form of a servant, being born in the likeness of men. And being found in human form, he humbled himself by becoming obedient to the point of death, even death on a cross." (Phil. 2:1).

His apostolic mindset explains how the One who owned all of creation could spend nights without decent lodging, and, although missing many meals, could feed 5000 at will. This mindset also explains what drove the Author of Life to will such an ignominious death.

Likewise, the Apostolic mindset resembles that of Jesus: it takes up its cross, subordinating its own personal pleasures to conform to His Word and will. The apostle thinks like Jesus.

PART 1: MINDSET AS A TOOL

To repeat, think of a mindset as a tool for making decisions, especially those that are mission-relevant. To help us navigate the ever-changing path toward a mission's accomplishment, people construct a set of pre-determined test questions, sequentially arranged to guide them through decision-making. This process is called an *algorithm*. The following well-known example demonstrates how an algorithm works.

How Processing Works

To help you understand how an algorithm works—the test questions it prescribes to determine the solution to a problem—permit me share this well-known example. It is designed to find out why a desk-lamp does not work.

To solve this problem, use the following set of "yes" or "no" test questions:

Test Question #1: Is lamp plugged in? Options:
1. Answer is "no". Plug it in to solve the problem.
2. Answer is "yes", Problem is not solved, so proceed to second Question.

Test Question #2: Is the bulb burned out? Options:
1. Answer is yes. Replace with a new bulb; problem is solved.
2. Answer is "no". Problem is not solved; proceed to next question.

Test Question #3: To light the desk, should we fix the lamp? Options:
1. Answer is "yes", because we have the skills, time, and tools. Repair solves problem.
2. Answer is "no". We proceed to next question

Test Question #4: Where to purchase new lamp? Options:
1. We spot one on sale at Wal-Mart.

Notice that by asking and answering the sequential questions, the problem is solved. As a result, we know the cause of our problem, and how to solve it, i.e., get the light on again.

Notice that this process begins with an initial state. It then proceeds through a well-defined series of successive states, each with its own one-at-a-time sequence of questions, options and instructions. The process arrives at a final state, which is defined as where problem is solved.

Perhaps you are computer savvy, and you see in this process a resemblance to that of a computer program; you are right. The system that John von Neumann outlined in 1945 was a similar, albeit, complex algorithm. Like the simple process above, the computer gets one instruction, performs it, and then gets a next instruction. The "questions" used for each step of process are kept in an area called "memory", along with instructions on how to ask them.

Since a mindset is constructed from a pre-programmed set of instruction, enabling it to make decisions that keep it focused on its mission, one might think that it is synonymous to another filtration process, called "world view". They are different.

What a Mindset is not

To expand our understanding of what comprises a mindset, let us examine two things that are different from it: worldview, and enculturation.

Mindset vs. World View

True; confusing a mindset with a worldview is easy; the resemblance is close. One constructs a worldview from a set of assumptions and beliefs about life and the universe. that enable one to view and interpret life.

The questions that form the protocols of a worldview are universal in scope. They define that which forms the bedrock of the subconscious mind. Only two things have proven to be effective in changing a mindset, emigration, and regeneration. They provide you with an overall perspective to view and interpret all of life with these core questions:
- Who am I?
- Where did I come from?
- Where am I going?

- What is true? What is false?
- Does God exist?
- What is His nature?
- What response does He require from me?

As you can see, a worldview operates at the deepest level of one's subconscious.

It is shaped by all surrounding influences. Religion, philosophy, ethics, morality, science, politics and all other belief systems also play a role in forming it. It is impervious to change; research shows that only the Holy Spirit is capable of changing it. It is so all encompassing that holding it is equivalent to living in the culture it defines.

However, a mindset differs from a worldview in several ways. First, it can be changed, whereas the worldview is almost impervious to change. Second, a mindset is mission-specific; it is designed to evaluate only the relevance and significance of any issue it confronts to the mission it seeks to accomplish; it does not govern all thinking. Third, a mindset can function in any culture.

Mindset vs. Culture

Again, the resemblance is close enough to suggest they are interchangeable.

The word culture, from the Latin *colo, -ere*, with its root meaning "to cultivate", generally refers to patterns of human activity and the symbolic structures that give such activity significance. Different definitions of "culture" reflect different theoretical bases for understanding, or criteria for evaluating, human activity. Anthropologists most commonly use the term "culture" to refer to the universal human capacity to classify, codify and communicate their experiences symbolically.

Culture centers on human activities, a system of shared beliefs, values, customs, behaviors, and artifacts that the members of society use to cope with their world and with one another, which they transmit from generation to generation through learning. Experts call this process, enculturation.

This is important; a kingdom mindset enables the apostle to penetrate the culture of any people-group on the planet. He can accomplish his mission why observing, adapting to, and respecting the tenets of their culture. However, his freedom to adapt to their attitudes and behaviors ends at the point that they infringe on his ability to accomplish his mission.

As a result, the people God has sent him to serve are able to perceive him to understand and respect them, and feel that they share the approach to dealing with problems and opportunities.

A Secular Model: MNC Mindset

The mindset essential to leading a Multi-National Corporation ("MNC") and the one an apostle uses are strikingly similar. Understanding the former's thinking will help you understand ours.

A Secular Global Mindset

The most essential goal of any business is to get people to give it money. To accomplish this it exchanges its resources (time, talent, technology, etc.) to create a product or service that customers perceive a need sufficient to shelling out their money.

Accomplishing this on a street corner with a fast-food product like "Double-Doubles" (a Trinidadian treat) is one thing; but to accomplish this simultaneously in several cultures and for many markets (globally) requires a very different mindset.

Mindset's Global Aspect

As individuals meet informational overload by incorporating a filtration process, likewise, corporations, being a collection of persons, do likewise. Therefore the mindset is a group of protocols by which a company organizes itself, distributes decision-making power and influence, as well as perceives and interprets the world about them.

Definition of Global Mindset

People operating with the secular equivalent of a kingdom mindset lead a Multinational Corporation ("MNC"). Therefore, let us examine how the MNC's global mindset functions.

As Percy Barnevik is the architect of The ABB Group, a global presence in the field of power and automation technologies, and its first CEO. He provides us with some of the traits of this mindset that a good global manager would exhibit:

- He is exceptionally open mindedness

- He maintains a profound respect for how different countries do things and why
- He is always pushing the limits of those cultures
- He never buys into this idea: "you can't do that in (blank) country because of the unions, or government 'red tape!'"
- He is always sorting through cultural information for opportunities to innovate.

As you can see, a global mindset is sensitive to the differences of other cultures and ready to adapt to this diversity. Notice that it combines an openness to as well as an awareness of diversity across cultures and markets along with a propensity and ability to synthesize across this diversity.

To appreciate the value of a global mindset, observe Microsoft's entry into the Chinese software market. Beijing presented Bill Gates with the opportunity for enormous sales. But there were also perils: rampant software piracy; fickle, unpredictable public policy tendency; and, a market whose size lags behind those of more economically developed countries.

Nevertheless, Microsoft's penetration into this vast Asian market worked because it saw events in China from a more integrative global perspective, and adjusted its profit-projections to longer time periods.

What made them successful was a balanced global mindset. That mindset, in terms of ministry is what makes the kingdom mindset so critical to a successful apostolic ministry.

What makes this global mindset so valuable? First, it enables the apostle to move into other cultures without becoming a prisoner of diversity. Second, it is able to build cognitive bridges across these needs and between these needs and the apostle's own experience and capabilities.

Summary

Was this secular model helpful? Let us take the principles learned back to our discussion of the global mindset the apostle uses—the kingdom mindset.

You will recall that we began by presenting a simple spiritual algorithm created by that youth group based on this question: What Would Jesus Do (WWJD)? As we conclude this introductory section, let me share with you another example of such a spiritual algorithm. It shows how valuable such a set of test questions can be to a true believer 'walking the walk". In doing so, it will help you appreciate the importance of a kingdom mindset to the apostolic ministry.

People embrace the WWJD algorithm because it enables them to compress a large amount of key processing data, thereby improving their ability to live the Christian life. It enables them to evaluate the issues they encounter using one simple question: *in this situation, here and now, what would Jesus do?* Face it, WWJD is a beautifully simple but effective decision-making tool.

It works because it is aligned with Biblical theology. If not, the results could be disastrous, as we learn from observing the bad algorithm made famous in Charles Sheldon's book, *In His Steps: What would Jesus Do*.

Ranked as the tenth-most-read book in the world it tells the story of a tramp who challenges a church of self-satisfied Midwestern congregants to live up to their declaration of faith.

Then, in their midst, the tramp drops dead. After the shock resides, the people and pastor, pledge to live for one year asking, "What would Jesus do?" It then details how they suffered, faced ridicule, but emerged victorious. His goal was to inspire other churches throughout the country to do the same.

Sheldon grew up in the Dakota Territory in a Christian home with Indians as his closest companions. After Brown University, Andover Newton Theological Seminary, and a brief pastorate, he took a pastorate in Topeka Kansas. His vision for his ministry was to preach "...a Christ for the common people".

To this end he then spent many hours each week following workers, the unemployed, freed slaves, etc. around. Soon, he published these sermons in a book entitled, *In His Steps*, which he subtitled, "What Would Jesus Do? The book became a national best-seller.

Sheldon's approach was to try to formulate a mindset that could enable any Christian successfully to navigate any fork in the road of life with a universal question. Nevertheless, his direction for processing this question proved that a mindset is only as valuable as the sound Biblical logic used to process it, and the goal it seeks to fulfill.

Charles Sheldon's legacy attempted to offer a universal question to resolve spiritual decision-making crossroad. , *In His Steps, What would Jesus do*, based on bad theology, led to disastrous consequences. Myriad liberal pulpits touted it as a spiritual algorithm, a dictum by which the Christian could practice his faith. Even humanists used it, since its message is sufficiently ambiguous. Anybody can something out of which to build a slogan and prompt people to follow.

Even now, liberal pulpits use it to promote their Social Gospel. Proponents of Liberation Theology love its humanistic "do-gooder" message. Why not—by denigrating Christianity's true message of salvation by faith through grace, and reducing our blessed Lord Jesus from being the Savior of mankind to a model revolutionary, on a par with the likes of the revolutionaries and megalomaniac, Karl Marx and psychopath, Che Guevara, it beautifully serves their purpose.

Nevertheless, the value of a good mindset remains a most useful tool for anyone. However, before we describe this to you, you must first understand what is meant by the term, "kingdom", as in Kingdom of God.

So, brace yourself; you are about to come face to face with one of the two most powerful organizations on earth, and locked in mortal combat for its control. They impact every event reported on each evening's news. Only one seeks to serve the best interests of the Christian.

Chapter 2

God's Perfect Plan: The Kingdom of God

If Pastors, evangelists, and teachers function with a church-mindset, what thinking guides the apostle? His is a kingdom mindset.

This question matters, because, in order to implement the nation-transforming strategy you are about to learn, you must acquire a kingdom mindset; it differs dramatically from a church-mindset.

In this chapter, I intend to explain this "kingdom mindset". To that end, I will inform you as to its Biblical and theological definition; provide you with insight into its nature and function, and even clarify what it is not.

As a result of what you learn in this chapter, as well as the knowledge you gained from previous chapter regarding the nature of a mindset, you will be able to appreciate our discussion in the next chapter on what are a kingdom mindset, and its role in an apostolic ministry.

PART 1: DEFINING "KINGDOM"

The people who heard Jesus and John the Baptist use the term "kingdom", possessed an understanding of its meaning sufficient to pass a college-level quiz. However, the rest of us must construct one. To this end, we will begin by examining the morphological meaning of the word.

Biblical Description of the term, Kingdom of God

Let us begin at the headwaters: analyzing the Hebrew root: *Malkut* and its Greek equivalent, *Basilea*.

Hebrew Roots:

Recall that we looked at the makeup of the Hebrew word for apostle to find the originally intended meaning. Here we shall gain similar valuable insight by looking at the root word, Malkut, "king".

Again, to refresh your thinking, recall the standard Hebrew word is comprised of three core consonants. This word is a noun, translated as "Kingship (Kingdom). Its core letters are *Mem + Lamed + Koph*. (I will not bore you by writing them backward (as the Jewish language would insist). By analyzing each, a picture of the true meaning of kingdom emerges:

- Mem ("Mah" is original pronunciation) is a letter shaped like waves of water. The pictogram suggests these ideas:
  1. "Glue"- that which holds all things together (glue was made by boiling hides and skimming the sticky floating residue, which they used as glue);
  2. "Unknown (because Israel bordered the Mediterranean Sea, a mysterious realm beyond the horizon where a ship could sink without a trace.
  3. 'Chaos" (as a storm at sea would produce for a ship caught in it).
- Lamed ("Lam") is a letter shaped like a shepherd's staff. This tool, vital to the shepherd, suggests these ideas:
  1. used to push or pull sheep in a desired direction;
  2. gave authority;
  3. also, could be used to bind oxen together
- Koph (Kaph): the shape of this pictogram is that of an open palm with the fingers extended upward, which was intended to suggest these nuances of meaning:
  1. Submission (as in surrender)
  2. Bending the will; and
  3. Subduing those within his control (Both ideas suggested by the image of the fingers bending to something held in the palm of one's hand)

From these pictograms, this aggregate meaning emerges: a kingdom is a territory within which those who legitimately belong to it enjoy an environment safe, stable, cohesive, without a fear of the unknown, and with a clear sense of divine direction.

The Hebrew word for the one who exercises the rule of a kingdom is "*Malek*"; the word employs the same core consonants. Therefore, we may conclude that this ruler of a kingdom is one who assumes responsibility to protect, provide, and lead forward those he holds power over, no matter what issues arise so that his people live relatively free of instability, chaos, trials, and the unknown beyond the borders of his domain.

Greek Equivalent: *Basilea*

While the Greek language enabled much more sophisticated communications, the essence of the word for kingdom remained relatively the same. However, the Greek term added this idea: the one ruling it, occupied the throne, lawfully; he was not a usurper.

Origin of the Word, Kingdom

Where did the idea of king and kingdom arise? Societies were originally organized around a set of commonly shared beliefs and practices; these identified them, gave them a sense of community.

Naturally, such a community requires order and protection from external threats. To accommodate its need for governance and protection, those with leadership skills emerged. As these people proved themselves, more power was vested in them by those depending on them, and being served by them. The earliest kings ruled city-kingdoms.

Similarly, after YHWH established His covenant with Abraham, Abraham called him "king". Later, YHWH revealed to Moses that He would be Israel's true king (Number 33:21; Dt. 33:5). So the Biblical concept of king/kingdom jibes with its secular counterpart.

However, in spite of the Bible providing us with a clear understanding of this term, theologians have managed to embrace different meanings of the kingdom of God.

Various Theological Definitions

Here are the four most dominant views; they represent nearly all of Christendom.

Two Dominant Protestant Interpretations:

1. A widely held view among liberal Protestant denominations is that the Kingdom of God is where people deal with social

problems; it has nothing to do with eternal salvation. Building the Kingdom is tantamount to tackling problems such as poverty, sickness, labor relations, social inequalities, and race relationships. First espoused by liberal theologian, Adolph von Harnack, this view is popular throughout mainline Protestant denominations. It is at the heart of the "Social Gospel."

2. Another view, popularized by Albert Schweitzer, sees the kingdom as something with absolutely no connection with life on this planet until the future time when history will cease.

Dominant Catholic Interpretation:

This view dominates all types of Roman Catholic and Eastern Orthodox Churches: the Kingdom is another name for the church. Augustine first publicized this idea.

Evangelical Interpretation:

This view, built from Scriptural analysis is so complex that we will devote the remainder of this chapter explaining it. George Eldon Ladd, in his acclaimed *Gospel of the Kingdom*, provided an early description of this view, along with an analysis of its Bible support.

How could so many views emerge? Part of the problem lies in the fact that the Biblical concept has a history as old as Adam. It gained substance as the Old Testament developed. With the emergence of John the Baptist, it really gained steam. After Pentecost, and Paul's unique tutelage by the risen Christ, the New Testament captured its meaning in depth, especially focusing on the two final phases, the "Age at hand," and the "Age to Come."

Permit me historically to trace the kingdom's development. This insight will enable us to focus in depth on the meaning of these phases.

PART 2: BIBLICAL DEVELOPMENT OF KINGDOM

Tracing the evolution of this concept, the kingdom of God, you realize how it was in the mind of God all along, and presented, at appropriate times, at each milestone of God's working with man throughout the history of the Old Testament. The confusion that greeted John the Baptist and Jesus need not have occurred. The religious leaders confronting them, following ideas foreign to those in the Word regarding the Messiah's true nature and purpose, caused this mess.

Kingdom's Evolution

Jesus explained (Matthew 25:34) that the Kingdom had existed from the foundation of the world. God was a King to Adam and Eve. He gave them dominion or authority to rule; they were his vice-regents in the Garden of Eden.

After the "Fall", He turned to Abraham who came to true faith in the King of Kings. Then Jesus made His faith the key to gaining entrance into that kingdom. Since these people shared Abraham's faith, they were truly his spiritual offspring. Every human soul that placed its faith in this hope became a member of this kingdom. As promised to Abraham, its constituents—His descendants—would become a great nation. Even kings come from this line (Genesis 17:5-6).

Generation by generation, Abraham's descendants multiplied until they emerged from Egypt, a nation based on that covenant made with Abraham, six million strong. Granted; it was a true kingdom. However, did YHWH lawfully rule it as their King?

Yes, Jehovah's (pre-incarnate Jesus) made a legitimate claim to this throne. He based His claim on two reasons that no political opposition could trump (or deny). First, He had created them by establishing a covenant of grace through Abraham, their progenitor.

Second, He had reached down when they were as helpless as a man in an iron lung and buried in grime and misery without a shred of hope. God then acted, reducing Pharaoh to despair, the religious leaders to charlatans, and the land to physical, moral, emotional, and economic shambles.

He then turned the hearts of every person they met to run to where they stored their life savings and heirlooms, and then press them onto the exiting Jews as farewell gifts. The buckets of precious gold, stones, and silver also bore witness of His ability to provide, preserve, and protect His own people.

Yahweh's power over Satan's dominion over Egypt, using its ten gods to wreck havoc on the people devoted to them, was such a powerful demonstration of the supremacy of His power that His people would never again have reason to fear evil.

Regarding His supernatural ability to care for the needs of His people, permit me this example. The escape required them to cross the most formidable desert—with daytime temperatures reaching nearly 130 degrees Fahrenheit, and nightly lows some 60 degrees lower. Remember, this group included elderly people and young babies; many would not survive such relentless heat. Therefore, YHWH covered them with a cloud. This reduced the surface temperature by about 30 degrees, and created a cooling breeze that chopped off another 15 degrees. As a result, they experienced, each day, a balmy spring experience. At night, YHWH lit a light a glowing fire several stories high; it raised the chilly nighttime air by about 20 degrees, making each as pleasant as he most pleasant Caribbean evening.

Therefore, Israel knew, from day-one, that they served a covenant-keeping, all-powerful, ethical, loving God totally committed to their rescue and destination to the point that He would destroy everything and everyone in their path.

Finally, in the Promised Land, He deposited each family into a fully built furnished home, surrounded by planted crops, vineyards, and pasture, and livestock.

Soon, God raised up a shepherd and invested him with ingenious musical and military skills, and blessed him with a heart so devoted to worshipping and serving Him that David became an archetype of Jesus. It was at David's palace atop a mountain called Zion that God declared it a permanent throne for His kingdom.

Then the kingdom that David had built began to unravel. First, those who occupied the throne of David after his death lacked his devotion to duty to his mission, and to the covenant God. Corruption, incompetence, greed, and evil caused that which the Shepherd-Psalmist had begun to crumble.

As a result, YHWH dismantled it, using the Babylonians. As the blood poured down the streets, God posted Jeremiah on a prominent corner of Jerusalem to remind everybody entering into Captivity of two important encouraging facts. First, that it would end. Second, afterward, He would launch a new plan enabling them to walk worthy, since trying to obey His covenant by law keeping had not worked. He would give them a new heart so they could live before Him as Abraham had (Jer. 31:31-33).

True to His word, and with the precisions of a Swiss watch, God gave them this heart. The means of this provision, along with the process, was announced one fateful day by John the Baptizer: *"Behold the Lamb of God."*, and *"the Kingdom of Heaven is at hand"*.

Unfortunately, the people hearing John announce those words—the Kingdom is at hand—were in such spiritual disarray that they could not appreciate or process them. As a result, they viewed these words as a threat to their hope. This is why so many of their spiritual leaders lashed out at this message. Sadly, even as He confirmed His message with supernatural works, they accused Him of using demonic power.

What were they looking for? From their words, we can piece together what they sought in a Messiah. They longed for another Alexander the Great; a Messiah riding into Jerusalem leading a massive army to drive Rome and all other unwashed from the city's gates.

In short, they were not looking for a spiritual kingdom comprised of citizens transformed by the Holy Spirit and equipped by Him to walk with God as Abraham had. No, thanks to very bad theological instruction they interpreted those verses in the Old Testament speaking about the kingdom of heaven to mean that the Messiah would establish a political kingdom capable of deposing and ruling Rome.

As a result, Jesus had His work cut out. So when He offered Himself as their king, the leaders of Abraham's natural seed (political Israel) completely rejected His offer to populate the kingdom with people possessing a new nature, modeled by Abraham, prophesied by Jeremiah, launched by John the Baptist, secured by the Cross, and empowered by Pentecost.

Granted, we have used many words to provide you with a clear picture of how this term, kingdom of God, developed to the moment Jesus makes it central to His message.

With this background we are ready to focus on the details of this kingdom, especially its two final phases as Jesus labored to clarify.

Uniqueness of Two Final Phases

"Present Age" Phase :

Jesus described all who trust in Him as Lord and Savior and permit Him to rule their life by obeying His will as revealed in the Word as members now of His kingdom as revealed in His Word. As such they enjoy the ability, (via the Holy Spirit) to understand both final phases. This is important because confusion could gain the upper hand since during this first, of these two final phases, the King permits evil to exist and influence people's thinking. It is a tense environment. As a result, the apostolic gift thrives.

"Age to Come" Phase

Jesus described this second phase as the culmination. It commences with His return to earth (Matt. 25:34). It is a future event, in which He assumes the throne of David in Jerusalem to rule, with His attendant saints, the world. His goal in this exercise of power is to enable this planet's inhabitants to enjoy peace, safety, freedom from pain, disease, worry, want, strife, and every human condition now ravaging every square inch of this planet.

How can the Kingdom of God be both a present reality as well as a future event? Let me illustrate. WWII was effectively ended on June 7, 1944, when the Allies successfully penetrated France at Normandy. However, the "mop-up" operation required another year to destroy Hitler and the Nazi regime. Then the victims and prisoners could be free and the world leaders sign the Armistice.

At Calvary, Jesus effectively secured the authority to rule the universe. However, as He told His disciples, it was necessary for Him to go the Father to secure the authority to impose His rule on every square inch of the planet. At the Ascension, after promising to return with the Father's authorization to establish it visibly on earth, He commissioned the Twelve Apostles to complete the "mop-up" operation. They, and those they commissioned, as well as those they appointed, have throughout church history, penetrated each culture, nation, and people-group to establish an environment where the church could secure people for kingdom membership by salvation, then equip with skills to evangelize, and disciple people.

Prior to Calvary, He had explained the necessity for going to the Father for this permission: the parable of the nobleman going into a far country (Luke 19:11-12). This point would be clear to His audience, since they had grown up under Herod. His rise to power paralleled that of the Nobleman in the parable. In 40 BC, Judea plunged into political chaos; much bloodshed. Finally, to resolve it, the Roman Empire lent its support to Herod and he won. However, while he had a place to rule (Judea), he first had to travel to Rome (a far country) to obtain Caesar's blessing, i.e., the authority to rule Judea.

The power and authority granted to His apostles was global, spiritual, and invisible. The Father's permission would make it global, spiritual, and visible.

We live in the period suspended between these two ages: Present Evil Age (PEA) and Age to Come ("Second Coming"). Christ, via His death/resurrection, makes it possible for us to enter the 'Age to Come' right now by salvation. This transforms the redeemed person from the kingdom of darkness to the kingdom of God (I Cor. 1.13). This is why the Apostle Paul described the true Believer as a person who lives "in Christ", i.e., able to experience here and now the power and quality of life reserved for the future Age (2 Cor. 5.17). We live between "now" and "not-yet" aspects of the Kingdom.

Will Jesus return? Yes! When? I do not know. In the meantime our ministry must be characterized as kingdom ministry in each nation or urban center, presenting the message that will not only transform individuals, but the society itself; confronting and Satan as the resident spiritual force and authority from whom to rescue one and all for the King we serve.

As you reflect on all this discussion, can you see why the concept could produce so many variant theological opinions and interpretations?

One of them, equating the kingdom with the church deserves further explanation. It provides us an opportunity to understand the nature of the kingdom by contrasting it with the church.

PART 3: THE KINGDOM VS. CHURCH

Even hymn writers confuse the two concepts. Consider these lyrics composed by Timothy Dwight:

> "I love Thy Kingdom Lord,
> The house of Thine abode,
> The church our blest Redeemer saved
> With His own precious blood"

The error of equating the kingdom with the church is a common one. Fortunately, the confusion is easy to clear up. Once you compare their features, you realize that the terms are not interchangeable for the following four reasons.

First, true Believers will inherit the Kingdom, thanks to the Father having bestowed the kingdom to His Son, and, He, in turn, bequeathed it to them. In contrast, the Scriptures nowhere describe them as heirs of the church. Saints maintain a unique relationship with the Kingdom. Since they will rule it with Christ, they must be considered as distinct from it.

Second, from Abraham, much of the Old Testament and Gospels take up the subject of the kingdom using prophecy and parables (Matthew 13: 2, 31, 33, 45-47). In contrast, the church was for all people in every generation prior to its revelation at Pentecost, a complete mystery, therefore, it would never have figured into Abraham's thinking (Romans 16:25, Ephesians 3:9, Colossians 1:26).

Third, The Bible markedly contrasts their characteristics:

Kingdom	Universal Church
Christ as King	Christ as Head
Saints as Citizens	Saints as Members of Body
Kingdom = physical reality	Church =invisible reality
Not Perfect: professing & true believers	Perfect: Only true believers

As you can see, the kingdom of God does not equate to the universal church. Nevertheless, they do enjoy a relationship.

Church and Kingdom do Relate despite Differences

When one sees the "big picture" of God's eternal plan, the role of the church and kingdom sort out. The plan to regain dominion of the world, in preparation for His return to rule from His throne had two objectives. One of them was to create a redeemed people-group to help Him rule from Jerusalem. To achieve this, He established churches, and those gifts mentioned in Ephesians 5 9: pastors, teachers, and evangelists. These primarily operate with a church-mindset. His other strategy involves subduing the earth, and this, the apostolic gift with its kingdom mindset shines. To appreciate that aspect, consider the analogy of Eden.

Eden was a microcosm of this combined global kingdom. He ruled it, shared fellowship in a vital relationship, with those He chose to enjoy, and maintain it. Adam's sin destroyed all of that. Nevertheless, it did not change or thwart His two-fold strategy.

With this introduction, permit me to help you to examine each of these strategies.

His People-Strategy

The first is to establish a particular "race" of people with whom to love, fellowship, and help Him rule. They are distinct as a race in that they share His likeness by natural birth (Imago Dei), and His nature by spiritual birth (regeneration). As sperm and egg produce an infant, repentance and faith produces a regenerated person.

What we know about this process begins with Abraham, the posterchild for this unique kind of faith. It ends with John the Baptizer, who defined the kind of repentance required to produce a regenerated person. Jesus, in His earthly ministry united both in His message: *"repent and believe"*. At first, He directed His message to Abraham's descendants, but His concept of Kingdom was so diametrically opposed to theirs that they completely rejected Him and His offer.

As a result, He rejected them, and commissioned the Twelve Apostles to preach grace to all races. Suddenly, the Twelve had thousands of regenerated people whom they had been mandated to develop into perfect, mature saints.

The result—the Church: its responsibility is to create regenerated people (via evangelism) and develop them into mature saints (via discipleship), qualified to rule with the King of Kings.

To accomplish this, the resurrected Jesus, worked through the Apostles (just as He had before the Cross), except now He indwelled each through His official "surrogate", the Holy Spirit. For this, He developed three primary ministering gifts: evangelist, pastor, and teacher.

His Territory-Strategy

As mentioned, He also had to build a place in which to share this life with those He chose and redeemed. After Eden, His kingdom became a virtual one. Then, with David, it became real and virtual. After the resurrection, it became virtual again. At His second coming, it will become real again.

Like the Jew, prior to 1948, the church of Jesus Christ exists globally, but without a tangible political territory able to qualify it for United Nations membership. In spite of this, in every nation, Jews maintained their faith and cultural identity, exerting tremendous influence on the culture, values, and vision of the nation in which they resided. Likewise, the true believer, living out His faith, serving the Savior, is able to exert influence that brings others to Christ, and preserves an environment conducive to presenting the Gospel.

As you can see from this brief description, it is a marvelous twofold strategy, with a mission for the church, and one for the kingdom, yet the two missions do enjoy a corroborating relationship. The apostle does preach the Gospel; his work of establishing a foundation; governing; confronting opposition, and thinking globally, paves the way for the pastoral and teaching gifts to establish churches and bring saints to maturity to rule with Christ at His return.

Now that we have nailed down a clear definition of the Kingdom, let us examine its unique nature. Since the kingdom is spiritual in nature, we must explain how an entity that remains invisible, can still be real. Otherwise, we have a virtual entity; an idea foreign to the Bible.

PART 4: NATURE OF KINGDOM: REAL OR VIRTUAL

To begin, let us compare our non-material Kingdom of God to its material, political counterpart. In doing this we shall see that this phase of the kingdom ("this Age") is as real as loaded .38, and not just a figment of someone's imagination.

All agree that in the "Age to Come" phase, the kingdom Jesus returns to establish will be sufficiently real to qualify for its own postal code. But now, many contend, "He rules but He does not govern." The implication: the kingdom of God is a virtual, albeit spiritual, reality.

I raise this issue for three reasons. First, a virtual kingdom skewers the mindset I require in order to fulfill my apostolic ministry; I emerge confused about what strategy my apostolic gifts should function in.

Second, a virtual Kingdom diminishes the role of all apostolic ministries, rendering it unnecessary, thereby strengthening the argument of those who advocate that this "office" vanished into the graves of its first-century apostles (which we have already demonstrated as not true). However, since the kingdom is real, the apostolic role, as the New Testament defined it, remains alive and well.

Third, a virtual kingdom offers only symbolic hope for the person who, neck-deep in calamity, turns to the Savior for supernatural help that Jesus promised when He urged us to pray for the Kingdom to "come".

No, a virtual kingdom hits me as a realm that resides just next door to "irrelevant", and just down the street from "make-believe". I prefer my ministry to take place in a real kingdom.

On the contrary, if this kingdom is as real in nature and function as that which resides in Buckingham Palace, our apostolic ministry is not superfluous, those who witness it appreciate its full dimension, and those who invoke "thy Kingdom come", experience immediate results.

To establish that the Kingdom of God is as real as the empire over which flies the Union Jack (British Empire) permit me to point out three traits they share in common. Each has an in-resident ruling monarch; each occupies real territory; and each fulfills its mission by operating a leadership system that is hierarchical and complex.

Both Ruled by Monarchs

The British path to a ruling monarchy typifies that of most monarchies. After Roman rule, the many communities of the British Isles, forced to defend themselves, organized into "kingdoms". Over time, the more powerful kings gobbled up the weaker ones. Then, when faced with the Viking invasion, they consolidated under a single throne, which they set up in England. In the mid-20th century, Elizabeth, at the death of her father, George VI, began a five-decade reign that, today, ably continues to function. Like other monarchies, the British throne bases its right to rule on criteria that rightly confirm the legitimacy of its right to rule, and transfer the throne.

At first glance, one might think that the British monarchy demonstrates its reality by throwing state dinners, or reviewing formally dressed militia. In fact, its ability to impose biblical virtues and values on his constituents strongly confirms its reality.

Nature of His Kingdom

Christ's kingdom is also able to impose a remarkable set of virtues and values over its subjects. Paul, in Romans 14:17 describes its primary characteristics, as evident on its residents as a full-dress uniform: "... *the kingdom of God is...of righteousness and peace and joy in the Holy Spirit.*"

The prominent characteristic of the kingdom is righteousness. The King reveals Himself as "the Righteous One" (Lev. 19:36, Deut. 25:1, and

Psalms 111:3). He individually creates each citizen, in the process, imparting His own righteousness to them.

Early on, in the Old Testament, He even called Himself, *Yahweh-Tsidkenu*, (Jer. 23:6) i.e., the God who is your right" This He accomplished on the Cross; it enabled us to be forgiven of our sins and to become rightly related to "the Righteous One".

This trait provides His kingdom with one of its most dominant characteristic. As a result, since it currently functions amid many people who do not share this nature, the marks of true righteousness, as Paul points out—peace and joy—become all-important identifiers to distinguish real members of the kingdom ("wheat") from the wannabe types ("tares").

Righteousness is such a marvelous gift! It not only cleanses us from all sin, but also gives us permanent "right-standing" with the King. Using a biblical metaphor for this righteousness, we wear it as a robe, even confidently into His royal presence.

Therefore, when Her Highness passes by, waving from her gilded carriage along a parade route, her subjects jubilantly shout "Long Live the Queen!", there is ample reason for their exuberance. This remarkable woman represents their kingdom. Their shared joy confirms a sense of belonging that unites and validates of the reality of the British monarchy, as a political kingdom.

What Qualified Jesus as King of Kings

Let me suggest seven reasons that support His legitimate claim to the throne of David as the King of Kings. They are as follows.

- He understood its origin—a promise made to Abraham (i.e., that his seed would reside in this perfect realm)
- He had a perfect understanding of every aspect of it: how to enter it (Matt. 5:20; 7:21); how to bring Divine help and authority to a situation (Matt 13:11), and the dual "time" aspects of it.
- He personally possessed the power to rule every aspect of it (including its invisible realm; all individuals and nations comprising it, as well as the environment in which it existed
- He was capable of solving any and every problem its people might encounter
- His rule extended even to complete authority over sin and death

- He possessed the ability to build a spiritual kingdom, and then transform it into a global physical entity (Rev. 21)
- He demonstrated the supremacy of His authority over the most powerful problem—death, but by surrendering His life to the Cross, and then regaining it from the Father, resulting in the resurrection.

Think about how compelling this truth makes the Gospel in this decade when each new day's headline announces some event trumps every preceding level of atrocity, tragedy, and evil.

No wonder people ask. "Where is all this going?" They are inquiring about righteous man's destiny. In the process they discover that the One in whom they have placed their hope and trust is worthy to rule every atom, organism, and soul in heaven and on earth with the same reality as we associate with a monarch as real as she who resides in Buckingham Palace.

Extent of His Rule

Jesus ascended the throne by His Father's will, having created the people (redeemed and unredeemed) and the place (all creation) over which He assumed the right to rule.

Adam's sin required Christ to take back His dominion; this he accomplished at Cavalry. His final words confirm the extent of His authority and power:

> "All authority in heaven and earth has been given to me. Therefore go and make disciples of all nations, baptizing them in the name of the Father and of the Son and of the Holy Spirit, and teaching them to obey everything I have commanded you. And surely I am with you until the very end of the age." (Matt. 28:18).

Permit me to point out four important things that this statement conveys.

First, notice that since "all authority" belongs to the risen Jesus, then Satan has zero authority!

Second, in the Father's bestowal of all power to the Son includes this phase of the kingdom:

> "which He exerted in Christ when He raised Him from the dead and seated Him at His right hand in the heavenly realms, far above all rule and authority, power and dominion, and every title

that can be given, not only in the present age but also in the one to come…(Father)…has placed all things under His feet and appointed Him to be head over everything…" (Eph.1:20-22).

As Paul points out, this truth is mind-boggling; therefore, apprehended by prayerfully asking the Holy Spirit to *"…open the eyes of your understanding"*.

Third, with that realization in mind, we return to the Great Commission (Matt. 28) above. Notice that since His authority was real, so was His offer to bestow "all power" on succeeding apostles until the work detailed in Ephesians 4:15 was fulfilled. Since that work (*"…until we all attain to the unity of the faith and the knowledge of the Son of God to mature manhood"*) remains even now incomplete, the apostolic role retains its central place in that divinely ordained mission.

Fourth, this authority was intended to gain global dominion by "going" and "making" disciples." The only way to gain access to it is to engage in His kingdom work. Therefore, this authority is predicated on obeying His command to *"…go and make disciples."*

As a result, the Kingdom mindset views the world and its authority in this light:

- The kingdom of God is a real organization, with a real king
- He wields absolute power; it was legitimately given to Him
- Satan has no authority in His midst;
- He has bestowed that power on His disciples and apostles
- Being able to access that authority is mine by divine decree no matter my role or limit of giftedness, I do share His authority.
- I do have His authority to take His ways and will into the world (Matt. 5:13-16)
- I am responsible to use this authority everywhere I go, and in every way I can.

The Kingdom mindset sees the world, as one in which there is a kingdom, as real as any political nation that exists with a true king over which He exercises absolute authority.

So what do these monarchs rule? Is the territory controlled by the British Empire more real than the territory over which the King of King presides?

Both Rule real Territories

At its zenith, the British Empire was the foremost power on the planet. It ruled over so many dominions, protectorates, mandates, colonies, outposts, and territories that it was impossible for the sun to set on some part of its 460 million inhabitants spread around the globe.

Thanks to its dominance, it created a political, linguistic, and cultural landscape that still affects the earth, long after its boundaries have shrunk.

Likewise, the Kingdom, beginning with twelve men assembled on Galilean seashore, moved that which John the Baptist had started to the Upper Room, and with the governance of the Holy Spirit, immediately expanded to thousands.

Within two generations, the successor to those Caesars murdering the Savior, then the Apostles, as well as massacring millions of true believers for refusing to worship them, Constantine, willingly handed over the keys to his Palace in Rome, and joyfully declared that he was now a disciple.

In this stunning act, the request Jesus urged His disciples to pray before the Father came true: "thy Kingdom had come." Within a few generations, the sun could never again set on the dominion of the Son of Righteousness.

However, we must again face the questions prompting this section:
- What is the nature of this kingdom?
- Is it real, like the British Empire, or is it a virtual territory?

These questions arise because the kingdom ruled by Jesus has no material border; it exists in parallel, although globally with all political entities seated at the UN. How, then, can we say it is a real kingdom? The answer lies in the material (matter) comprising both types of kingdoms.

The Nature of Matter

Scientists, early in the 20th century, made a succession of discoveries about the atom, matter's essential building block. First, they discovered it to be comprised of sub-atomic particles, protons, neutrons, and electrons. Later they learned that these comprised of smaller particles, called quarks.

As the century closed, they found a still smaller group of particles comprising these Quarks; they called these smallest units, made only of vibrating energy held together by a "frequency." They called it, a "string". This discovery signaled the end of the trail; particle physics had unraveled the mystery of the atom. From these strings, quarks form. These, in turn, create protons, neutrons, and electrons that produce the atoms that comprise the 118 elements of the Periodic Table.

When a foremost expert in Particle Physics was asked what had been required to get the first string to vibrate, he replied, "sound; preferably one generated by a spoken word". Reading this, I immediately thought of that spoken word that caused the creation of the first string, which, then formed into quarks, and these into atoms, and these into elements, and these into compounds, and these into substances: *"...Let there be light"* (Gen. 1:2).

The Lord God set the frequencies of every "string's" vibration to a specified pitch; as a result, in six days, the resulting 118 atomic elements coalesced into all the forms of matter to create the material universe. Every social entity, including the British Empire exists in this realm we call the material universe. However, is that the only universe?

Could a parallel universe exist comprised of a type of "matter" in which its most essential components vibrated at different frequencies?

With that thought in mind, consider this Bible verse: *"Then I saw a new heaven and a new earth, for the first heaven and the first earth had passed away."* (Rev. 21:1)

How will that take place? I do not know. However, I can suggest a plausible scenario. The One whose spoken words created all matter (therefore the material universe), in order to create a new parallel universe will need only to reset the frequency of those vibrating "strings", the essential building blocks of all atoms, and the nature of matter will be changed. By speaking a new word, Christ will 'retune' the frequencies of the smallest sub-atomic "strings" to produce the new matter comprising the new heaven and earth.

Likewise, this concept of a dual kingdom universe enables me to understand the nature of the Kingdom of God in this current phase. We know that it does exist, and that created matter can be made to function in it, because the Lord Jesus, during His resurrected ministry, demonstrated His ability to function in both realms.

How else could the God-Man, nail-prints and all, walk through the front door into the Upper Room without having opened it, or walked up the stairs?

It exists as a parallel universe, as real as that on which my automobile travels, and my house stands. However, because of the frequency of its strings, it is invisible to the naked eye. As a result, it endures a "bad rap", providing critics the opportunity to pronounce its invisibility to be tantamount to "unreal".

His Kingdom now, although invisible, is as real as an ocean wave.

Both Oversee Complex Hierarchical Organizations

To rule a vast empire such as the British Empire requires an enormous system of national, regional, and local administrative, judicial, financial, and educational governmental branches to ensure that the needs of its Dominions, Colonies, Protectorates, Mandates, and other territories are met and maintained on a sustained basis.

Likewise, the kingdom of God operates a global organization with many interlocking layers. Daniel discovered this as he mourned that he was unable to understand the latter part of the prophecy God revealed to him. He received two visits from angelic leaders from the invisible kingdom of God. One was Gabriel (Dan. 8:15-17), and the other Michael. One explained that he had come from fighting the satanic counterpart in the opposing spirit kingdom that ruled over Persia, and would leave the brief meeting with Daniel to fight the spirit-prince of Greece.

Thus, we see the realm of the Kingdom of God does operate with a hierarchy, including Archangels (Jude 9). Archangel means, "to be the first (in political rank and power)"; he holds the highest office in the heavenly hierarchy.

The Ministry of Angels

The invisible realm is constantly described in the Bible as something present in our midst, not as a distant reality. Angels do not appear occasionally in the Bible; they manifest themselves continually! There are, in this day, "...all spirits sent to minister to those who will receive salvation?" (Heb. 1:14). Wow! Every true Believer enjoys his own angelic protector.

How Angelic Sphere is Organized (Col. 1:16)

As the British Empire, in its hey-day, exercised its power to influence the direction of the affairs of the nations under its dominion, so the Kingdom of Heaven maintains its hierarchy that exercises influence over nations and affairs of states within them (Dan. 10:13).

Angels form an organized, structured society with different hierarchical levels of authority, which according to the above quoted chapters of Daniel (9 and 10) were directed to exert profound influences on the political entities ruling the earth. As an example, consider the archangel, Michael, (Dan. 10:13) who governs over the spiritual affairs of Israel, ready to wage war against incoming onslaught from demonic forces.

Likewise, Satan's kingdom of darkness is also organized; its hierarchy is comprised of "…principalities, powers, governors of the darkness of this world and spiritual forces of wickedness in the heavenly places". These beings, created by God, rebelled with Lucifer, and as Jude describes it (verse six), they "did not retain their lofty position" (Jude 6), and are now agents of the adversary, bound under his dark dominion and serving in Satan's rebellious undertakings.

My apostolic ministry requires me to enter into the midst of this spiritual struggle between the angels and demons. The Lord will provide me an invitation to travel to a country; there I will minister to the leaders of the nations during the daytime, and to all those who will listen at night. I share the sevenfold strategy to transform their nation that you are about to learn. I confront evil forces, casting out demons; I also demonstrate the power and love of God to bring wholeness via a ministry of physical, moral, and psychological healing.

At every occasion, the army of righteous angels assembles to take my words and helpful works and use them to accomplish a purpose that God intends about which I may or may not be aware. Since a demonic battalion controls the nation in which I minister, as soon as the meetings commence, war breaks out in this invisible realm.

Sometimes it spills over into the material realm; audio-visual equipment breaks for no apparent reason; an unruly person shows up to attempt havoc. You would not believe half the stories I could tell! Do I always understand the "big picture" of what is going on? Hardly! However, the apostolic gift serves the Savior in ways I shall never comprehend. Further, I do not need to understand everything; my calling is to be faithful to use the gifts as He directs. He is the coach; I am a player, being directed by him to play the position assigned to me.

Still, I understand that in my public ministry, much more is going on at the invisible level than meets the eye. How do I know this? Examine that passage in Daniel 9 and 10 with me again.

First, notice that on a visible level a political kingdom is engaged in a serious internal political struggle. The government is that now controlled by the Persians. Nebuchadnezzar, but his inept grandson had originally controlled it Belteshazzar lost it to Cyrus. It is within the leaders of his regime that this political struggle takes place that Daniel 10 records.

Notice that in this struggle, conflict will occur on two fronts. On the visible front, inside the royal "Board Room", a debate rages over this issue: should the Jewish captivity end? Should they be allowed to return to their land to rebuild Jerusalem?

The debate heats up; nobody is neutral. Some insist that they must set the Jews free. Others promise that doing so will be over their dead bodies; the Jewish captivity must continue. One suspects that this side harbors a financial motive.

On the invisible front, the angelic forces are at work. Their motive: to fulfill the promises made by Jeremiah that after 80 years, the Captivity would end and the people would be permitted to return to the Land of Israel. Leading this attack is a strong angelic warrior, Michael' God commissioned him to protect the interests of Israel on His behalf. He has a counterpart a demonic leader of magnitude whom Daniel calls "the King of Persia" (Dan. 10).

Get this picture: while the conversation heats up in the Kingdom "Board Room", we discover that in the parallel universe surrounding it, the battle wages; and there are no Marquis of Queensbury rules to ensure safety and civility. No, this is a battle as fierce as that waged at Waterloo! Who prevailed? As Daniel reports, Gabriel proved victorious since Israel was allowed to exit the nation and return to Jerusalem.

I say this with full confidence; because in a few verses after this account, we learn that in another battle, waged between the angelic forces led by Gabriel and the demonic leader known as "the King of Greece", the battle proved to be fierce, exhausting, and in doubt until the very end.

Now can you appreciate the turmoil that swirls about the apostolic ministry? We are invited by the leaders of that nation to come and minister. This is God sending us on a mission of His choosing in order to accomplish His purpose. There we preach the Word. Suddenly spiritual war breaks out! Of course, much of it remains invisible to the naked eye;

but like the invisible wind making its presence known by shaking the tree branches, the reality of spiritual warfare becomes evident to every person with a regenerated spirit. Sure enough, the demons show up. No problem the blessed Lord vanquishes them. Then Satan throws illness, and despair at us, taunting God to "prove His power. No problem; the blessed Lord makes many 'comers' whole. It is a war; just as exhausting.

The apostolic ministry traverses both realms, a collaboration with the unseen aspect of the kingdom. Is this invisible realm real or virtual? Ask Philip, one of the first leaders in the Jerusalem church; he understands this collaborative process.

After evangelizing Jerusalem and Samaria, an angel told him to go out on a desert road to keep a divine appointment with an Ethiopian eunuch, a prominent political leader of that African nation (Acts 8:26).

How did he know where to go and what to say except that the scene had been orchestrated from the invisible realm of the Kingdom? Was not this Ethiopian chosen because his salvation was strategic to the Divine plan to evangelize that nation, thereby expanding God's Kingdom there? He was a man with royal connections.

That man, regenerated, and full of the Holy Spirit, after his life-changing encounter with Philip, returned to his home, where, history shows, he helped transform his nation, restoring its domain to Jesus, its rightful Lord.

Sometimes, this collaboration requires the apostle to go where he would otherwise not go, do things he has never done before because they violate his culture and experience. Case in point: (Acts 10) Peter had never entered a Gentile's house, nor eaten non-kosher food. In Acts 10, we find God urging him to do both, in the house of Cornelius.

Peter obeyed his apostolic calling; and the man and his household came to saving faith. As a result, this ministry paved the way for a later apostle, Paul, to move into and transform the Gentile world with the Gospel.

This Kingdom Mindset is so valuable; it enables me to see all aspects of my ministry. It equips me to view the invisible realm in which I serve as real as the material realm in which my body exists. It informs me that no ministry, however routine, is only what it appears to be on the surface; that behind it all, at invisible level, tremendous, destiny-shaping events are occurring. This protection from guardian angels accounts for the many times I, my family, traveling companions, and in-country hosts have been rescued from dangers and pitfalls capable of destroying lives, and wrecking reputations.

This kingdom mindset also keeps me mindful that, at every turn, a fallen angel (Rev. 12:7, 9) can appear, and wreck havoc or create deception.

As we close this section, permit me to explain how this divine and spiritual organization is led.

How the King Governs the Kingdom

Since the New Testament uses the terms it is easy to get confused as to which Person of the Godhead indwells the Believer. In addition, since the New Testament writers used the terms *indwelling* Christ and *indwelling* Spirit, one might become confused as to which Person of the Godhead actually indwells the Believer. Both have the attributes of God (eternality, omnipresence, omnipotence, and omniscience). What revelation resolves this riddle?

The Lord Jesus promised to return and indwell the true believer. He then sent the Holy Spirit. Therefore, the Holy Spirit literally indwells the regenerated spirit of a true believer, authorized by a mandate. He imposes values, imparts His power, and illuminates. However, he governs as a proxy; He legally acts on behalf of the Son.

Likewise, regarding the Kingdom of God, the Son governs its activities, but does through the Vice Regency of the Holy Spirit. The Son now governs His kingdom through the Holy Spirit.

On behalf of the King of Kings, the Holy Spirit provides in-resident governance for everything relevant to the Kingdom.

CONCLUSION

How amazing to be loved by a God who conceives a life for us as magnificent as the Kingdom of God offers. It began in the Garden; God enjoying and pursuing a loving relationship with the two people He had granted dominion over the earth and everyone and everything within it. Sin thrashed this idyllic existence. Nevertheless, He began a global plan that would restore dominion to people who shared His nature, beginning as a person, Abraham, and then through him, to raise up a nation, under Moses, and nurture it until, under David, its influence cast a shadow over the entire political world.

Then, when Solomon's seed began to corrupt it, He raised up prophets to advise the people; the true kingdom will now become a spiritual domain, and later, the spiritual domain will impose its full stature and authority on the physical realm, creating a new heaven and earth—Eden Two.

Like political kingdoms, it is a covenant community. Unlike other invisible realms, it is just as real as are its physical and political counterparts. An on-site monarch rules it. Through His governance, he deals with every task, problem, and opportunity that can arise on any square inch of this global community. He oversees a vast organization of spiritual leaders who engage in destiny-altering responsibilities every day over a territory that dwarfs the British Empire at the height of its power.

Within its reach, the church brings individuals to salvation, then maturity, so they can rule with Him that final realm described in Rev. 21. Yet the kingdom is not the church

In some ways, it is an enigma: its current prospects are extraordinary, capable of changing a nation. Still its glory lies in the future. It is invisible but real, moving toward a state of being both real with that which is now invisible, quite evident.

How can the true believer live in this dual universe? How can he be part of an earthly nation, people-group, or culture, while, at the same time, functioning as a citizen of the Kingdom of God? The international banking industry provides a beautiful clue.

When a person is engaged in a type of international business that requires the services of an international bank, especially when he must enter into a financial agreement, involving financial instruments such as bank guarantees, or loans, a contract must be signed.

Let us assume that he is dealing with a major bank, such as Credit Lyonnais, one of the top fifty banks. The person or corporation he is doing business with is, let us say, a resident of Paris. However, he is in Los Angeles. The bank requires that he sign the contract so that the courts of France can prosecute to get any non-payment type complications resolved. Since the court only has jurisdiction in France, and he is signing in Los Angeles, how can that contract be enforceable?

International banking law has devised a solution. In the Los Angeles branch, a small space located where the contract is to be signed has been deeded by the USA to France. It is only about nine square feet, but standing inside of it, the businessperson's signature is considered to have occurred on French soil. On the other end of the transaction, the French counterpart exists, enabling the USA to process those who violate the contract signed while standing in that nine square feet owned by the US although on French soil.

The true believer, and the apostle function in a dual universe, one in which, they operate within political boundaries, subject to its laws, culture, and language. Still, they operate in the other realm that will hold their actions just as accountable, and possessing a much greater capacity to prosecute problems for solutions.

Now that we have a solid grasp of what a mindset is, and what the kingdom is, let us proceed to construct the kingdom mindset.

CHAPTER 3

Wrapping Our Brain Around This Kingdom Mindset

RECALL THESE LYRICS OF the chorus of Roger Miller's 1965 best-selling song?

> Trailers for sale or rent
> Rooms to let...fifty cents.
> No phone, no pool, no pets
> I ain't got no cigarettes.
> Ah, but two hours of pushin' broom
> Buys an eight by twelve four-bit room
> I'm a man of means by no means
> King of the road.

Influenced by the Hippie Movement, the song lampooned the productive/responsible lifestyle by honoring that of a bum. To celebrate his carefree lifestyle, marked by leisure, self-sufficiency, and indulgence (i.e. friends, fine cigars, and endless travel), it crowned him "King of the Road".

While this glimpse into the mindset of "His Highness of the Highway"—the Hobo is interesting, it cannot provide us what we need: an in-depth view of the characteristics of the apostle's most important tool, his Kingdom mindset?

PART 1: COMPREHENDING THE KINGDOM MINDSET

A mindset is like a custom-programmed internal computer in that it is built from pre-determined mental instructions. With it, the apostle can make decisions, spot problems, opportunities, strengths and challenges along the ever-changing path he has been divinely assigned to travel. As we said earlier, its function resembles that problem-solving tool which a computer programmer uses to develop software.

In his divine preparation, the Holy Spirit reveals the most essential things he must focus on to stay "on-mission". He must remain ever mindful of these areas:

- He is sent: As such, he must make sure that he remains sensitive about his heart, sin, and personal conduct. Remember, the only one who can disqualify an authentic apostolic ministry is the apostle—therefore, be ever mindful about walking with integrity.
- He is to govern
- He is an ambassador
- He is to confront and subdue evil
- He is to lay a foundation:
- He is to bring a message
- He is to tear down, and restore to wholeness
- He is to build a team
- He is not a pastor
- He is all cultural
- He maintains a global perspective

For each of these, by experience and the Holy Spirit's guidance, he will develop a set of protocol questions that enable him to remain "kingdom focused". Many of these test questions are more complicated than the simple set we used to solve the mystery of a non-working desk lamp. Nevertheless, the process he uses does resemble that set of protocol questions discussed earlier.

Previously, we suggested that the apostle's kingdom mindset functions like that of a person overseeing a large Multinational Corporation ("MNC"). As we revisit the qualifications that make for an effective CEO, notice the similarities between the secular and apostolic counterparts:

- Both must strive to maintain an open mind at all times, and to be ever mindful of the diversity within the cultures he seeks to penetrate and serve.
- Both must be adept at improvising, innovating, and synthesizing.
- Both must remain vigilant to understand the culture; how it operates, does things, and why; and continually sifts through all

incoming data for ways to innovate, and penetrate the culture God has sent him to serve.
- Quitting because of the opposition, political and otherwise, that confronts him is not an option for either role. The apostle's reason: God sent me; He will work it all out.

Again, each of these will require its own set of protocol questions not unlike those we used to fix a lamp that does not throw light.

For each of these traits, the apostle will develop a set of protocol questions that filter through all incoming data to keep him focused and his mission on task. To do this, he will train his mind to examine each new piece of information, process it to extract that relevant, and beneficial to the execution of his ministry. The process will become intuitive. He will employ a sequence of questions, options and instructions based on his countless experiences, and "*Rhemas*".

Now that you have an idea of what comprises a kingdom mindset, permit me to analyze two apostles whose ministry exemplified this gift at its best implementation. The exercise will help you understand the ministry that God called me to fulfill.

PART 2: JOHN AS MODEL OF KINGDOM MINDSET

Certainly, no finer servant of the living Lord ever drew breath. John the Baptizer's kingdom mindset enabled him to prepare Israel to receive the Jesus as King of Kings. In the end, it killed him.

The ministry of this last Old Testament Prophet was apostolic. The Bible says he was sent from God (John 1:6). To appreciate his approach to the ministry, it is first helpful to understand the Old Testament prophet whom he epitomized in speech, lifestyle, and appearance, Elijah.

Recall that Elijah was the prophet who fearlessly confronted the political base of Israel, as well as the false prophets who held her people in a spiritual strangle hold, while warning the people with a single message: "Repent, and return to the God of Abraham; judgment is at hand" (2 Kings 1:8ff). Likewise, his New Testament counterpart, John the Baptist, cried day and night: "Repent, for the Kingdom of Heaven (promised to Abraham) is at hand."

It appears that both chose to speak to their nation as an outsider. John's decision proved effective; from this vantage he could speak directly to individuals befuddled by the terrible contemporary times; he could proclaim his kingdom message with maximum clarity, and provide a way to apprehend it by faith with the least obstacles; his only props, the Jordan River and a listening audience. Like Elijah, he confronted people and called them to a faith-response with passion.

In addition, his ministry was foundational. Recall that the purpose for which he had been called was to "prepare the way of the Lord," i.e., laid a foundation for the Lord Jesus to launch the first of the two final phases. This helps me appreciate the uniqueness of his ministry. The people who responded to his ministry must be truly and totally committed the Messiah he was about to present.

Easy believe-ism would not suffice; hence, the straightforwardness of his message, Repent.

Since the Jordan was considered ceremonially unclean, therefore, his message really was:

- Consider yourself a non-Jew, crossing again into the Promised Land.
- Consider yourself unclean—place no confidence in your Jewish heritage, consistency in practicing Judaism; strip all religious advantages from your hope. Count only on this: my repentance was completely wholehearted and genuine.

His method was designed to lead a heart, mind, and will through the same regenerative process that Jesus later outlined in the Beatitudes. Beginning with a conviction of being very impoverished in spirit (lost sinner), the penitent was ready then to become pure in heart, and recognize the King of Kings when John later pointed Him out as He passed by and announced, "Behold the Lamb of God that takes away the sin of the world!"

Further, John's ministry was global in scope. He spoke to anyone and everyone; by positioning himself outside of their culture, he could appeal to every citizen in the nation.

Finally, it was transformational. By confronting evil, and demanding a complete, unfeigned faith- response, his spiritual fruit had an excellent chance of remaining transformed.

While, we will not investigate each quality listed above, let us conclude by examining one final quality, his ability to build a team of ministering leaders. Is it not ironic that of the first four apostles chosen by the Lord, half (James and John) had first been disciples of John the Baptist. Many of his disciples remained loyal; two he sent to inquire of Jesus regarding questions related to Jesus' Messianic ministry. Decades later, Paul encountered a remnant band of John's disciple and helped them become true Christian believers, become baptized and filled with the Holy Spirit as followers of Jesus.

As you can see, this outstanding man of God truly ministered with a kingdom mindset. Jesus sang his praises. He was a remarkable apostle-prophet, in spite of a flaw that proved common to the religious world that Jesus faced.

Flaw in John's Kingdom Mindset

The flaw in his thinking surfaced while he was in prison, awaiting the fate of Herod for having confronted him about the sin of murdering his own brother in order to steal his wife, as described in Matt 11:1:1-3 "Are you the One, or should we seek another? Recall that we alluded to it in the previous chapter.

Remember, John had no access to the wealth of information available to the Twelve after the Holy Spirit instituted in the Upper Room some fifty days after Jesus' Ascension. (This is why, after extolling his virtue as the greatest of Old Testament prophets, Jesus added, "yet he was the least in the Kingdom of God").

Therefore, when John sends two of his disciples to ask Jesus this question, we must appreciate its context: "Here I am in prison, about to lose my life. Based on my understanding of what the Kingdom is, your actions do not seem to fit my mould. Therefore, I seek clarification, because if you is not the Messiah, what is the meaning of all that I have done?"

When you view his questions from this context, you see that it reflects an understanding of the kingdom widely shared by his contemporaries and based on a whole lot less information than we possess.

Recall that earlier we described the Kingdom as occurring in two phases: "now" and "afterward". Many people, hearing Jesus, were knowledgeable that the Messiah would establish His rule on earth, but failed to distinguish the timing. As a result, they were looking for kingdom to replace the oppressive occupation of the Romans, i.e. "now".

In John's case, he figured that if Jesus was truly the Messiah, He would perform works connected with a political deliverance of Israel - or at least the deliver him out of prison.

Jesus sends back an answer: "I am the Messiah; my works prove that, since they are exactly as Isaiah prophesied. Nevertheless, my power, at this time ("now" phase) will be foundational, and spiritual. Later, I will return ("afterward" phase) bringing the kind of universal political deliverance you have in mind".

To repeat, we should not be too harsh on John. His error was a common one in that Jewish society. For four centuries, the religious leaders had promised them that the appearance of the Messiah that Daniel had described was impending. Theologians had also told them that He would emerge with the military might and resources of Alexander the Great and Caesar Augustus combined. They were looking for relief from the awful tyranny they lived under by way of a political solution (military in nature). Having their heads full of such bad theology regarding the Messiah, they completely misunderstood Jesus' strategic approach His ministry.

Nevertheless, that does not make John a bad apostle. His record confirms him to be a stellar model

PART 3: JESUS AS MODEL OF KINGDOM MINDSET

Both John the Baptist and Jesus proclaimed, "The time has come…kingdom of God is near." What if they had proclaimed: "The Kingdom…is 2,000 years from now?"

It would not only have been erroneous, but it would have spelled the end of their favorable response from the people. In truth, the Kingdom had definitely begun; it was operational; and it would continue to be so, indefinitely.

In fact, the phrase was well known and its meaning understood thusly: "God is going to send us a leader to throw off Roman rule and install David on Herod's throne."

Therefore, from the outset of his ministry Jesus was forced to challenge their thinking and clarify. A war of words commenced that finally cost Him His life.

Thanks to the Gospels, we have much insight into the nature and purpose of the kingdom form the narratives that describe the ministries of both John and Jesus. Thanks to the New Testament, we already understand what the Kingdom is, and how it differs from the universal church, our purpose now is to examine the phrase by which Jesus introduces

His ministry for clues that will add to our understanding of the mindset shaped by it:

> "After the death of John the Baptist, Jesus entered into Galilee, preaching the Gospel of the Kingdom: repent and believe, for the Kingdom of God is at hand" (Mark 1:14).

This verse offers much insight we can later use to construct a Kingdom mindset. Of course we have the benefit of hindsight to help us understand a concept that was brand new to those who initially heard its announcement.

Clues of His Mindset in His first Sermon

Message Analysis

It is important, first, to understand his teaching emphasis. He did not primarily preach repentance, i.e., "You are a sinner and you need to repent". He did speak to this. However, His message included another aspect: "The Messiah is coming" therefore; repentance is your only appropriate response.

An apostolic pulpit performs two tasks. First, we must boldly confront a languishing people-group with this Good News: the anointed One, capable of transforming your lives at every level has sent me to tell you: He is at hand; ready to tackle your problems.

Therefore, for our efforts to be effective, we must always proceed with this reality firmly in mind: we could not transform anyone or anything; that power alone resides in Him. Only the Savior, working through the precious Holy Spirit can change a life, and yes, a nation. Therefore, our task is to lift Him up; make people realize that He is their solution, and that we are only messengers of this truth. To do otherwise would be to attempt to share and pilfer His glory.

In addition, we must make clear that the key to accessing His magnificent help lies in true repentance; it perfectly prepares the way for transformation to begin. However, true repentance involves more than just turning from sinful practice, i.e., "turning over a new leaf", i.e., changing one's ways. To appreciate this word's connection to the kingdom mindset, permit me to share these insights regarding its meaning.

"Repent"

Confusion arises from this problem from making "repent" and "turn" interchangeable terms; not so in Greek. Notice that the normal idea, "to be sorry" and the true action for repentance actually involve different words.

This word, *metanoeite*, means, "to turn, look in the opposite direction, and thereby change the view of one's mind and heart". Our English word derives from the Latin, *"repoenitet"*, meaning to be sorry; the Greek has a word for this, *meameloma* (Mt. 27:3). The distinction matters, because the Bible reveals that God repents (Joel 2:13: (*"God is...and He repents..."*). Certainly God cannot sin therefore in His repentance (like ours), He changes His mind.

Repentance is the gateway to a kingdom mindset as well as entering into its benefits. It is wonderful to feel sorry about your sin, but repentance is not a "feeling" word. It is an "action" word. Jesus told us to make a change of the mind, not merely to feel sorry for what we have done. Repentance speaks of a change of direction, not a sorrow in the heart. We cannot come to the kingdom of God unless we leave our sin and the self-life.

John's selection of water baptism as an appropriate response to the kingdom message sheds much light on just how deeply must be this decision to repent if genuine change is to occur. He chose a ceremony that forced one, dramatically, to demonstrate a change in thinking in at least three radical ways to force one to action.

He borrowed a ceremonial washing used by Gentiles who wished to become Jews. Therefore, for a Jew to enter those baptismal waters was essentially confessing that he was as far away from God as any Gentile; and needed to get right with God. In my opinion, for this to take place would require nothing less than a genuine work of the Holy Spirit.

Jews considered the Jordan River to be unclean. Think about it; in a culture that made ceremonial cleanness the key to everything, imagine how hard it must have been for a Jew to plunge beneath its murky waters? Only the Holy Spirit could supply such power over the human will. The river also signified something else: repentance is returning to "square-one", the Jewish spiritual roots—when they crossed this river to enter the Promised Land.

Clearly, John's baptism had two goals in mind: to force a genuine demonstration of repentance, and to signal that it occurred because of supernatural prompting. However, in Jesus' case, He was not baptized because He needed to repent of sin; no, He entered Jordan to show that His kingdom ministry fully aligned with people as sinners—these are the very ones He came to save. John, in his public introduction to Jesus, makes clear this identity with sin: "Behold the LAMB of God that takes away the sin of the world".

"Kingdom at Hand"

By this phrase, Jesus meant that He was the key to the deliverance Israel was waiting for; and would require His supernatural action; and that this sought-for salvation was now, in their midst, available.

In our case, a kingdom mindset thusly translates this truth: He is at hand to begin to make a complete change, which begins at the roots of its thinking. Our message informs and promises salvation, but it is a prelude. We are completely dependent upon the Holy Spirit to "baptize" our words so that our words become transformed into His words; i.e. a person hears them as from His mouth and heart. Suddenly, the people wonder, "is this spiritual kingdom real? Can I trust my future, and my life to live in it, i.e., applying its principles and Laws?" It is at this point that the use of signs and wonders are so helpful, because they enable people to see power originating from this kingdom is real; Jesus is at its center, King, and Lord; and they can completely put their hope in it.

When the Savior preached this theme he added two phrases: "near", and "time is fulfilled". Regarding the first, He meant to share the good news that divine help was as available ("near") as the back of one's hand; therefore, His promise was real, versus being on the order of something imaginary, i.e., not to be taken as truth.

By the second, He meant that His and John's ministry signaled a true sea change. To make this point He chose a Greek word that does not mean chronological time (*chronos*), but *kairos*, a decisive moment, which equates to "a strategic opportunity that demands a decision". Therefore, His message could be thus summed up: "This is a strategic moment; the Kingdom of God is right here in your midst. Therefore, this is an opportune time; it demands action; do not let it pass you by".

"Believe"

Jesus added another component "Believe". The Greek word He used, *pisteuo*, means much more than "to agree with one's mind".

Many people then (as now) believed in Jesus. This preposition ("in") suggests that one accepts His statements as intellectually accurate. However, this type of faith will not transform anyone. No, the Savior's word goes further. It means to not only to accept its truthfulness, but to put one's trust in it, i.e., allowing the heart to embrace it as applicable to the point of finding joy and comfort in resting in it, and conforming one's life to this reality.

As you can see, kingdom preaching is not about moral renewal. It requires one to take Jesus at His Word, and then build a living relationship by depending on Him to do what He promises in the Book. Only when a mind is so transformed, can the culture in which they live become transformed.

Audience Response Analysis

Let us now probe the response of the synagogue congregants to the first sermon of Jesus for clues as to their thinking regarding the Kingdom of God: "And they were astonished at his teaching, or he taught them as one having authority, and not as the Scribes" (Mark 1:22).

To appreciate the impact of His message, permit me to share the meaning of these words. The Greek word, *explasso*, means to have one's thinking completely and forcefully reshaped; if one's thinking was a person, it would be lying motionless on the canvass by an opponent's punch.

The Greek word, *ekousia*, means this: the audience is totally convinced of its truthfulness (therefore, does not need further confirmation from a quoted expert source) as well as is completely "sold" on this idea; he feels that his words and actions are based on good logic.

We will, in a later chapter, discuss kingdom preaching in detail, but for now, see its impact when anointed by the Holy Spirit. We bear witness, that the strategy you are about to learn has had, in this same anointing, a similar impact. People are astonished at its uniqueness, freshness, and sense, although quite different from what they can to the meeting thinking they would hear. In addition, they sense, that in the principles, and laws, they are for the first time, hearing God's prescription for their sickness.

CHAPTER CONCLUSION

Why was it easier to lasso a Tsunami than to keep "What Would Jesus Do" from becoming the alpha-topic of every talk show, and sermon?

The answer matters because it provides a breath-taking insight into what makes the apostolic mind "tick"; how he employs his and his Kingdom Mindset. Permit me to refresh your thinking with some elementary facts relevant to it.

Recall a few chapters ago we discussed why a mindset is so helpful: First, life throws more information than any brain is capable of processing; to preserve sanity, we must develop a way of systematically filtering out the relevant stuff from the extraneous. Second, we humans were created with four core needs: hope, belonging, significance, and meaning/purpose. Since gratifying those eats up about 23 or every 24 hours, we need to sift through an on-going incoming stream of data for that which will help us with these top needs.

Enter the mindset; this device enables us to filter all incoming data, using an elaborate set of protocols. Functioning like algorithms, they simplify one's decision-making process. It provides an early-alert system to spot approaching problems, and tag information that appears to be innocuous for possible future review.

You can see how this serves the apostle. A highly sensitive kingdom mindset enables him to stay on mission until he has accomplished that for which the Holy Spirit has called him to do in a specific place. It is such a valuable "tool", and for these reasons. First, his primary role is that of governing. Surely this requires him to prioritize.

Second, he is sent; therefore he needs to maintain a finely tuned sensitivity to all incoming data so that he is able to deal with cultural implications, and not commit some *faux pas* with the potential to derail his mission.

Third, his mission has a clearly defined ultimate outcome

> "Then I saw a new heaven and a new earth, for the first heaven and the first earth had passed away, and the sea was no more. And I saw the holy city, New Jerusalem, coming down out of heaven from God, prepared as a bride adorned for her husband. And I heard a loud voice from the throne saying, "Behold, the dwelling place of God is with man. He will dwell with them, and they will be his people, and God himself will be with them as their God. He will wipe away every tear from their eyes, and death shall be no

more, neither shall there be mourning, nor crying, nor pain anymore, for the former things have passed away." (Rev 21:1-4 ESV)

Therefore, this kingdom mindset enables him to focus vigilantly on incoming data for early signs of people, and ideas relevant to his mission, as well as threatening opposing forces.

Regarding enemy threats, he has no choice. He must fulfill his mission in the midst of a destiny-defining war raging between Jesus God and Satan to control of every square inch of creation, and minute of time. This mindset keeps him "on his toes".

With the Ascension, the Twelve, in partnership with the risen Son of God, operating through the governance of the indwelling Holy Spirit, the fulfillment of the Kingdom took a decided turn toward the final stage of fulfillment.

Since the apostle becomes directly engaged in this ongoing process, he requires a kingdom mindset in order to have a prayer of successfully doing his part.

CONCLUDING BOOK TWO

The popularity of the WWJD (What would Jesus Do) movement proves the value of employing a mindset to filter through the entire information one encounters daily in order to stay focused, alert, while maintaining a proper perspective.

Interestingly, their strategy was not the first of its kind.

At the turn of the twentieth century, a proponent of the social Gospel, Sheldon, wrote a book In His Steps, subtitled: what would Jesus do. He tells a story about a pastor who sees a hungry homeless man and wonders what Jesus would do in this same situation. It helped many people to process the call of Christ to" follow Me" as insisting that each day one should find some social situation needing an infusion of cash or kindness (or both).

However, it greatly misunderstood the Biblical mandate for discipleship, and reduced the Savior to a merciful, kind philanthropist; and it led to the development of Liberation Theology, a view espoused today by those who reject Jesus as God, the Bible as truth, including all it says about sin, salvation, heaven, and hell. That attempt to filter the walk was a disaster.

However, centuries before, a book did successfully lay out the tenets of a mindset that enables a true believer to mould his daily existence to conform to the Biblical standards laid down by the apostles on how to walk the walk.

Three medieval German monks began a serious investigation into how to live each day with a mindset focused on living for Christ by trusting and obeying Him.

Later, one of their colleagues, Thomas, who lived in a small village called Kempen, 'journaled' his devotional thoughts, then collected and published a hundred such principles and observations. The title stated clearly the purpose for presenting this litany of how-to instructions for daily walking the walk. It was called, *"Imitation Dei"*, Imitating God its author, Thomas a Kempis.

Therefore, we must not dismiss the importance of a properly constructed mindset.

Without doubt, the apostle's best friend is a Kingdom mindset. It enables him to filter all the information he encounters each day, so that he stays focused, and alert. It serves him like the WWJD helped the young people in Holland Michigan to stay focused on living a life of obedience to the Savior they loved.

To this end, we have presented what a kingdom mindset is how it differs from worldview and how it influences leadership. We have also established that although the kingdom of God is, in part, invisible, it is nevertheless as real as rain.

This mindset also helps an apostle to stay focused on the goals that he is called by the King of Kings to accomplish. What are these?

The pursuit of the answer to that question will move us to our next destination on our learning journey. In Book Three we will discover the intentional vital outcomes that result from a fully engaged apostolic ministry.

Book III

Essential Outcomes of Apostolic Ministry

Chapter 1   Fear of the Lord as an Outcome

Chapter 2   Outcome: Divine Favor

Chapter 3   Shalom as an Outcome

Introduction: An Overview of Our Discussion on Outcomes

AS IT BEGAN ITS descent toward a Florida runway, one of the commercial airliner's landing gear's warning light suddenly went 'dark', indicating either a malfunctioning landing gear or a burned out light bulb.

The investigating Third Officer sized up the problem as probably due to a burned out light bulb, since the landing gear had worked about an hour ago.

After working up a sweat trying to coax the bulb loose from its socket, he solicited the help of the Co-captain. Finally, even the Captain jumped in.

Was the bulb burned out? We will never know, because, as the entire crew focused on extracting it, the unattended commercial airliner slowly descended into a swamp, killing all on board. Sadly, no child of a passenger need ever have been orphaned if only those in the cockpit forgot what the purpose for which they were there.

Airplanes fly to safely land, and efficiently disembark all people and belongings. Outcomes, such as these, are 'take-aways'—the benefits people seek from an airline or a ministry such as ours.

Since outcomes are as vital to a successful project as the sun is to a plant growing tasty tomatoes, why do we find it easy to lose our focus?

For some, the problem arises from confusion as to the nature of the gift. They view an "Apostle" as a title, a General Officer in God's Army. To these, the title is intended to garner prestige, or legitimize them wielding power over constituents. Some use it exploitatively; they remind us of that New Testament character, Simon Magnus, a magician who sought the tools of this gift to build a substantial revenue stream. Others use the title with no malice or selfishness intended at all.

For others, the gift serves as a model for the type of missionary gift-set exemplified in the ministries of pioneer missionaries as Hudson Taylor? These insist that we all calm down, take a deep breath, and reconcile ourselves to the reality that this once premier ministry gift, as demonstrated by the Twelve, now only serves as a model for pioneering cross-cultural (missionary) ministry.

In truth, the true apostolic gift is a set of spiritual gifts, possessed by one called by Christ to accomplish a set of personal outcomes intended to supply qualified leaders.

Observe the dogged determination of our Lord to fulfill His apostolic ministry. After beginning at the Jordan River, He moved like a 747 turning from the Tarmac onto the runway for takeoff.

He turned at the border of Israel deliberately to propel Himself onto the Cross. His passion never waned. Like the Pied Piper, He marched with the Twelve through a seamless succession of encounters until He entered Jerusalem in triumph. Everywhere, He restored sight, cured leprosy, raised the dead, and opened hearts to Truth—and much more.

When, in triumph, He entered Jerusalem, He left behind a seamless stream of wholeness, wisdom and joy. Every seed needed to transform the world was taking root. Jesus, as a bonafide king moved through its main street with deliberation to Golgotha. In death, He wrecked Hell, putting death to death, only to emerge and ascend to heaven, the resurrected Lord of Lords.

In each successive generation, the qualities Jesus modeled have marked those exercising this gift. I feel privileged to be among those so anointed in this generation. Nevertheless, it is not as if I had won a prize; it is a call to fulfill certain outcomes. What are the foundational personal outcomes the apostle seeks to accomplish? As I list them, realize that we consider them important enough to devote a chapter to each.

In Chapter 1, we will describe the first personal outcome we want people to embrace: to understand and act upon the Fear of the Lord. This is critical for the apostle to be able to influence the three Institutions that govern any society.

In Chapter 2, we will explain the first result of embracing this first outcome: walking in the fear of the Lord results in Divine Favor. This outcome, we describe by its Hebrew name, "Esheri", is strategic to securing resources smashing strongholds, winning friends and influencing decision-makers.

In Chapter 3, we will detail the second outcome from walking in the Fear of the Lord: "*Shalom*". While Bible students recognize this as the Hebrew word for Peace, it means much more: wholeness, completeness, and a sense of centeredness.

With a solid knowledge of these outcomes, a thorough understanding of the nature and purpose of the apostolic gift, and the kingdom mindset that governs its thinking, any mystery about this gift, its purpose, and intended outcomes will begin to vanish.

Therefore, store all items under your seat, return it and your tray-table to an upright position, and make sure your seatbelt is securely fastened. This learning journey is preparing for take-off.

Chapter 1

Fear of the Lord as an Outcome

INTRODUCTION

Thanks to C.S. Lewis, we have an insight into the phrase, "fear of the Lord" that a child could grasp.

In his allegory *The Chronicles of Narnia*, Lewis creates a make-believe world resembling heaven (Narnia). Children enter it through an upstairs Wardrobe. Christ, portrayed as an imposing lion, named Aslan, rules it.

Mr. and Mrs. Beaver, (talking animals) prepare Susan and Lucy to meet Aslan. At first sight of him, Susan exclaims, "Oh no! I feel very nervous about meeting a lion!" The Beavers then explain that it is normal to approach Him trembling in one's boots.

Lucy then asks, "Is he safe?" In Mr. Beaver's reply, we gain a breathtaking insight into the meaning of this phrase.

"Safe? Of course not! He *isn't* safe! But he is good. He's the king, I tell you!"

To transform a nation the apostle impacts the three institutions (government, religion, and home) governing it. Proverbs describes "the fear of the Lord" as integral to a healthy and wholesome life. It is just as strategic to changing these institutions.

Therefore, to help you appreciate its critical importance to our apostolic ministry, permit me to analyze this phrase's meaning so you can understand this attitude and how to use it to act in a manner pleasing to the Lord. Then you will know why it tops our list of <u>must-achieve</u> outcomes.

PART 1: ANALYSIS OF THIS PHRASE

> "The fear of the Lord is the beginning of knowledge; fools despise wisdom and instruction."

The apostolic ministry is foundational; God uses these people to transform the soul of a culture using a divinely designed strategy. What makes this ministry effective?

Spiritual transformation occurs as people make wise decisions. Two factors account for such wisdom. The principles we share provide prudent guidance. However, each wise choice stems from an attitude the Bible calls "the fear of the Lord". It functions so determinately that every wise thought owes its existence to this attitude.

Since our apostolic ministry depends on wisdom and this attitude is its prerequisite, we must understand it. We begin by analyzing the above Biblical phrase. It must be important; the Book of Proverbs makes no sense without it.

Mining for Meaning

1. Analyzing the Phrase

If the phrase used as a word was intended to define a material thing, i.e., a butterfly, analyzing the component words "butter" and "fly" would not be helpful. A butterfly is quite different than something constructed from a small insect (fly) and a dairy product (butter).

Likewise, the component words of this phrase, when considered independent of each other, do not add up to its intended meaning. Yet, in order to understand its meaning, we must consider them separately.

"*...fear*": the Hebrew language uses two words for "fear". One, "*moira*" means the kind of terror when a bus crosses a freeway lane and careens head-on toward you—unqualified terror-stricken dread. The other, *yirah*, includes a strong element of fear, but it tempers this negative with this positive idea, reverence, holding in awe.

"*...of*" preposition meaning something originates in another, therefore, proceeds from it.

"*...YHWH*": God uses this name in connection with His covenant. It marks this aspect of His nature: His name offers a clue as to His nature, "I AM THAT I AM". This is His personal name. It means that the individual rightly related to Him (party to the covenant) has constant, continual, and complete access to all His power, knowledge, and compassion. It was designed to express the fact that He is always closer, more caring, and more committed to this individual than is humanly possible because He views a covenant-person to be more precious than life itself.

Now that we understand the nature of the YHWH from whom this "fear" originates, we see that the above second meaning of "fear" is intended. The fear that strikes terror and repels us is not possible. No, the meaning intended here is the kind of fear represented by the Hebrew word, *yirah*. It means to maintain a healthy dread of offending Him (i.e., violating His Word), while maintaining a warm affectionate love. Two words come to mind as accurately describing best word to describe its component emotions: we hold Him in <u>reverence</u> and <u>awe</u>. Such feelings can stem from only one thing—a covenant relationship, since, as the Bible shows, unsaved people have no fear of Him.

Therefore, what makes this "fear" possible is that it grows out of a relationship. We know and love Him because He first loved us. That remains the single best motivation to prevent a true believer from choosing anything but Yahweh's will, as well as seeking to do whatever He directs. This is why people in a covenant relationship make Bible study to a high priority, because they discover His will and act on it in an effort to maintain a relationship that pleases the God who loves them more than they love life apart from Him.

Now that we have an idea of the meaning of this phrase, we need to determine its relevance and value to everything in the Christian life. For that we will analyze its most important occurrence in the Bible. This verse is like an algorithm for the Book of Proverbs. To understand any of its hundreds of life-principles so useful to dealing with life, one must interpret them in the context of the meaning of this four-word phrase. Surely this was Solomon's intention. He uses this verse with the phrase as the key to all knowledge that only a person in a covenant relationship with YHWY can enjoy.

2. Contextual Analysis: Examining Proverb's Pivotal Verse

We shall explore two key clauses. The first is this:

> "The fear of the Lord is the beginning of knowledge; (Prov. 1:7a)

As we analyzed each word in the phrase, we will now examine each key word in the above clause. As we have already examined the meaning of the first phrase, "*the fear of the Lord (YHWH)*, we will now analyze this phrase in the context of this verse, since it is one of the most pivotal verses using this phrase in all of the Bible. To that end, let us look at these two chunks: "*is the beginning*" and "*knowledge*".

..."*is the beginning*":

The phrase, expresses two important principles:

- It is the first thing; fearing God is the literal first step of true wisdom, and
- It is the foundation of all true wisdom.

Therefore, a proper reverential response towards God is foundational; without it one has not made the first step in attaining wisdom.

"*knowledge*" (Hebrew word, "Dah-ath") It means knowledge that is practical, i.e., useful to gaining practical know-how or solving problems using lateral thinking skills, i.e., "*connecting the dots*").

In getting a job, facing a crisis, or working through a problem, nothing is more practical than being able to apply principles, laws, and concepts, learned by experience, and life-long learning to changing a life, or marriage, or business, or any aspect of life.

Therefore, from this Hebrew word we learn that the knowledge necessary for the covenant man to prosper in life begins with the attitude embodied in this phrase (the fear of the Lord). This is where all wisdom begins. It is the first step toward wise actions. To confirm the legitimacy of this interpretation, permit me to show you three Bible verses that express this same truth.

In Proverbs 3:7 we read, "Be not wise in your own eyes; fear the Lord, and turn away from evil." Notice that the key to properly enjoying life under God's care begins with this attitude: do not put your trust in anything but the Lord.

In addition, the writer of the Book of Ecclesiastes makes a similar point. He sums up his assessment of life apart from trusting YHWY as "vanity" (literal Hebrew translation" "vapor")? This word expresses a life lacking this essential attitude for gaining access to the answers of life. His point: without this fear of the Lord, life is all smoke and no substance.

Also, in the Psalm One we find a similar assessment of a life lacking this fear, which he calls "the ungodly" since he has no interest in maintaining a relationship with the LORD by delighting in the Word as a means to pleasing Him. He likens such a life to a piece of worthless chaff. Ouch! What a candid description of a lifetime of worthlessness captured in this metaphor: his life has no more substance than a miniscule morsel of debris that no one either values or respects; its whole existence is described as "swirling", i.e., existing in meaningless perpetual motion.

Beyond these three passages, throughout the Bible, we find the confirmation of this same message: the fear of the Lord is foundational: without this attitude, there can be no hope of gaining access to the kind of information that can save, and enhance your life.

Now, permit me to analyze the second part of this verse. For openers, we discover another disturbing fact about this attitude—it is not only the source of wise knowledge, it also has its source. To fail to tap into that source is tantamount to blocking access to this most essential and valuable information. This bad attitude prevents access to a life-changing one.

Now, permit me to analyze the second clause of this verse so pivotal to introducing the message of the Book of Proverbs:

"...fools despise wisdom and instructions." (Prov. 1:7b)

In our analysis of the first half of this verse, we found that this attitude that opens up access to life-changing knowledge because it equips one's attitude with a sense of awe and reverence robust sufficient to motivate him to choose obey YHWH (and His Word). It also enables one to reject a path contrary to God's expressed will. The reason this reverential attitude is foundational: it represents a set of values that functions as an algorithm for the process integral to acquiring and understanding knowledge (wisdom).

Now, in this second clause of this pivotal verse, we discover that the attitude that prevents one from ever gaining access to true wisdom and knowledge is also driven by an attitude—it despises such answers to life's most important questions. To appreciate this, we need to catch a glimpse of the meaning of four key words.

"fools" (Hebrew: "ev-eel,"): the root means, "to be perverse". In this sense, the word "perverse" means to be completely confused to think, that which is truly "right", is wrong, and vice verse. What is at the root of such twisted thinking? Obviously, the motive is spiritual; therefore, it stems from an attitude of impiety that leads to these outward expressions: mocking when found guilty; argumentative (defensive); and licentious.

Suddenly, it becomes clear: this attitude stems from a personal realization that God truly exists; and that this person realizes his accountable to Him. Such thinking drives this person to reject Him.

Therefore, a person is a fool because deep within his soul he has said: "I reject the notion of God's existence, and my accountability for my actions. I choose to live my life as I please." These next three words support this conclusion.

"*despise*" (Hebrew: "boo-ze). This word's literal root meaning: "to trample under-foot". The word as used in the Bible means to despise, hold in contempt, hold as insignificant, and show despite toward someone or something.

"*wisdom*" (Hebrew: "Cha-kam") is "knowledge that knows how to use what He knows to solve problems and take advantage of opportunities. It enables him to discern truth from error, and use what he learns to influence the quality of his life. Therefore, a proper reverential response towards God is not only the foundation, but also the first step in attaining wisdom.

"*instructions*" (Hebrew: "mu-sar"). The root meaning: the kind of correction and admonition commonly shown to children by their parents. It is associated with these terms: disciple, chastening, and correction. They share in common two motivations: to provide helpful, useful information in a situation where it is obvious needed; and to realign one's attitude toward a legitimate source of such information as being respected, and sought out for counsel.

Now that we have a good idea of what each key word of this second clause means, let us step back for insights into how this information helps us appreciate the truth revealed in its content.

Hebrew scholar, Franz Delitzsch, feels that the phrase's foremost insight is the contrast it exposes between two contrasting attitudes: the fear-attitude, vs. the fool-attitude. The attitude employed by the "fearer" motivates him to sink wise counsel and instruction.

Conversely, the fool attitude despises these same values and has not a shred of desire to embrace and act on such values. His goal is to establish his own autonomy in the face of God's sovereignty. The only moment when he ever seeks true wisdom is when he knows that his survival depends on it; and even then he despises its source—God's mercy extended even to unsaved people because He knows that even unregenerate people need enough knowledge to survive in life, even when they reject its true source: the covenant God.

Hebrew scholar, Bruce Waltke, adds another helpful insight. He asserts that the reason a fool rejects the idea of reverencing the Lord is because he is incapable; his heart is consumed with pride. Thus, in those rare moments when he feels it in his interest to apply true wisdom, we cannot hope that he will revere the creator of this knowledge; his nature will prevent him.

SUMMARY OF PART 1

As we close, let me summarize what we have learned regarding this pivotal verse.

What is this *fear of the Lord*? The child of God bends himself humbly and carefully to his Father's law by that affectionate reverence. It does this because it understands that His wrath is so bitter and his love so sweet. As a result, it develops an earnest desire to please him, and an apprehension about the danger of coming short from his own weakness and temptations—a holy watchfulness and fear, "that he might not sin against him." (Heb 12:28, 29.)

This attitude influences his thinking. As a parent, he seeks to train up his family under its influence. (Gen 18:19; Eph 6:4) because he knows that is the source of the wisdom one needs to life abundantly and avoid its most subtle temptations.

Why then do multitudes around us *despise wisdom and instruction*? Because *the beginning of wisdom* — "*the fear of God* — is not before their eyes." (Psa 36:1.) They know not its value. As a result, they scorn its obligation and despise the blessing that results from it. Result: they rush toward ruination.

I have learned to make this my prayer: May thy childlike *fear* be my *wisdom*, my security, and my happiness!

The Bible describes this *fear of the Lord* as "loving reverence" for God expressed in submission to His will with hatred of evil, awe that results in "worshipping submission." It is an attitude formed by embracing three sets of values:

- An objective revelation of God's moral law (Psa. 19:7-9; 34:11),
- The subjection submission to that revelation (Pro. 15:33), and

- A dread of the wrath and judgment of God (Deut. 6:13-15; Job 31:23)

When the mind properly focuses on these values, these results occur: i) submission to God; ii) obedience to His Word and will; iii) rejection of evil; and, iv) a concerted effort to live in constant fellowship with Him.

This *fear* has two aspects: rational and non-rational. Its rational aspect is constructed from the objective revelation that can be learned (Psa. 34:1) to provide a standard for moral conduct powerful enough to motivate a person to behavior aligned with biblical principles. Its irrational aspect is built from emotionally balancing two emotional responses: on the one hand they believe the promises, therefore love Him.

Simultaneously, they believe the threats His Word makes for disobedience, and fear Him.

The wisdom literature of the Old Testament is adamant: this attitude, the fear of the Lord, is foundational; it is the prerequisite to gaining wisdom and knowledge, the cornerstone for practical holiness and skillful living.

In conclusion, Bruce Waltke is right: "What the alphabet is to reading, notes to reading music, and numerals to mathematics, the fear of the Lord is to attaining the revealed knowledge of this book."

No wonder this verse is quintessential to understanding every proverb in all of Wisdom Literature.

Now the wisdom of C.S. Lewis comes into sharp focus: the Lord of our salvation is One in whom we can rest assured of His righteousness, but we must not live without a sharp eye on His fierce anger when disobeyed.

Does any relationship better describe the meaning of how one practices this attitude (*fear of the Lord*) than that of a child to a parent? The true believer, a child of God born of the Holy Spirit, holds an affectionate reverence for the living God who possesses both fierce wrath and perfect affection.

This knowledge moves him to bend his will to obey humbly and carefully his heavenly Father's law. It springs out of an earnest desire to please Him, and an apprehension of willful disobedience. He is like a godly son, being trained up by his loving Father's influence.

This childlike fear is his security his source of happiness.

PART 2: A GLIMPSE AT A "GOD-FEARER"

When we perceive a person to conduct himself in a wise manner, what observable qualities move us to draw such a conclusion? We now take up the discussion of those qualities essential to making wise decision or performing wise actions.

The wise person has a lot of Knowledge
- Facts: He has invested time to become knowledgeable. He then makes them available to help others becoming knowledgeable. Such knowledge is learned in a formal setting, such as a class, and using books.
- Experience: Experience provides "facts" too numerous and too subtle to be recorded in books. They can only be gained by applying essential principles learned in books. As a result, one gains a knowledge only learned via real-life experiences.
- People Knowledge: By observation, he learns to understand how they think; what motivates them, and how to predict how they will react.
- Empathy: he knows how other people feel and how they internalize their feelings. He also knows how to relate to others in a therapeutic way.
- Thinking skills: he possesses a competence to deductively analyze any situation:
  i) To use acquired collateral thinking skills to draw data from disparate sources and use them to reach a logical conclusions;
  ii) To discern the motivations behind actions as well as real issues when masked by emotional explanations; and,
  iii) To find the right balance in a debatable situation that leads to something that is the most beneficial to greatest number of people.
- Values-based Outlook (Philosophy). This person has internalized a set of rules (values), and guidelines (virtues) by which He uses to guide his thinking. He holds himself accountable to apply them in making decisions and solving problem.
- He is competent to ferret out from all the data regarding a situation at hand that which is the core issue that which matters the most and the best solution for all involved.

- He is a coach and mentor; He is not content just to know, but seeks to help those about him to know the underlying causes and solutions that He owns by personal discovery.
- He is not afraid to step back and test his ideas against reality, and the possibility that He could make a mistake.
- He is consistent: there is consistency between his current thinking and past-observed behavior.
- He is not egocentric: He does not believe He has the last word on a subject or the corner on truth. Test: confront him with an argument that disagrees with hers and watch how He steps back to consider the plausibility of that argument.
- He is self-disciplined; He does what is necessary without being prodded.
- He tends to operate objectively: Without involving emotions, and with an honest, open mind.

A pastor friend told me that while visiting a home he encountered two pet dogs. One stuck its muzzle near, a look on its face as if it had not seen him in years and had missed him every moment since. His fur was silky soft. His personality was that of a cuddly Teddy Bear.

The other lay in the corner, a look on his face as if he was in a severe state of depression.

He barely moved his eyes to glance at the one who had just entered the room. Soon, the reason for his depression became obvious. The other dog sucked all the warmth and friendliness from the room.

Reflecting on this story, I thought of the above characteristics of the man who fears the Lord. As I re-read them I thought, who would not want to be around such a person. Compare that to the egocentric, self-centered personality that marks the attitude shaped by rejecting the Lord's leadership in one's life.

Can you appreciate the benefits that accrue to developing this Godly demeanor resulting from the attitude that "fears the Lord"?

Remarkably, it flows out of a character, resulting in a to-die-for life. Think about only two of its golden benefits. First, this attitude makes one a life-long learner. Therefore, he develops skills and insights, therefore make his resume very marketable. The career that results generates sufficient resources to support a comfortable lifestyle. Second, this attitude also renders him a good listener. As a result, people are drawn to him; his opinion is sought out. People value his friendship. Rather excellent pay-offs for such a right attitude, eh?

In contrast, consider the fool. He is egocentric, did not train himself, nor prepare himself, therefore, his relationships are marginal; his skills render him minimum wage jobs; and people are generally either put off by his conversation, social skills, and willingness to 'get along'. Therefore, like chaff he enjoys no permanent achievement. He is perpetually 'blown' about by every wind of doctrine or new idea coming along. He is the product of the last book he read and it was probably either a TV Guide, or a comic book.

Now that you realize what a rich life results from this amazing attitude, does it not motivate you prayerfully to ask Him to strengthen your resolve to live by this attitude?

In our apostolic ministry, we are constantly on the look out for people who demonstrate this splendid, Godly attitude. They are the lifeblood of our ministry. By modeling this God-fearing attitude, they become strategic to our goal of influencing the institutions comprising those cultures He seeks to transform.

PART 3: RELATING THIS OUTCOME TO OUR APOSTOLIC MINISTRY

All apostolic ministries have as a mission that which Paul lays out in his introduction to the Book of Romans:

> Him we have received grace and apostleship for obedience to the faith among all nations for His name (Romans 1:5).

Notice that he points out that we are to influence the culture we are called to confront in order to bring about varying stages of faith. Some will embrace Christ; others, will treat our ministry with respect, and others feel constrained to offer us tolerance.

At whatever level they connect with the Gospel we preach, people will be able to find a place they can comfortably position themselves. They can proceed toward true faith and allegiance to the Savior from a starting place. Think of this process as if it was water descending a channel continuously and progressively from one rocky level to the next.

As you will discover, our apostolic ministry seeks to fulfill three outcomes (fear of the Lord; divine favor; and shalom). However, all progress begins with this first one. Therefore, our first task is to help people understand and align with the fear of the Lord. It leads to second outcome: divine favor, which, in turn, leads to the third: shalom, wholeness.

How one maintains their relationship to God affects their way of life; proper fear will result in a blessed life. However, right morals are not the result of knowledge spawned by viewing life wisely, because, one has taken the first step toward true wisdom—fearing the Lord.

In seeking to help the people in this first goal, we are engendering wisdom as well as exposing and reducing foolishness and an unwillingness to learn. Bad thinking is as damaging to the institutions comprising a society as malaria is to that society's public health.

You see our goal is not just to bring individuals to saving faith, but impact society so that they encounter God in a covenant-based relationship (covenant of grace, i.e. salvation by grace through faith), but begin to use divine wisdom to tackle the issues plaguing their way of life.

Therefore, our apostolic ministry presents Biblical answers to the questions regarding life. The theme of such preaching can be summarized as follows: to enjoy life is to live it under His care, utilizing His creation properly. Without this, life is vanity. Knowing how to use the resources God properly has brought into our life requires wisdom that derives from fearing the Lord. Therefore, this outcome is foundational to our apostolic ministry. Of course, many are skeptical that the turn from meaninglessness begins with a reverential attitude that precedes everything else both temporally and logically. The breakthrough comes when they begin to embrace the truth of the Bible we preach and act on this principle by faith. Then, like a canoe moving down-stream, they begin to move to answers, blessing, and finally change that is substantial and sustainable.

Recall the definition of a fool that we offered earlier: a fool is one who tries to establish his own autonomy in the face of God's sovereignty, pragmatically employing a measure of wisdom and knowledge for his own survival, all the while despising it. In his heart, he resists the idea that the fear of the Lord is as essential to life as the alphabet is to reading.

Living wisely because of one' mind is fixed on fear of the Lord is equivalent to acting according to values.

The church in this postmodern world is flabby and lacks a witness. At the heart of these problems lies the lack of Godly fear. This is one of the root sins of the evangelical church; this accounts for its moral flabbiness and ineffective witness!

How lamentable that not too long ago Christians considered being known as God-fearing people to be a badge of honor. However, somewhere along the way we lost such respect. Now the idea of fearing God, if thought of at all, seems like a relic from the past. Granted that the phrase might seem old-fashioned, but the Spirit of Christ can make it important in the thinking of a God-fearing person.

Ironically, when that occurs, that person has no one or nothing else to fear. Is not this near the point that Isaiah was making in this passage?

> "The Lord spoke to me with his strong hand upon me, warning me not to follow the way of this people. He said: "Do not call conspiracy everything that these people call conspiracy; do not fear what they fear, and do not dread it. The Lord Almighty is the one you are to regard as holy, he is the one you are to fear, he is the one you are to dread, and he will be a sanctuary (Isa. 8:8-11)

To that end, let us explore some other ways in which we apply this principle of fearing the Lord as an outcome of our apostolic ministry.

Teaching the Church Not to Fear

Why does the flock of God struggles with fear? Luke 12 points to at least four things that we are prone to fear. First, in verse 4: we are prone to fear death—especially death by persecution: *"I tell you, my friends, do not fear those who kill the body, and after that have nothing more that they can do."*

The second fear is mentioned in verse 11: *And when they bring you before the synagogues, the rulers, and the authorities, do not be anxious about how you should defend yourself or what you should say.* In this verse, we discover the fear related to public shame. We are prone to be anxious about what others will think of us if we do not have the right thing to say.

Third, in verse 22 and 23: Jesus makes says to His disciples, *'Therefore I tell you, do not be anxious about your life, what you will eat, nor about your body, what you will put on. For life is more than food, and the body more than clothing'."*

Jesus' point was that we are prone to worry about whether our basic physical needs will be met—food and drink and clothing and shelter.

Reasons for Not Fearing These Things

Therefore, as we see from these verses, in every case Jesus wants us to be free from fear. So He says:

1. Death is not the worst, hell is. Moreover, God will keep you out of hell and care for you with detailed tenderness—the hairs of your head are all numbered.
2. The Holy Spirit will teach you what to say in an hour of public testing. You will not be left alone.
3. Your Father knows your daily needs and is far more inclined to give you what you need than he is to feed the ravens and clothe the lilies, but look how he takes care of them!

Therefore, Jesus does not want us to fear. That means no fear of death, no fear of public shame, no fear of poverty and want. He wants us to see that God is the kind of God whose people do not need to fear.

The Fourth and Deepest Fear vs. 32

As He concludes His message recorded in Luke's 12th chapter, He says, *"Fear not, little flock, for it is your Father's good pleasure to give you the kingdom."*

His point: we fear that God is not the kind of God who really wants to be good to his children. This is a fear that rises up in the hearts of those of us who are prone to feel that God does not want to be gracious to us, that he does not want to be generous and helpful to us. We are prone to think of God as one who is irked with us—ill disposed and angry.

Sometimes, even if we believe in our heads that God is good to us, we may feel in our hearts that his goodness is somehow forced or constrained. We feel as if we are being maneuvered like a judge after freeing a person he knows is guilty because a clever attorney just pointed out that to incarcerate would violate a legal technicality.

Therefore, Luke 12:32 is a verse about the nature of God. It is a verse about the nature of God's heart. It is a verse about what delights Him and He takes pleasure in doing.

> *Fear not, little flock, for it is you Father's good pleasure to give you the kingdom.*

As we have learned, the fear that comprises the fear of the Lord is not unlike that which a child has toward his father; it registers in his brain as either reverence for him or terror at offending him.

Fortunately, the Bible distinguishes between them by assigning a word to define each. Fear as terror is generally expressed by the Hebrew words *magor*, and *pacadh*, and by the Greek derivative word, *phobos*. For fear as reverence it uses the Hebrew word, *yirah*, and in Greek as *eulabeia*.

All fear stems from the same source—love, either for our interests, or for God's. Self-love engenders fear when something occurs which could deprive us of something good or whereby some evil could befall us. We fear deprivation, or the evil itself, and whatever or whoever would deprive us of that which is good or whereby evil could be inflicted upon us. Not all self-love is evil. For example, we are required by the Word to love our neighbor, therefore it is not sinful to fear deprivation and evil. Adam experienced a true fear of God prior to the fall. Fearing death, and pain is perfectly acceptable. However, when this fear moves us to use evil means to acquire something that is good, or avoid evil, it becomes bad. Usually, in such an instance, we fear man rather than God, therefore, keep not His commandments.

In this moment we are guilty of fearing him who can destroy the body, rather than him who is capable of destroying both the body and soul in hell (Matt. 10:28)

The key is to remain cognizant that our soul is dependent upon the Lord out of a serious regard for our own salvation. This fear, properly channeled, enables us, when we present the Gospel of grace to persuade them to believe and to be saved. This fear stirs the redeemed person to fear, "… lest, a promise being left us of entering into His rest, any of you should seem to come short of it" (Heb 4:1).

Understanding Filial Fear (Yirah)

As we have previously mentioned, the filial type of fear *(Yirah)* is a holy inclination of the heart its source: the Holy Spirit. God generates it in the hearts of true believers, whereby they, out of reverence for God, take pains not to Him in all things.

The unbelieving hearts knows nothing of this. "There is no fear of God before their eyes" (Rom 3:18). Thank God, that in regeneration the heart of stone becomes pliable, eager to obey the Lord, and sensitive to that which the Spirit has revealed to his soul. This is so universal that an early mark of salvation is a new and profound respect for the Savior that expresses itself in a desire to serve Him.

In regeneration, however, the heart of stone is removed and a heart of flesh is received which is soft and pliable, and is very readily moved upon beholding God, dependent upon the measure in which God reveals Himself to the soul. If God is perceived as being majestic, a motion immediately arises within their soul—a motion that is becoming to the creature in respect to God.

In contrast, the unconverted heart directs his fear to seeking his own interests, by his own means, without regard for the spiritual or moral consequences. Why not he either finds no delight in God, therefore, has any desire to fear Him or his experiences terror at the thought of God moving against him. He may be terrified of God, but he cannot fear Him rightly.

However, as the Holy Spirit takes up residence in the redeemed soul, God puts His fear in that heart, that enables such a person to depart from His love (Jer. 32:40).

This source is the Holy Spirit; in this function He is called "the Spirit of knowledge and of the fear of the LORD" (Isa 11:2).

Because of the ministry of Holy Spirit, all saved people understand, possess, and act upon this filial type of fear. As a result, they are called God-fearing people. "...the same man was just and devout" (Luke 2:25); "...devout men" (Acts 2:5).

Filial fear is engendered by reverence for God, because thanks to the Holy Spirit's illumination, they are able to see the Lord as eminent, glorious, and majestic within Himself (1Chron. 29:11). The closest that "natural man" can get to this is to hold contact with the living God as terror inducing; he can never tolerate His majesty. Praise Him for the work of the precious Spirit of God through whom Christ reconciles to the Father, enabling them to simultaneously love and revere Him. "Serve the LORD with fear, and rejoice with trembling" (Psa 2:11).

The Fear of God in Believers

True believers are enabled by the Holy Spirit to perceive that the fear that the Lord has made us aware stems from Him. They experience joy, acquiescing in it, striving to trust and obey Him. Their hearts are gladdened because they realize that this new viewpoint regarding fear validates their saving faith; as a partaker of it, they become servants of God, thereby described as "...Thy servants, who desire to fear Thy name" (Neh. 1:11). They experience this, also, when, out of true fear of disobeying Him, they confront a sin habit, and find it losing its grip upon them. They also experience this, as they prayerfully trust Him to fulfill a promise made to them in His Word. In their newfound desire to please him, their prayer resembles that of David, "Unite my heart to fear Thy name" (Psa. 86:11).

Incentives for the Fear of God

A lively fear of God diminishes sin's ability to control us. What incentives does God provide us to keep our hearts focused on Him? In His Word, we learn that all perfections to meet our every need are in Him, and He is in us (Ex. 15:11). We also learn how dreadful is His wrath upon those who do not fear Him (Psa. 90:11). Further, in the Word we learn that His goodness is designed to lead us to repentance, in order that we fear His name (Deut. 28:58). In addition, realize that the fear of God is the fountain of all the holiness, which delights you. Finally, meditate on this: the Lord has pleasure in those who fear Him (Psa. 147:11)

As you apply these principles, you will find that sinful lusts will lose their potency, corruptions that surface will readily be subdued, you will be stopped in the middle of sinning, and you will find yourself inclined toward the practice of all manner of virtues. "The fear of the LORD is the beginning of wisdom" (Pro 9:10); "The fear of the LORD is the instruction of wisdom" (Pro 15:33); "The fear of the LORD is clean" (Psa 19:9); "The fear of the LORD tends to life:" (Pro 19:23); "...perfecting holiness in the fear of God" (2 Cor. 7:1).

Serious Consequences of Not Fearing God

As we conclude, permit me to share three terrible consequences of not fearing the Lord:
1. God will give you a fearful and trembling heart as long as you do not fear Him, so that you will find neither rest nor safety anywhere — rather, your own heart and conscience will be continually tormented (Isa. 2:19).
2. As you approach the end of life, He will visit you with His terror, as He did with Belshazzar (Dan 5:6).
3. After death, the terror of God will surround you, since you exist in the midst of His wrath, anger, oppression, and consternation, eternally. In the instant you breathe your last, you discover what it means to "...fall into the hands of the living God" (Heb 10:31).

Dear reader, does such knowledge not move you to repentance? Receive the salvation freely offered to you in Jesus Christ; experience a new, healthy fear of the Father, as the indwelling Holy Spirit will provide you.

CONCLUSION

The great preacher, William Brake put it well, "how lovely it is when man delights himself in God and when God finds pleasure in man!"

Will Rogers was famous for his laughter, but he also knew how to weep. Once he entertained hospitalized rehabilitating polio victims and people with broken backs and other extreme physical handicaps. Suddenly, in the midst of their roaring laughter he exited to the rest room. When his traveling assistant entered to hand him a towel he found Rogers sobbing like a child, and beat a discreet retreat. In a few minutes, Rogers re-appeared, as jovial as before.

Someone has observed that you can learn what a person is really if you know three things about him: What makes him laugh? What makes him angry? What makes him weep? The Bible contends, that in addition to these, this, too, is telling: What/who does he fear?

This attitude is pivotal; no apostolic ministry has a prayer of success without inculcating this most important attitude. It is the key to the character development of Christian leaders.

Chapter 2

Outcome: Divine Favor

Acres of Diamonds tells the story of Russell Conwell. He coveted security, and 'lit out' his front door in furious pursuit of the wealth to acquire it.

Years later broke, and disheartened, he returned the humble four walls from which he had sped in search for fortune. Coming to terms with his situation, he began to acclimate to his home. In the process, while planting a garden for spring vegetables, he spotted a stone he recognized. It turned out to be one of many diamonds in the rough.

The fortune that had eluded him—he had chewed up the best decades of his life—was, all along, smack in the midst of the place he raced to escape. He was not the first of such fools.

His contemporaries rejected Jesus' Messiahship because they sought an invincible Alexander-the-Great-like leader marshalling a juggernaut of crack militia, ridding them of the tyranny of Rome and silencing the corrupting influence of those non-kosher Hellenistic ideas. What drove their thinking: the same thing that propelled Conwell out his front door: security to be and do what they wanted in short, peace, freedom, and security. Like people of the Renaissance, they pined to recreate that era when life was superb—in King David's world.

The problem is, if General George Patton, leading the 9th Army, had rolled into Jerusalem with 20th century weapons, and every Roman beat a hasty retreat back into its surrounding seven hills, every Jewish inhabitant's life would not have fundamentally unchanged.

Fortunately, for them (and us all), Jesus knew this, and refused to only provide them with those things He knew would satisfy their deepest spiritual needs. He knew what was needed to enjoy *"Zion-like"* living—

that finest Jerusalem neighborhood built by David for the Messiah to ultimately inhabit.

As a result, every true believer does enjoy a quality of life of one inhabiting Zion. It is a blessed life. Those possessing it are said to enjoy "divine favor". The Psalm designed to introduce the life that the entire Book describes and praises begins, "How blessed is…" Since there are two Hebrew words for 'blessed', the one used in Psalm 1:1, *esheri* is the one we shall explain so you can understand the second outcome we seek to accomplish in our apostolic ministry.

Our goal in this chapter will be to clearly define it, and then demonstrate its strategic importance to godly living as captured in the first Psalm. We will then point out people making vain and horrible attempts to gain it wrongfully. Finally, we shall show you why *esheri* (divine favor) is vital to our apostolic ministry.

PART 1: DEFINING DIVINE FAVOR: NOT EQUIVALENT TO LUCK

A newspaper ran this ad: "Lost dog--brown fur, some missing due to mange. Blind in one eye; deaf; lame leg due to recent traffic accident; slightly arthritic—goes by the name of 'Lucky.'"

Why is it that the entire human race is eager to get a date with the proverbial Lady Luck?

The moment man figured out that he owed his existence to a Creator; he realized his accountability to Him. He then devised the first belief system to curry Divine favor without cramping his freedom to do as he pleases. Today such religions abound. The devices they use to provoke supernatural influence (amulets, etc.) generate billions in profits. Conjuring divine favor is one of the biggest businesses on the planet.

We encounter such belief systems in each culture we serve. The favor they seek to curry they call luck. People prize it as a treasured possession and constantly seek after it. Although they may have never ventured more than a few miles from their home, they use 'luck' to curry favor for bigger crops or safety much like people sidle up to a Roulette Table.

While the world's idea of luck does not exist, I could give you a definition of that which the world calls luck that does exist. It occurs *where preparation meets opportunity*. Unfortunately, this definition will not satisfy one trying to blow on a pair of dice in a gambling casino. He does not want to associate 'luck" with diligent preparedness and staying constantly on the look out for approaching opportunities; he prefers to think of luck as a fickle 'divine' influence to be enticed without regard for human effort.

Praise God, the Gospel we preach offers something as real and useful as rain. It goes by the Hebrew name, "*esheri*"—"divine favor". It is fickle-proof; anyone can access it. We consider it critical to our own effectiveness. Helping others to understand and gain its benefit is one of our most important ministry outcomes.

Meaning of the Other Word for "Blessed"

There are two words for "blessed" in Hebrew. We are probably least familiar with the word *esheri* and more acquainted with the word *barak* or *baruk*. They are not used for the same purpose, nor are they synonymous. Whenever a person is blessed (*barak*), YHWH always initiates this blessing. It originates with God; He is its divine source. One person cannot *barak* himself or another person. A person cannot receive a *barak* type blessing from another human. Only God can give this type blessing.

On the other hand, one person can issue an *esheri* blessing upon another person. You can receive the *esheri* blessing from another person. Whenever I ended a service, I gave a blessing. Sometimes I said, "I bless you." When I say this, I can only mean the word *esheri*. It is one human being blessing another. It would never be appropriate to use it to bestow a blessing on YHWH. For that consider adding, "*and may God richly bless you.*

The *barak* blessing is given to man by the grace of YHWH. It is undeserved and unearned. Only God is so gracious to bless this way. However, *esheri* is happiness, a blessing that results from positive action (i.e., preparation meeting opportunity). Let us lay out other examples for you. Listen to Psalm 119:1: *Happy/blessed (esheri) are the undefiled in the way that walk in the Torah of YHWH.*

Thus, *esheri* is not that type of undeserved blessing resulting from the grace of YHWH. The *esheri* blessing results from observing Yahweh's Torah! Those who hear and obey the Torah are blessed . . . they are *esheri*!

In the New Testament, in His words, we call the Sermon on the Mount; it begins with the introduction of *esheri*-"blessed." (e.g., How blessed are the...). *Esheri* is the Hebrew equivalent for the Greek word translated "blessed" in the Beatitudes. It speaks to a state of mind that a person should have.

To appreciate the connection between appropriate human effort and divine favor, we need turn to the first Psalm. It lays out the life enjoying divine favor, and contrasts it with a life seeking to achieve its quality of life without a personal relationship with the living YHWH.

PART 2: EXAMPLE OF ESHERI: PSALM ONE

Ezra, when compiling the Psalms, chose two as the perfect gateway into the warm, heartfelt thoughts of devoted poets—the first and second psalms.

He chose the second to provide a key to understanding the relationship of covenant people to the God of Abraham.

He chose the first psalm to provide a model by which the reader could evaluate his own personal spiritual journey, and finding areas to model his life after.

> Blessed is the man who walks not in the counsel of the wicked nor stands in the way of sinners, nor sits in the seat of scoffers; 2 but his delight is in the law of the Lord, and on his law he meditates day and night. 3 He is like a tree planted by streams of water that yields its fruit in its season, and its leaf does not wither. In all that he does, he prospers (Psa. 1:1-3)

Permit me to guide your thinking to a clear understanding of this first strophe.

Overview

"Psalms" means "Praises," and the keynote is here struck at the very outset. Only the Blessed man's praises are acceptable to Him. The word "Blessed" used here, as in so many places in Scripture (like Matt. 5:3-11), has a double force. It is most signifies that this favor determines the quality of one's life. Without it, one is doomed to a meaningless and worthless existence.

In addition, this favor is always bestowed on a personal and individual basis. Only that one who lives in a right relationship to Him enjoys His divine favor, because only his praises are acceptable to heaven's throne.

In the first strophe (stanza—vs. 1-3) the Holy Spirit gives us a portrait (by which we may honestly compare ourselves) of the man on whom the Divine benediction rests, the only man who can worship the Father "in spirit and in truth." The outstanding features in this portrait of the "blessed" man may be briefly expressed in three words: his separation (v. 1), his occupation (v. 2), and his fertilization (v. 3).

Verse 1

"Blessed is the man that walks not in the counsel of the ungodly." The Spirit is here describing the character and conduct of the "blessed man."

The first characteristic of the "blessed man" is his walk, a walk in separation from the wicked! Piety begins with separation from the "far country." Where does it begin: he rejects all counsel flowing from unbelieving mindsets.

The flaw in such counsel is that it stems from a mind and heart that lacks the fear of the Lord. This renders such advice worthless and harmful, because it encourages one to act by self-will to serve this goal: self-pleasing. The blessed man shuns such help because he has learned by meditating in the Scripture and delighting in its insights that it truly is

a "lamp unto his feet and a light unto his path." His desire and his determination are to walk by the wholesome counsel of God, and not by the corrupt counsel of the ungodly.

The "blessed" man's self-isolation from such worldly counsel is expressed three ways.

First, he "walks not in the counsel of the ungodly," that is, according to the maxims of the world. Joseph provides us a good model in the way he declined the invitation of Potiphar's wife.

Second, he does not "…stand in the way of sinners." He refuses to associate with them; but, instead, fulfills his need for communion with people who share his righteous nature, as Ruth did, by choosing life with Naomi.

Third, he does not "…sit in the seat of the scornful." He does not take comfort or seek joy in the recreations of the world. He prefers the presence of the Lord to the "the pleasures of sin"—as Mary found at the Lord's feet.

Verse 2a

"But his delight is in the Law of the LORD"

The opening "But" points a sharp contrast from the last clause of the previous verse. Unlike the unsaved, he finds his delight in the "Law of the Lord". The expression, expresses an emphasis on its divine authority.

It shows that he is no longer at enmity against God (Rom. 8:7). As a result, this delight marks him as having received the Spirit of Christ (who said, I delight to do Thy will of My God (Psa. 40:8). The unregenerate delight in pleasing self, but the joy of the Christian lies in pleasing God. It is not simply that he is interested in "the Law of the LORD," but he delights in subjection to God's will, which is obtainable, nowhere else.

Verse 2b

"...and in His Law doth he meditate day and night."

Thereby does he evidence his "delight" therein: where his treasure is, there is his heart also! Here, then, is the occupation of the "blessed" man: he determines to please God, therefore, in order to obtain a better knowledge of His will, he mediates day and night in God's holy Law. Thereby extracting its insights and nourishing his soul.

His "meditation" herein is not occasional and spasmodic, but regular and persistent: not only in the "day" of prosperity, but also in the "night" of adversity; not only in the "day" of youth and strength, but in the "night" of old age and weakness. Meditation is to reading what mastication is to eating (Jer. 13:16).

It is as God's Word is pondered by the mind, turned repeatedly in the thoughts, and mixed with faith, that we assimilate it in order to obey it (Josh. 1:8). The Psalmist could thus appeal to God—can you: "Give ear to my words, O LORD; consider my meditation" (Psa. 5:1).

Verse 3:

"And he shall be like a tree planted by the rivers of water, that brings forth his fruit in his season; his leaf also shall not wither, and whatsoever he doeth shall prosper" (Psa. 1:3).

Here we have the "blessed" man's fertilization. However, notice very carefully, what precedes this season of productivity (prosperity):

1. There must be a complete break from the world—separating from its counsel or policy, from fellowshipping its votaries, and from its pleasures; and,
2. There must be a genuine subjection to God's authority and a daily feeding upon His Word.

These conditions precede fruitfulness. Therefore, let us examine each phrase and clause of this verse in detail.

"He shall be like a tree."

His life enjoys strength and stability; therefore, not a reed, or a creeping vine. He is very stable; no storm moves him; he grows heavenward; and what he shares is totally needed by the world about him (like trees exhaling oxygen, and men inhaling it). This tree is "planted" by someone else (tree does not plant itself), therefore, under the care and cultivation of its owner. This metaphor assures us that those who delight in God's Law are owned by God, cared for and pruned by Him.

"Planted by the rivers of water"

This is the place of refreshment—rivers of grace, or communion, of renewing. Just as a tree derives life and fruitfulness from the adjacent river, so the believer, by communion, draws from the fullness there is for him in Christ.

"That brings forth his fruit…"

His life lacks fruitless branches, since it is connected to the true Vine.

"In his season"

Neither do all fruits do not appear in the same month, nor are all the graces of the Spirit produced simultaneously. Trial calls for faith, suffering for the exercise of patience, disappointment for meekness, danger for courage, blessings for thanksgiving, prosperity for joy; and so on.

"His leaf also shall not wither"

Notice that his fruitfulness is mentioned before "his leaf". It is to draw our attention to the fact that faith precedes fruit. If we do not bring forth fruit to God's glory, his profession (leaf) is a mockery. This order is reflected in this testimony regarding Jesus: He was mighty in deed and word (Luke 24:19), and describing His ministry as "he began to do and teach (Acts.

1:1), because of his fruitfulness, his "leaf", i.e., his living vitality becomes visibly evident.

"And whatsoever he doeth shall prosper"

This necessarily follows, though it is not always apparent to the eye of sense. Not even a cup of water given in the name of Christ shall fail to receive its reward—if not here, certainly in the life to come.

Let us again press the order of these three verses. To the extent we fall into the sins of verse 1, so will our delight in God's Law be dulled. Likewise, as far as we resist subjecting to His will, so shall we be fruitless. Nevertheless, a complete separation from the world and wholehearted occupation with the Lord will issue in fruit to His praise.

PART 3: BAD EXAMPLE OF ESHERI: GAD AND ASHER

Numerous times, YHWH warned Moses to warn the Israelites not to become influenced by the pagan worship that was the predominant type of worship in the Promised Land. After all, this was the reason God drove them out of Canaan. However, many within the camp, when settled in their new homesteads, began to corrupt their souls by involving themselves in the pagan religions of the former inhabitants.

We can trace this tendency back to Jacob and the family he formed from his association with Laban.

Laban, his father-in-law was a conniver and a crook—made his living gaining advantage via unethical behavior. Laban tricked Jacob into marrying Leah first, in spite of his love being for Rachel, the younger daughter. They went to war, trying to win Jacob's affections.

When Leah became barren, she sent her female servant, Zilpah, to bear even more children for Jacob through Zilpah. It is very likely that Bilhah and Zilpah both may have been pagan worshippers and we will find out later that Leah definitely worshipped pagan gods. When Zilpah bore her first two children in behalf of Leah,

Leah gave them both pagan names. Gad's name was based on a Syrian and Babylonian deity, "Fortune". This "Fortune" is the same deity that is spoken against by Isaiah 65:11-12. Here it is referred to by its nickname, "Gad". Leah was literally saying: "The god, Fortunah, has come and blessed me so I am going to honor him by naming my son the nick-name of Fortunah, which is "Gawd".

Asher's name means "Happiness"; he was named after a Canaanite fertility goddess and the wooden cult symbol that represents her. I find it shocking and amazing that two of the twelve tribes of Israel undeniably bear pagan names.

As a result, when the Tribes that bore these two names entered Canaan, they found a valley used for the worship of Fortunah named after them (Joshua 11:16-17). Unfortunately, Joshua had commanded them to drive these people out (Josh. 13:5-6).

It must have felt quite strange for the people of the tribe of Asher when they went into the land and found that the Canaanites were worshipping the same god that they were named after. Maybe that is why we read in Judges 1:32: Result: Neither Tribe drove out the inhabitants... so the Asherites dwelt in the midst of the Canaanites, the inhabitants of the land, because they did not drive them out.

Gawd and Asher, and they were already corrupted before they even went into the Promised Land. Moreover, when they did finally go in to possess the land that had been promised to their forefathers, they felt comfortable among the pagan worshippers because of their own names. They were the product of an unrighteous example that went all the way back to Laban.

How easy it is for one generation's unrighteous influence to pass to the succeeding one, until it ends up an unrighteous influence upon thousands of future generations.

PART 4: DIVINE FAVOR'S CONNECTION TO APOSTOLIC MINISTRY

It is interesting that the first money Congress allocated was for military intelligence. George Washington felt it was important to know the enemy.

The apostolic ministry, since it is the first to penetrate spiritual territory controlled by Satan, experiences fierce combat with the spiritual enemies of our Savior. In this spiritual warfare we enjoy the proactive support from the living Lord. It is called Divine Favor. To help you appreciate the extent of this blessing, permit me briefly to list the benefits that the Bible describes as derived from divine favor.

Our list includes these:
- It shields our ministry against threats we cannot see (Psa. 5:2)

- It ensures our ministry will not end up sparking anger and tears Ps 30:5
- It confirms the legitimacy of our ministry (Deuteronomy 28:13).
- It confirms the promises that the Bible makes about it (Psalm 119:58).
- It facilitates us gaining a good reputation with heaven and those who control the institutions we seek to penetrate (Proverbs 3:3-4).
- It confirms the legitimacy of our plans (Proverbs 11:27).
- It builds our brand (Proverbs 22:1) "A good name is to be more desired than great riches, Favor is better than silver and gold."
- It frees us to objectively critique and rebuke wrong doing—the outcome will not prove negative to our ministry (Proverbs 28:23)

Can you see why this outcome enjoys such a high priority in our planning and ministry?

CONCLUSION

Metaphors can be so helpful, as this example illustrates. Beulah Land was a place that the Old Testament prophet Isaiah tried to fix in the minds of the distraught Israelites for whom he wrote would sustain them, emotionally, as they descended *en masse* into bondage under the thumb of Nebuchadnezzar.

This place is not unlike that place that secular literature describes as Camelot. Except this biblical place is where no mythical king rules (King Arthur), but the true and living King of Kings personally resides and exercises absolute power and distributes His blessings to every inhabitant. True believers enter it now via physical death—it is the Presence of the Lord. However, when Christ returns, it will exist as the New Jerusalem, where He reigns over all, along with those washed in His blood.

This is that place that the true believer keeps in mind as his final destination after death—when he enters into the true heavenly "Promised Land" Beulah Land was like Zion, the place where the truehearted Jew wants to return from wandering the earth.

To appreciate its value, we only need to study how a well-known hymn writer, Edgar Page Stites described it in a hymn by the same name.

Permit me to share with you the chorus:

> O Beulah land, sweet Beulah land!
> As on thy highest mount I stand,
> I look away across the sea
> Where mansions are prepared for me
> And view the shining glory shore
> My heaven, my home forever more.

The following passage of Isaiah mentioned inspired the sentiment behind these lyrics

> "Thou shall no more be termed Forsaken; neither shall thy land any more be termed Desolate; but thou shall be called Hephzibah and thy land Beulah; for the LORD delights in thee, and thy land shall be married." (Isa. 62:4)

The verse is in reference to the return of the Jews from their exile in Babylon in which the Jews shall no longer be called Forsaken, but Hephzibah (My Delight Is in Her), and Jerusalem shall no longer be called Desolate, but Beulah (Married). This implies that the Jews have turned back to the worship of God.

The idea that this hymn presents is this: Heaven can be seen from Beulah Land. We cam trace this idea to John Bunyan's Pilgrim's Progress. There he writes, "Therefore it is, I say, that the Enchanted ground [i.e. Heaven] is placed so nigh to the land Beulah and so near the end of their race."

When I think of these metaphors, I envision our apostolic ministry being anointed by the Holy Spirit to become His instrument, enabling many to experience all of His blessed outcomes, including true divine favor.

Chapter 3

Shalom as an Outcome

INTRODUCTION

SINCE THE BIBLE LOVES to use metaphors, it describes life as God intends it to be for those in fellowship with Him with these: Beulah land, "Eden", New Jerusalem, and Zion. Each depicts a realm wherein man and God live in true harmony, free of sin's influence. All of these metaphors share, in common, this idea: they exist as a community that enjoys a marvelous quality of life. That quality is embodied in the word, *shalom*.

You get an idea of the importance of this word when you realize that the Hebrew (*shalom*) and Greek (*eirene*) words are used almost 500 times in the Bible. Also, since many different English words are needed to translate them, you realize how complex is their meanings. If you look up the word "peace" in a dictionary, you will find it defined by a negative connotation: peace is described as a state absent of confrontation, violence, etc.

However, the Hebrew word *shalom* goes far beyond that described in the Oxford dictionary. It encapsulates the Hebrew vision of a human society, so ruled by the Messiah that every aspect of life (including the non-human aspects) exist in such integrated harmony that wolves and lambs feed together, and lions, no longer carnivorous, munch straw like oxen (Isa. 65:25). Walter Brueggemann (*Peace, pg. 205)*) rightly points out that the Hebrew word meaning includes hope in a future time when all aspects of the ecosystem flawlessly function as God intends when the Messiah rules.

For this reason, this outcome is strategic to everything we seek to accomplish.

However, to appreciate its importance, you first need to understand the meaning of the word as used by the Old Testament language (shalom), as well as that of the New Testament and Greek (*eirene*).

PART 1: ANALYZING THE WORD'S MEANING

Ancient Roots

We begin with the ancient formation of the word, shalom by analyzing its three main consonants, "Shem", "Lamed", and "Mem" as Hebrew alphabetical pictographs.

When I "connect the dots" by organizing the meaning of:
- Shem (white teeth as a cliff, i.e., Gibraltar) plus
- Lamed (shepherd's staff, i.e., leading, protecting and yoking) plus
- Mem (the unknown, as is the ocean beyond the horizon)

This meaning emerges when I organize these meaning fragments into a composite picture: Like Gibraltar, *I will protect and guide you by yoking you to Myself as I lead you into the unknown so that you experience safety, security, and wholeness.*

Lexical Report

Surely the ancients got the meaning of this word right, because when the word was added to the first lexicons, the root word, *sh-l-m*, conveyed the idea of entering into a state of wholeness and unity. However, they did add three insights. First, this state was achieved by the actions of someone else. Therefore, one enjoys it as state to which one has been restored. Second, the word occurs in the intensive active aspect known as Piel.

Therefore, this state of wholeness and unity can not be disturbed. Third, this state is achieved by the payment in full of a debt.

For these reasons the word was soon identified with salvation since the redemptive relationship results from the divine payment for sin, thus restoring man and his Lord to a relationship with no pending conditions. No wonder Paul summarized the Gospel as the Gospel of Peace (Eph. 6:15).

In the context of the Gospel, Shalom is the result of God acting because of a covenant relationship to purchase our righteousness and place us in a state of harmony with God by grace.

Therefore, this type of peace has its source in Him who speaks *shalom* to His people (Psa. 85:8). This is why Paul calls Christ *"our peace (Eph. 2:14),* the one who, as Messiah, delivers wholeness to those He saves.

The word also has an eschatological aspect. When Jesus returns to establish His reign as the Prince of Peace on earth, the planet will experience righteous wholeness and fulfillment.

Pulling It All Together

As mentioned earlier, when we hear the word "peace" we usually think of a state free of war or strife but the Hebrew meaning of the word shalom has a richer meaning.

The verb *shalam* literally means to make whole or complete. The noun *shalom* has the more literal meaning of being in a state of wholeness or with no deficiency. The common phrase *shalu shalom yerushalayim* ("pray for the peace of Jerusalem") is not speaking about an absence of war (though that is part of it) but that Jerusalem (and by extension, all of Israel) is complete and whole and goes far beyond the idea of "peace".

Think of it as the deep, inner sense of tranquility and fulfillment that comes from a life well lived in the heart of God that He created us for.

In our apostolic ministry, we focus on this outcome because we know that peace cannot be found by any other means. Solomon proved that living in perfect circumstances could expose how empty our inner life really is. Only Jesus who is our Peace can deliver true peace that passes understanding to the human heart.

When the Holy Spirit plants this true peace within a human soul, and they experience its extraordinary sense of an inner sense of safety and provision, that new life is capable of enduring through the most horrendous situations.

Describing this state to one who has never tasted it is like describing color to someone who has been blind from birth. It is not easy to define. It is something you have to experience to appreciate. Where is that life? It is in Him alone (I John 5:11-12), and only by learning to feast on him as the Life itself, will we ever know the reality that our hearts desperately long for.

Remember, YHWH promised Abraham three blessings: a son will be born (despite his and Sarah's age); a land will be given to them so that all of them can live together with Him in posterity; and, for the rest of Abraham's life, the LORD promised him that he would live in the state of *"shalom"* (Gen. 15:15). The meaning is clear; God intends for him to spend the rest of his life at peace with all people, and with Him.

Now that we have a clear idea of this word's meaning, let us now pursue its source.

PART 2: SOURCE OF THIS PEACE

Every member of the Godhead participates to provide it. God the Father is the God of peace.' I Thess. 5:53, I Cor. 14:43, and Phil. 4:4.

God, the Son as the 'Prince of peace' (Isa 9:9), purchased this peace by shedding His blood (*"having made peace by the blood of his cross."* Col 1:10). This atonement is typified in the sacrifice Aaron made for the people when he entered into the holy of holies.

God the Holy Spirit administers it as an integral part of the 'fruit of the Spirit.' Gal 5:52. The Spirit enables the true believer to find the well of God's peace.

Thus you see whence this peace comes - the Father decrees it, the Son purchases it, and the Holy Ghost appropriates it to our hearts.

Because peace flows from regeneration, the unbelieving heart cannot experience it. When he claims to possess it, its source can be traced not to the work of God in salvation but to events occurring that produce what the world calls happiness. This form of "peace" is counterfeit. The marks such false peace include the following:

- A confidence resembling that of the foolish virgins masquerading as peace
- A peace that rejects its twin, holiness (Deut. 29:19), and
- A peace that is unwilling to be tested; it fears exposure as a vampire hates light.

If these indicate a false peace, what signifies true peace?

Signs of True Peace

Here are some signs of genuine peace:

1. It flows from union with Christ. In this, it resembles a 'shoot' grafted onto a tree for nourishment. By being in Christ we have peace. John 16:63.
2. It flows from a heart submitted to Christ who, on the throne of the human spirit acts as a High Priest, thereby bringing peace to our soul. Remember, if Christ is to be our peace, he must first be our Prince (Isa. 9:9). He pacifies the conscience after subduing everything controlling it.
3. It follows trouble. Having counseled couples for decades, I have observed this pattern of experience: i) they get into the grasp of a spirit of bondage; ii) humbled, they cry out for forgiveness and His deliverance; iii) He forgives and 'speaks peace to their soul'. This that "balm of Gilead' that the Bible speaks about; in reality, it is the golden oil of peace that the Holy Spirit pours into broken hearts.

Do all Saved People Possess this Peace

No sadly, they do not experience *shalom* although they possess title to it by grace. Again, from my pastoral experience I have observed these reasons why true believers do not experience His peace:
- Satan entices them to sin, thereby destroying their peace;
- Believer looks at weight of sin and concludes "forget-it" and loses sense of peace;
- People stop trusting and obeying, causing their peace to cool

If you slacken the strings of a violin, the music is spoiled; so, if Christians slack in duty, they spoil the sweet music of peace in their souls.

PART 3: RELEVANCE TO OUR APOSTOLIC MINISTRY

Why is this outcome so vital to our ministry, therefore strategic? Permit me briefly to describe these reasons.

Relevance to our Goal of Nation-restoring

Shalom is integral to our ministry because we seek to restore the nation to wholeness. A society characterized by shalom embraces the core values of peace, justice, and enjoyment of all relationships, centered in relationship with God.

Often we enter situations ravaged dominated by injustice. As the impact of this peace begins to be felt, the community of true believers begins to speak truth. As a result the institutions that govern the society (which we shall discuss later) begin to improve.

Because *shalom* connotes the complete well being of a society or community, it connects it with justice; a shalom community is a just one. It also renders the society a covenant community since it results from God's covenantal commitment to His people (Ezek. 34:25; 37:26)

To appreciate how true peace from God can influence a community, notice in the final chapters of the Book of Revelation a diverse group of people from every tribe and tongue, yet experiencing life within a perfect Christ-centered community.

Therefore our goal is to impact and transform the culture with God's *shalom*.

This diversity in unity that will fully characterize God's people at the end of time gives a snapshot of God's intention for His community now.

Diversity in unity as a model for God's people has its basis in the nature of God. God reveals himself in Scripture as one God in three persons: Father, Son, and Holy Spirit. God's very nature may be conceived in terms of diversity in unity. This view of diversity in unity seems to be an important part of what it means to image God, fulfilling God's intention for humanity.

The story of humanity, however, shows that the shalom envisioned by God for humanity and established at creation was marred in the fall. The marring of shalom in a society leads to many kinds of injustice and division.

Our Goal: Restore Shalom

In His covenant with Abraham, God made it clear that His larger plan is to bless all nations by restoring shalom.

Jesus fulfilled God's intention of bringing shalom to the nations by becoming "a light for revelation to the Gentiles and for glory to [God's] people Israel."

Jesus focuses His new community around two central ideas:
- His expanded concept of neighbor to those outside one's own cultural or ethnic circle, even to those he now regards as his enemy; and,

- His focus on reconciliation

Recall how, in the Upper Room, as the Holy Spirit appeared, and people began to speak in tongues they did not understand, how He was making the Body of Christ inclusive.

The early church progressively came to realize that the witness of Jesus might reach the ends of the earth, ultimately, a spiritually unified community in which God's spirit dwells in anticipation of that eternal vision of "a great multitude of worshippers that no one could count, from every nation, from all tribes and peoples and languages, standing before the throne and before the Lamb." (Rev. 5)

Therefore, we seek the outcome of *shalom* to enable us to strengthen the culture by including people from all categories, who although diverse in language or customs, nevertheless are united in worship for Christ, and a dedication to make Him known to all people within their borders.

Relevance to our Healing Ministry

First, it relates to our healing ministry. Recall that two of the primary aspects of meaning for this word are "completion" and "wholeness". The purpose of healing and deliverance is to reverse the savagery of the evil one by visiting them either with sickness or invading their souls by his minions.

What are we doing when the Holy Spirit uses us to confront disease, invading germs and microbes? We are setting people free, restoring them to wholeness.

Remember, we are at war, spiritually, as we partner with the Savior in building His kingdom. Satan has infested the realms we seek to serve with illness, injury, and disease.

Then, into this arena we come preaching the Gospel that sets people free. Within this message we proclaim deliverance from sin's penalty and filthy grip, and, using our apostolic tools, begin to eradicate this evil that holds people's bodies, minds, and souls in bondage—we bring shalom.

So, like Jesus said,

> "But that you may know that the Son of Man has authority on earth to forgive sins"—he said to the man who was paralyzed—"I say to you, rise, pick up your bed and go home." (Luke 5:24)

Likewise the exercise of our healing and deliverance gifts demonstrates the supremacy of our God over the forces of demonic influence and illness.

Therefore, healing and deliverance are integral to bringing shalom to the people our apostolic ministry serves. By exposing them to the message that delivers peace, we are introducing people to wholeness and completeness.

Relevance to our Deliverance Ministry

Recall, that one other nuance of the meaning of Shalom is "safety and security". Surely for one possessed or oppressed by demonic spirits, life as "shalom" must seem as remote as the corner of Main and Seventh Street in downtown Mars.

Such possessed persons live in constant fear from self-mutilation and tyranny by the evil spirits who control and manipulate their lives so self-destructively. Then by His leading, we show up and they learn that Jesus can free their souls, minds and bodies by His grace.

For many, the offer to become whole is most compelling. As a result, the territories in which we serve take on the look of that small region of the Decapolis after the Gadarene sat, clothed and in his right mind after Jesus had delivered him from so many controlling evil spirits that it took an entire herd of swine to carry them away (Matt. 8:28).

Thank God that the Gospel we preach offers people protection from evil spirits, and deliverance from their encroaching tentacles! To distinguish between the needs expressed in these two aspects of our ministry, consider healing to restore to wholeness, and deliverance to restore people to security and safety of wholeness. Are these not two ways in which this outcome becomes relevant to our apostolic ministry?

Relevance to our Kingdom Building

Paul describes the kingdom as righteousness, peace, and joy (Rom. 14:17)

> For the kingdom of God is not a matter of eating and drinking but of righteousness and peace and joy in the Holy Spirit. (Rom. 14:17)

As we have discussed, the kingdom of God reflects His nature. Therefore, He upholds peace, joy, and righteousness and projects them as values that His citizens must have. Let us examine the value, 'peace'. Its contribution to kingdom building lies in its ability to create 'well-being', one of those nuanced meanings of *shalom*

We seek to help people develop 'kingdom-mindedness'. The importance of this is twofold. First, we want them to experience true salvation, which includes experiencing true joy (as our text above points out), and genuine peace. This latter includes that which the Cross-provides—the peace of God—to those once estranged from God and His enemy. Thanks to the perfect work of the Son, the Father makes peace with us at salvation, and offers peace to us through the sacrifice of Jesus.

When Jesus appeared on the scene, the Jews, at first, wondered if He was their long awaited Prince of Peace. Then the disappointment settled as He, instead of urging them to rise up against the Roman empire, he asked them to carry the shields of Roman soldiers for an extra mile (Matt. 5:41). His intention, of course, was to dramatize that He had come to deliver peace to the human heart that so transcends any kind of peace that the world has to offer (John 14:27) that once the Holy Spirit instills it, you would not care who sat atop the political throne of a nation or the world.

This message is also relevant to our message, because everywhere, we encounter masses who seek to 'purchase peace' by ingesting drugs, entertainment, or alcohol just to experience some relief they consider as peace (although it is not). Then, they act on the message we bring, and experience true peace that is not an illusion.

Therefore, we hold seminars, and minister through healing and deliverance in order that they can find perfect peace by keeping their minds stayed on Him (Isa. 26.3); the essence of a kingdom mind.

Relevance to our Prosperity Message

The Bible addresses the issue of prosperity, even making promises to the true believer, as He did Abraham, Joseph, and all those that continually meditate on the Word, that whose who trust the Lord will prosper.

The key to prosperity is stated in the Bible with the straightforward clarity of a mathematical formula: "but Godliness and contentment is (leads to) great gain (prosperity). This contentment is a form of peace, thereby, establishing the relevance of this second fruit of the Spirit (the first is sanctification). Permit me to share this story to illustrate.

A man in the throes of financial collapse threw himself humbly upon the mercy of the Lord. In this terrible moment, the Holy Spirit came alongside his hurting heart to advise him that he needed to relinquish his concerns about his financial matters, and, for the moment, he advised, become content with what you have. The man then threw himself upon this living God in a new and totally surrendered way.

In an instant, the Spirit of God washed him from head to foot in His peace. God also whispered that he would extricate him from any self-destructive solution such as bankruptcy. Twenty minutes later a man knocked on his door and said, "I feel awkward to mention this, but do you have a financial need. You see I feel that the Lord wants me to bless you with this financial gift. He then placed an envelope in the man's hand.

The key to true prosperity is twofold. First, it reflects a process. The Hebrew word, "*tsalech*", (translated as "prosperity"), is promised. However, rather than dropping out of the sky as if a large bag of cash, it occurs because the person begins at a point of need, seeks the mind of the Lord regarding what to do next, and then acts on the counsel the Holy Spirit provides. After repeating this process consistently, at each decision-making opportunity, this individual finds himself steadily progressing toward true prosperity.

Second, throughout the process, the man maintains a spirit of contentment of God, triggering the release of divine anointing; thereby transitioning the needs he had from the spiritual into the natural realm. Suddenly, money loses its control over him, since he now sees God—whom he has placed his complete trust—as his supplier. This contentment is a form of peace relative to his finances that has nothing to do with what is in his bank account.

As you can see from this example, peace places an important role in the attainment of true prosperity—the one that the world promotes: "give me a financial gift and you will be forcing God to bless you with wealth." The flaw in such thinking, of course, is that it shifts the emphasis from trusting in God to taking pro-active steps to solve your financial problems by your own strength for yourself. The Kingdom path to prosperity involves trusting the goodness of God for whatever we need. It is not about us, it is about Him.

On the other hand how wonderful to tell many thousands over the decades of our ministry that prosperity begins with being rightly related to Him. The telltale sign of this is the peace that expresses itself as contentment. I bear witness that those that begin properly soon drink from wells they did not dig and live in houses they did not build.

Ah the wonder of this peace "...that passes understanding? It opens the spigot to God's blessings that discontent and selfish ambition and the love of money kept blocked. Seeking first the kingdom of God has a way of 'anxiety-proofing' the heart from worry, doubt, and ungodly ambition. What a privilege true believers enjoys. Unlike chasing money as the world's system implores, they pray, gain the mind of the Lord and obey, and then watch as God brings the things they need into their hand.

Peace, expressed as contentment, enables us to pursue the Lord, rather than the things He can provide. I have observed that whenever I do this, I find myself running away from the very blessing attempting to overtake me.

This peace looks at His promise, e.g., I will never fail you, nor leave or forsake or abandon or relax My grip on you (Heb.13:5). When I surrender and trust Him I often find myself doing the opposite of why my emotions recommend. But, shortly, afterward, I find the blessings and abundance forthcoming. Then the truth hits me, all of this is happening to me because I have kept my eyes focused on the things above; and the peace I am experiencing confirms that my decision was correct.

How such experiences have strengthened my confidence as I encourage people to seek Him for all their needs, even to the abundance that the Bible calls prosperity.

Remember, Eve tried to teach Adam that he could have the things of God WITHOUT GOD, resulting in the great fall. Satan was cast out of heaven for much the same reason. Therefore, if someone seeks to "get something from God" he makes two mistakes. First, as a true believer, they already enjoy Divine favor. Second, none of His blessings (including financial) are to be had apart from a trusting relationship with the Savior who shed His blood at Calvary so that His people might have life and have it more abundantly (John 10:10).

Experiencing the peace known as contentment, I acknowledge the favor obtained through my shed blood and give only in Obedience to My Spirit and I begin to experience unmerited favor and financial blessing—a form of Godly prosperity that reaches beyond money to every area of my needs.

Shalom as an Outcome

Relevance to our Ministering Processes

Face it apostolic ministry is pioneering. We venture into territories unknown to us, and with a message unknown to those we share it with. This can be a cause for angst. Thank God that we have His peace to provide stability and confirm our decisions. Permit me to explain each of these contributions of peace to our work.

First, peace acts as an anchor, stabilizing our ministry. What is the key to experiencing this peace?

Two clues (from Peter and Paul)

Peter reveals that peace derives from the knowledge of His Word that we possess, and is occupying our mind as we face trials. Grace and PEACE be yours in abundance through the KNOWLEDGE of God and of Jesus our Lord (2 Pet.1:2).

Paul makes a similar point:

> Finally, brothers, whatever is true, whatever is noble, whatever is right, whatever is pure, whatever is lovely, whatever is admirable— if anything is excellent or praiseworthy—think about such things. Whatever you have learned or received or heard from me, or seen in me— put it into practice. And the God of peace will be with you. (Phil. 4:8-9).

The point they both speak to is this: the peace that you can partake of is in proportion to the knowledge you have of God that occupies your mind when you face trials.

This counsel is particularly helpful when we face a decision, or an impending need for resources. In such moments, we try to focus on His past faithfulness. Then, in such peace, we ask for His supply. When He delivers, we praise Him for having met our need, and having taught us, again, the value of being anchored in a reality that surpasses the natural realm!

As I write this, I think of a ship parked off shore of our nearby harbor. Suddenly, by divine illumination, I realize what enables it to remain undisturbed by the constant onslaught of waves—it is anchored. Then I pray, "Lord do not allow any waves approaching me steal my peace".

In that moment I experience a reality that Isaiah describes:

> You will keep him in perfect peace, him whose mind is stayed on You because he trusts in You (Isa. 26:3).

Yes, perfect peace anchors us, therefore, the ministry to which we are called.

Second, peace acts like an umpire, guiding our path correctly. What a waste to pursue this arduous ministry without regard to whether or not we were obeying Him, i.e. following the path that He directs. How will we know that our way is His? Peace! It acts like a referee, officiating His will not unlike those that keep players from fouling in a game popular in our homeland that we call football, but people in the US call soccer. Paul describes it this way:

> And let the peace of Christ rule in your hearts... (Col. 3:15).

Upon reflection of what I just wrote, this sports analogy came to mind as I thought about the word translated as "rule". The Greek word, *brabeuo* means, *"to be an umpire"*.

The word *"umpire"* being a sports name, helped me examine how the umpire works in sports. The rulebook defines an umpire as one having the authority to make decisions about whether or not the action on the field conforms to the rules that govern it. That moment I realized that peace umpires the decisions we make as we conduct our ministry.

How does peace become a decision maker? Let us suppose that you face a dilemma—a career change, or signing a contract, etc. You turn to the Lord for direction and you wait until He approves a decision by placing His peace within your heart.

This is how peace "referees" our decision-making process. I can honestly say our ministry has enjoyed His blessing because of the decisions He affirmed by the peace He placed within our hearts.

While I am at it, permit me to add these ways in which the *shalom* of God helps our ministry:

- It gives boldness at the throne of grace. When the Spirit whispers peace, we go to God with boldness, as a child to his father. (*Unto thee, O Lord, do I lift up my soul.*' Psa 25:5).
- It fires our heart with love to Christ. Peace is the result of pardon. He, who has a pardon sealed, cannot choose but love his prince.
- It quiets the heart in trouble. The enemy may invade our 'palace', but not our peace: When worldly troubles assault us, our mind may be in peace and quiet. (*I will lay me down in peace, and sleep.*' Psa 4:4). David experienced the tragedy of his own son

trying to destroy him (2 Sam. 15:50); yet, this verse shows that his trouble with his son could not rob him of the peace with God. This is a peace worth getting.

Small wonder, then, that when we feel we have lost this sense of His blessed peace we fall before Him to ask that He, the Prince of Peace, show us what caused the loss of Your peace that we may confess our sin and need, so you can then restore that peace we need so desperately to serve You.

This is also why we make war continually with sin so that it has no dominion over us (Rom 6:i); and why we do not ask for its supply based on our merit but upon His shed blood (Rom. 5:5); and why we try to walk closely with Him. It is because we know that peace derives from cleanliness as Paul said (Gal. 6:16).

We preserve this peace as a treasure more precious than a bag of large diamonds.

CONCLUSION

The Hebrew word *shalom* is understood around the world to mean peace. But peace is only one small part of the meaning of the word. *Shalom* also includes completeness, wholeness, health, peace, welfare, safety soundness, tranquility, prosperity, perfectness, fullness, rest, harmony, the absence of agitation or discord.

Sar Shalom (Prince of Peace) is one of the descriptive names the Bible uses to indicate the ministry and personality of the Messiah: Isaiah 9:6 - The Son of God is completely perfect in all things.

So in essence, when you speak out the word SHALOM - you are not only proclaiming peace, but also all the above meanings of the word over that person - that is a mighty blessing!!!

Someone has said, "No wonder the Jewish people are so blessed. Every time they greet someone with "Shalom" they are, in effect, pronouncing all of the rich spiritual benefits imbedded in the full meaning of this word.

When spoken with the level of sincerity it enjoyed in Jesus' day, it gets even better. To address an oncoming friend with the greeting, 'Shalom Aleichem' (literally, "Peace be upon you") obligates the greeter to help with any situation the person addressed is going through at the time. For example, we exchange greetings and you tell me your son has injured himself with a knife; I am thus obligated to come to your house and meet any remaining need until his wound mends. Yes, that also included a need for financial help.

Does that help you appreciate the significance this world held for Jews? Certainly it helps me understand how powerful the promise is imbedded in it when Christ, through the promises in the Bible, conveys 'peace be upon you' to me — how that resonates!

It also warms my heart as I hear a pastor, at the close of a worship service say to his people, (quoting Numbers 6:24-26): "*The Lord bless you and keep you. The Lord make His face shine upon you and be gracious to you. The Lord lift up His face upon you and give you SHALOM in the name of SAR SHALOM - the Prince of Peace*".

Now, knowing what you know about the rich nuanced meaning of this word, is such a benediction not a that is a blessed way to start one's week?

Many years ago, a wealthy patron looked for a picture he felt depicted perfect peace. Finding none, he promoted a contest with a substantial prize. He appointed judges to analyze every canvass of the many entries that had poured in. Finally, only two submissions remained; he had rejected all others.

The first one unveiled portrayed a mirror-smooth lake reflected lacy, green birches under the soft blush of the evening sky. Along the grassy shore, a flock of sheep grazed undisturbed. Surely, this was the winner.

Then as the final painting was unveiled, the people gasped. It seemed so unlike the other depictions of peace.

The canvass held this scene: a tumultuous waterfall cascaded down a rocky precipice; the crowd could almost feel its cold, penetrating spray. Stormy-gray clouds threatened to explode with lightning, wind and rain. In the midst of the thundering noises and bitter chill, a spindly tree clung to the rocks at the edge of the falls. One of its branches reached out in front of the torrential waters as if foolishly seeking to experience its full power. A little bird had built a nest in the elbow of that branch. Content and undisturbed in her stormy surroundings, she rested on her eggs.

After much debate, all judges agreed, this mother bird, with her eyes closed and her wings ready to cover her little ones, manifested the peace that transcends all earthly turmoil.

Our apostolic ministry seeks this Shalom for those we serve. We pursue no more important outcome.

Book IV

The Apostolic Toolbox: Tools Essential to the Apostolic Ministry

Chapter 1	Fasting & Prayer: Tools Used in Tandem
Chapter 2	Deliverance
Chapter 3	Healing: Part of the Deliverance Toolkit
Chapter 4	Exorcism: Part of the Deliverance Toolkit
Chapter 5	Repentance as a Tool
Chapter 6	Kingdom Preaching as a Tool

"Find the right tool and the job is half done"

Introduction

THOMAS CARLYLE WAS RIGHT, "Man is a tool-using animal." Historians have perpetrated the myth that politicians shape our civilization. The truth is that tools and those who create them mold our world.

Can you imagine a world minus the invention of writing? Each generation begins without the benefit of any record of its history, or accumulated wisdom since no way exists to record or pass on any information.

The invention of the horse collar (or oxen yoke) rates high on my list because of important inventions because it was the first use of non-human energy to transport people and goods as well as pull a plow. As a result people spread over the Mediterranean area, and food production increased.

Others may argue for the invention of fire, but I contend that anyone, after observing trees burned by a fire started by lightening could have figured out how to transport and preserve enough glowing embers to warm their home.

Top Choices: Forbes' and Mine

Here are my tool and inventor top choices. First, consider Euclid's Elements (300 BC), without these we could not measure flat surfaces, figure distances, or venture out onto the ocean since his principles made possible navigation. Without his principles, life in this century would resemble the fifteenth.

Alongside him, I nominate the tenth century (AD) mathematician, Sridhara for giving us the numeral, zero. Without him we would need to be bare-foot to count to twenty. Without his invention, science, mathematics, business, and all other fields of endeavor would be unrecognizable. Can you imagine a world without computers? Its essential code is comprised of the numerals ones and zero.

My third choice: Sir Isaac Newton's varied mathematical and scientific principles governing the natural universe. His book, *Principia*, may be the most influential book to science; it describes his discovery of the concepts underlying classical mechanics. Without his breakthrough thinking, Neil Armstrong could never have set foot on the moon's surface. Newton helped birth our scientific revolution.

So much for my choices! Recently Forbes magazine created its own list of the twenty hand-held tools that have impacted civilization and shaped history the most. I found their selections insightful, especially since my horse-collar made the top five. The other four included the knife (#1), followed by the abacus, compass, and pencil, and my first choice (#5).

Tools influence everything we do, including writing this book. Could I get these hundred thousand words on paper with only a pen and pad of paper? Yes, but the chore would be arduous. Thank the Lord for these tools—my computer and Internet access to the world's largest online research library—they simplify my task!

On the other hand, could I conduct my apostolic ministry without the tools we are about to discuss? No way it would be as impossible as trying to steer a ship without a rudder, or building a fence without a hammer.

Mapping our Learning Journey

This discussion about apostolic tools now before us is inevitable because once you understand the intended outcomes (BOOK THREE) of the apostolic ministry, then this question logically follows: "*What tools are required to produce these outcomes?*" To answer it, we will detail the Tools so essential to the Apostolic ministry they define and distinguish it from the other four categories of giftedness highlighted in Ephesians 4:11, 12.

Each chapter details one of them. Two tools enable us to transform and restore a nation's hearts—*preaching* and *repentance*. Four additional tools—*healing, exorcism, fasting,* and *prayer*—confirm our ministry's anointing, and pinpoint how the supernatural, transforming power is generated.

The following overviews sketch each tool's discussion. We will focus on them according to the way they support our ministry. We shall segregate their treatment according to their area of usefulness: generating spiritual resources deliverance, and pulpit ministry.

CATEGORY ONE: TOOL-KIT TO GENERATE RESOURCES
OVERVIEW OF CHAPTER 1
FASTING AND PRAYER: TOOLS USED IN TANDEM

We take up those gifts that are essential to generating the power from on High needed to supply the resources, without which we could not hope to fulfill our apostolic calling. Because these two tools work in tandem we will consider them together as a single chapter. However, to facilitate your understanding of this chapter's presentation, we will focus on each separately.

Fasting

In this part of the chapter, you will learn why we consider fasting strategic to breaking strongholds, preparing hearts for repentance, making important decisions, and preparing for spiritual warfare. In the process of fasting two things occur. First, He draws closer to us in order to answer our prayers. Second, we draw closer to our mission; our focus sharpens; we see Him and His plan for our ministry more clearly. Fasting causes our confidence to soar.

Prayer

In this part of the chapter, you will learn that, as faith needs a life of prayer in which to grow and keep strong, so prayer needs fasting to fully develop. You will also learn these principles: i) in the Kingdom, there can be no effectual faith without prayer; ii) Prayer gains its power to move heaven by its closeness to Word and the Spirit's Presence; and, iii) Fasting aids the development of that closeness. By enabling us to blot out all the extraneous stuff we are free to focus on Him, His Word so we can gain insight into His will for us.

As you can see, these tools were meant to be used in tandem. In fact, our deliverance meetings utilize both of these gifts. With one hand, through prayer, we grasp the invisible. With the other hand, through fasting, we let go of the visible. Our apostolic ministry leaves us no choice but to lay hold of the power that will put demonic forces to flight. Therefore, prayer fasting is one of our most often employed tools.

CATEGORY TWO: DELIVERANCE TOOL-KIT
OVERVIEW OF CHAPTER 2: DELIVERANCE AS A TOOL

Christian deliverance occurs when God rescues someone from bondage, oppression, hardship, or domination by evil. He brings deliverance. "Deliver us from the evil one," (Mat 6:12-13). While we devote a chapter to each of the healing and exorcism tools, we felt it important to discuss first the issues they share deliverance in common, thereby laying a foundation for both of these discussions.

When people received deliverance from entanglement with Satan, it takes the form of exorcism. When God frees them from infirmity, disease, etc., it is called healing. The use of these two supernatural tools serves another useful purpose; they demonstrate the reality, viability, and relevance of the kingdom of God, thereby helping it to be respected and pursued. Considering all of these "value-adds" together, you begin to see the strategic role these tools serve the apostle.

We use them extensively because wherever God calls us to serve; Satan enjoys a chokehold over so many lives, including those who line the aisles in our Crusade meetings

Therefore, this chapter will help you understand the relationship of deliverance to the healing and exorcism gifts, along with an understanding of the hindrances preventing it, the steps that will bring it about. You will gain know-how about what this category of ministry is all about.

OVERVIEW OF CHAPTER 3: HEALING AS A TOOL

The purpose of healing is to restore the harmful effects inflicted by the Evil One on a person's body or mind. In our meetings we encounter problems scary to behold. Nevertheless, people turn to the Savior for healing who, continues faithfully to respond to their needs. After decades, we bear witness that He has shown Himself to be so faithful and merciful, not only removing the consequences of evil, but also restoring the individual to wholeness.

In this chapter we present the purpose, and process of healing. You will also meet a man who influenced my thinking in this area. Finally, we will share with you our efforts in research and dealing with some of the top causes of death. We consider these 'immune-deficiency' problems, chronic and infectious diseases as preventable and curable. You will see how through the gift of healing, the laying on of hands and the spoken Word, God has left the church a way to destroy the works of Satan.

OVERVIEW OF CHAPTER 4: EXORCISM AS A TOOL

As the healing gift offers the promise of freedom from disease and disability, so this gift promises deliverance from malevolent invisible spiritual forces seeking to impose Satan's sinister wills. This is why exorcism was integral to Jesus' earthly ministry.

Therefore, we discuss the origin of demons, how they use sexual enticement and fear casting. You will learn why they inhabit human bodies, and why cultures that Jesus sent Apostles to confront were throttled by the dominating influence of the Evil One and his minions. Also, you will learn about the territories of influence that demons inhabit and over which we have control.

This makes the apostolic tool of exorcism to be vitally important! For these reasons and a host of others, we thank God for anointing us with this apostolic tool. Over the years it has enabled the Lord to impact cultures with His presence, leading many to deliverance.

CATEGORY THREE: PREACHING TOOL-KIT
OVERVIEW OF CHAPTER 5: REPENTANCE

No aspect of our apostolic ministry is more important than preaching the Gospel. What moves hearts to embrace our individual message of salvation as well as act on the principles and Laws of our transforming message? Nothing occurs at the deepest spiritual level until the Holy Spirit acts in power; and only one thing prompts Him to action—repentance. Hence this is the tool used in tandem with the preaching gift.

It is the key to the Holy Spirit's transformation of a sinner by grace; it sets in motion a divine process that enables the repentant sinner to replace all God-dishonoring, Christ-belittling hell-bound perceptions and dispositions and purposes with those that treasure God, and exalt Jesus with a spirit that has been transformed by the Holy Spirit—born again.

As you can see, this renders repentance a most important tool in our apostolic ministry. Therefore, we need to understand its meaning and more important implications.

In this chapter we will explain its importance to the ministry of Jesus, what it is, how to distinguish it from theological counterfeits (especially, the example of Cain), and how to make it a way of life.

Repentance is the first and foremost response the Gospel of the Kingdom demands from an individual. Therefore, we consider repentance one of our most important apostolic tools.

Jesus, as He ascended to glory commissioned His Apostles to transform lives through preaching that makes repentance central to its message and the intended pivotal response. His mandate remains relevant for His Apostles in this 21st century.

OVERVIEW OF CHAPTER 6: KINGDOM PREACHING

Preaching is as vital our apostolic ministry as a paddle is to a canoe. We have no choice since the One who commissioned me to apostolic ministry made it the centerpiece of His own Messianic strategy.

We use two venues to exercise the preaching tool: sermons from church pulpits, and seminars from secular platforms. Often we have addressed Parliaments and hosted luncheon meetings.

In this chapter you will learn what preaching is, i.e., what distinguishes kingdom preaching. You will also gain an appreciation of its intended outcomes. We will analyze their sermons to discover how John the Baptizer and Jesus modeled kingdom preaching.

SUMMARY

How grateful we are for the provision of these tools! They are as vital to our apostolic ministry as an operating system to a computer. Without them, our efforts to fulfill our calling would prove to be a waste of time, producing many unintended outcomes.

Two scenes, taking place at the same time illustrate my point. As the French Revolution gutted that great nation, and blood stained the cobblestones of Paris in a vicious, crazy, misguided attempt to change a nation, American inventor, Eli Whitney was perfecting his cotton gin, and creating a new way to mass-produce machinery using interchangeable parts.

Notice how these tools transformed the world, in a way that the politicians could never deliver. One built a great new nation, while the other crippled an old nation for a century.

So, thanks to the invention of writing, please watch as we explain the tools we use to fulfill the outcomes essential to our apostolic ministry.

With this introduction, let us proceed to discuss each one of these tools.

Category One: Tools for Empowerment

CHAPTER 1

Fasting & Prayer
Tools used in Tandem

WHAT DO CERTAIN FOODS (e.g., rice and beans), and some tools, like a fishing pole and line with attached hook share in common? They work well when used in tandem. This is certainly the case with two tools used to confront spiritual forces in our apostolic ministry: prayer with fasting.

The idea did not originate with us. The Apostles asked Jesus why their faith failed to extricate the demons trying to burn that epileptic boy. His reply: Your faith was insufficient. He then explained how to gain the kind of faith that makes demons run: "*this kind comes out (only) by prayer and fasting*" (Matthew 17:21).

To grasp His meaning, we must understand the nature of biblical fasting, and intercessory prayer. Then we will understand how they generate the faith to move mountains and cast out demons from an innocent boy.

PART 1: REGARDING FASTING

John Chrysostom (350 – 400 AD) was such a masterful preacher that Constantine chose him as his pastor. This Godly leader encouraged all true believers to fast, including the Emperor occupying a pew.

Extolling its benefit, John said (and we paraphrase): "*When you hear about the fast, do not be afraid of it as if it were a fearsome commander: it is not terrible for us, but for the evil spirits. Has the evil spirit possessed you? Show him the face of fasting, and the one—scared stiff and tied, as it were, with iron chains—will become more motionless than a stone, especially at the sight of prayer, the tool that works beautifully with fasting."* How does this happen?

It happens because God uses fasting to quench and refocus your heart before Him in order that you can once again begin to give Him the attention He desires, deserves, and seeks. In the process, He draws closer to you, eager to answer your prayer.

Fasting enables our ministry to not only accomplish our mission, it helps us refocus, i.e. get back on mission. Also, it helps us once again to see Him close enough to view His visage radiating agape love. As a result we once again lock onto His intended mission for us. Therefore, we consider this fasting as a tool as strategically important as a hammer to a carpenter. Permit me to explain why.

A reason to fast: to break a stronghold

Have you ever caught yourself thinking aloud, "Man, I never seem to 'catch a break'; maybe God is no longer for me. For example, here I am, really needing His help with this huge problem. I pray and pray, but nothing happens. What is the deal?"

In our ministry, we often encounter people who have drifted into some sort of compulsive behavior. They passionately want to stop, yet, failure rules. They cry out. They then confess to us that they feel He is ignoring their prayers. We then point them to the example of Israel in dealing with the Benjaminite's (Judges 20).

This incident began (what else) with gross sin: Benjaminite men raped a woman from the opposing tribe and in the process, caused her death. To resolve this mess, people from other tribes came to ask the Benjaminite's to produce the guilty people for judgment. The tribe resisted preferring to go to war with Israel. At this point, the Israelite leaders twice sought the mind of God as to how to fight their brothers: "Who of us shall go against the Benjaminite's?" Judah stepped up.

Now at this point, one would assume that Judah/Israel's victory would be guaranteed. They had asked Him what to do. He had told them what His will was in this matter. They then prepared to obey. Sounds like a prayer aligned with His will, right? Then why did the army of Israel failed twice? Only after their third attempt at battle did they achieve victory. What made the difference? Here is a clue: on the day before their third attempt they fasted that day until evening (Judge 20:26b). Using fasting, they moved the battle into a different spiritual realm. As a result, they smashed Satan's stranglehold.

This is another reason why we consider the spiritual discipline of fasting as a vital ministry tool. Since we are sent into situations desperately in need of a spiritual breakthrough situations, battles are inevitable, without this tool, our ministry would be a disaster.

Trust me; we have seen this pattern too often. A spiritual obstacle or conflict looms. Then the person facing this obstacle tries to handle matters in a biblical manner. Often they will lay a scriptural promise before the Lord via prayer, asking Him to answer it in their situation. When they turn to us for counsel we discover that they are being thwarted by a spiritual stronghold that requires a strenuous spiritual response, including fasting.

Another reason to Fasting: To Prepare a Heart for Repentance

Sin requires repentance; and repentance requires sorrowfulness. People confess to us: "I know that I need to confess, but I do not feel emotionally sorry for my sin. Repentance does not depend on feeling sorry enough, but it does require one to look so deeply into one's soul that you see your guilt for what it really is—a monstrous, monumental offense against His holiness. However, sin dulls the senses. As a result, people tell me that they do not feel able to reach a level of Godly sorrow sufficient to trigger genuine repentance. Praise, Him, there is hope. Learn how from Moses.

God directed him to establish a national Day of Atonement to remember the salvation provided by God that enabled them to leave Egypt. Each family shed the blood of a lamb and placed the crimson liquid on their doorframe. It pictured true salvation, achieved by the Lord Jesus on the cross, the true "…Lamb of God that takes away the sin of the world." Since they owed their salvation, and the blessed existence resulting from it, God wanted them never to forget this monumental event. So He directed Moses to establish an annual Day of Atonement—for them to reflect on this.

However, sunrise on Yom Kippur does not automatically ensure that one's heart will feel like repenting. Recognizing this, Moses instituted a fast on the preceding day:

> "...deny yourself [fast] and not do any work... because on this day atonement will be made for you, to cleanse you. (Lev. 16:29-30).

Notice the principle: denying yourself leads to afflicting your souls in such a way that the will surrenders to His will. As a result, the heart is ready to address those areas that the individual struggles with, and needs to confess.

By starving the flesh, fasting produces the power we need to master the tyranny of self. The joy of forgiveness is the fruit of true repentance. However, this joy may owe much to the way fasting prepared the heart to repent.

Another Reason for Fasting: Ministering with Invincible Power

It is important to get this principle in mind: fasting, in the final analysis, is not about resisting food; it is about gaining dominion of yourself so you can control your destiny. This is especially important when you are involved in a ministry that requires exercise of your spiritual gift. Fasting, in this case, enables you to fulfill the pre-requisite for using it effectively, gaining control over your personal life. We speak from experience!

Our apostolic calling requires us to move into brand new national situations, and use our apostolic gifts to gain spiritual dominion. Our need is like that of the athlete. In order to conquer his opponent and achieve victor, he must first get into physical condition. For this to occur, he must gain mastery over every appetite or inclination that preventing his progress. The battle continues daily, relentlessly.

How does the apostle gain self-mastery to exercise his breakthrough gift-set to achieve dominion, especially, in light of this reality: every day our flesh confronts our spirit for control of our will. What can we do to give us the edge over our flesh's power?

Permit me this example. If an athlete seeks to increase foot speed, one exercise will surely produce this result: jumping rope. Likewise, one spiritual exercise guarantees your spirit the strength to gain dominion over your "old nature"—fasting.

It is the only way you can train your flesh to become subordinate to your spirit's desires. To repeat, it is not about withholding food; it is about subduing the flesh to the spirit so that through us, the Holy Spirit can gain dominion in the area where He calls us to minister. Fasting, gives us the ability to minister as a royal viceroy—wielding power that leads to Him ruling and reigning.

Another Reason for Fasting: To Make Important Decisions

Like our first-century counterparts, our apostolic ministry requires decisions that carry momentous consequences. The Twelve, on two occasions recorded in the Book of Acts, fasted before making serious decisions. In each situation, they linked prayer with fasting (Acts 13:4; 14:23). As the record reveals, they viewed fasting not to take one's eyes off of food and worldly pleasure, but to sharpen their focus on the Savior who was guiding them.

Where did they get this idea? Our Lord Jesus said fasting would be necessary for his disciples after he ascended. "The time will come when the bridegroom will be taken from them; then they will fast," (Matthew 9:15). So, the early disciples remembered the words of their master and thus they made fasting vital. The outstanding work God accomplished through them speaks for itself.

As an example, the Twelve, after also, a period of praying and fasting:

> "While they were worshipping and fasting, the Holy Spirit said, 'Set a part for me Barnabas and Saul (Paul) for the work to which I have called them.' So after they fasted and prayed, they placed their hands on them and sent them off," Acts 13:2-3.

John Calvin also learned from the Biblical examples. In this regard he said this: "In general we must hold that whenever any religious controversy arises, which either a council or ecclesiastical tribunal behooves to decide; whenever a minister is to be chosen; whenever, in short any matter of difficulty and great importance is under consideration: on the other hand, when manifestations of the divine anger appear, as pestilence, war, and famine, the sacred and salutary custom of all ages has been for pastors to exhort the people to public fasting and extraordinary prayer." Calvin, Institutes, IV, 12, 14

Another Reason: To Prepare for Spiritual Warfare

Fasting, combined with prayer, provides us two of our most powerful weapons in conducting spiritual warfare and deliverance. It is powerful in seeking God to intervene. No, it is not a device to manipulate Him; but we have observed that fasting moves the Savior to fulfill His intended will in an important situation.

Another Reason: to Draw Close to Him

As we mentioned at the outset of this chapter, fasting a tool designed to gain access to His presence, when sin has quenched our fellowship with Him. Fasting is not intended to punish our flesh, but to focus on God. We should not fast to lose weight, but rather to gain deeper fellowship with God.

Summary of Fasting

Why then do we fast? When we are unable to repent, solve problems, smash strongholds, prepare ourselves for ministry, sharpen our focus, we use this divinely given tool to move us into a spiritual realm where the Holy Spirit can work in our human spirit to resolve problems, and gain the benefits listed above.

We do not fast for the wrong motive—self-interest. As Richard Foster writes, "to use good things to our own ends is always a sign of false religion" (*Celebration of Discipline*). This problem is inherent; hence Jesus' first commentary of fasting was to warn about doing it because of a wrong motive (Matt. 6:16-18).

No, he must initiate fasting. In the final analysis, we are sustained by His word (Matt. 4:4). When approached in the proper way, fasting is feasting. It can produce ministry breakthroughs that otherwise might take decades to bring about.

PART 2: PRAYER WITH FASTING: TOOLS IN TANDEM

A moment ago, we introduced you to that pathetic scene with the father and son and the disciples powerless to heal the boy. We return to it to discover the divine antidote for powerlessness:

> "Then came the disciples to Jesus apart, and said, 'Why could not we cast him out?' And Jesus said unto them, 'Because of your un-

> belief: for verily I say unto you, if ye have faith as a grain of mustard seed, nothing shall be impossible to you. Howbeit this kind goes not out but by prayer and fasting.' "-Matthew 17:19-21

As Jesus was being transfigured, nine Apostles remained below to ministering to the ever-present crowd. Their failure to free the epileptic boy from demonic control was dismal. Placing myself in their 'shoes', I imagine them saying, "What went wrong? Did we not approach this situation as in the past? Did He not anoint us with this ability?

Such speculation is unnecessary since Jesus pinpointed the problem's source: their lack of faith. What rendered their faith ineffectual? They faced a very intimidating display of satanic power. Like Peter sinking into the Sea because he took his eyes off of Jesus, their faith shrank to such a degree they were ineffectual. However, the moment provided them (and us) with a teachable moment. He explained the remedy for restoring their faith to being able to send demons scurrying: *"This kind goes not out but by fasting and prayer."*

Do not miss this insight: the faith sufficient for a healing ministry requires sustenance, and that is supplied through the exercise of fasting. Andrew Murray (*With Christ in the School of Prayer* captured the Savior's lesson in a nutshell: *"(As) ...faith needs a life of prayer in which to grow and keep strong... (so) prayer needs fasting for its full and perfect development."*

Truth is; in His counsel we learn three principles regarding fasting and prayer.

First, He reveals that faith can grow, and cultivating it must become a priority. When Jesus healed the two blind men, He said, *Believe ye that I am able to do this? They said unto him, Yea, Lord. Then touched he their eyes, saying, According to your faith be it unto you.* (Matt. 9:28, 29).

- In His statement, we learn these great truths:
- In the Kingdom, people exercising varying degrees of faith;
- There can be no effectual faith without prayer;
- Prayer gains its power to move heaven by its closeness to Word and the Spirit's Presence; and,
- Fastness produces that closeness, by blotting out all else so we can focus on Him, His Word, and obtaining His mind so we can pray according to His will.

In the face of such faith, no situation can remain resistant; it will pry anyone loose from the grasping clutches of demonic control.

How can you make faith grow? Faith can only live by feeding on what is Divine, on God Himself. Therefore, in adoring worship, we wait before Him. In that precious silence our soul is able to yield itself sufficiently that God is able to reveal Himself. As a result, we get to know Him more intimately. We lay His promises, recorded in His Word, before Him, asking Him to speak it to with the Holy Spirit's loving voice. How can the power to believe Him fully not fire our faith to move mountains and cast out demons? What we contend here, church history confirms to be true: men and women of powerful faith are those who spend much time in prayer. With the kind of faith in hand that this kind of prayer develops, nothing is impossible to you.

But the key to its power lies in the way in which individuals bury their 'Self' by allowing Him to become everything through them. This union is not easy to foster. What exercise accomplishes this degree of Oneness? Fasting causes us to focus on Him and forget all else; suddenly we are alone with Him, then at one with Him, and we emerge from this process exercising a faith that routs demons, heals sickness, and makes minds and hearts truly whole.

Second, in His counsel to the Apostles, we discover a second valuable principle: As faith needs prayer for its growth (first principle); so prayer requires fasting to act in great power.

To repeat, with one hand, through prayer, we grasp the invisible. With the other hand, through fasting, we let go of the visible. Nothing connects human nature to the world of senses like its need for and enjoyment of food. Fasting, in denying this, strengthens our spiritual resolve to pray for such mighty things as smashing strongholds, and breaking sin's chains.

The process is simple; we use our hunger for food to motivate us to yearn, instead, for the Lord Jesus to become more important in our life. In the process we discover that fasting serves to confirm our resolution that if we can forego a few meals to obtain His will, we are a little better prepared to struggle with evil.

Our apostolic ministry necessitates that lay hold of the power that will put demonic forces to flight. Therefore, prayer fasting is one of our most often employed tools.

CONCLUSION

We have learned the value of this tool; how time and again, it has proven to be a modest price to pay to obtain the prize of exorcism and healing as well as direction and divine favor, all because we have practiced our Lord's advice: "this kind goes not out but by fasting and prayer".

Category Two: Tools Used in Deliverance Ministry

Chapter 2

Deliverance

DELIVERANCE IS SUCH AN enormous part of our apostolic ministry that we once considered making it part of its name (ultimately, we did not). Deliverance includes both healing and casting out demons.

Both are important to confirming our message. The one (healing) ensures people that the Jesus we preach can transform any condition involving the human body and mind into wholeness. The other (exorcism) demonstrates to people that they can be set free of the bondage of Satan and live free of his constant attempts to recapture and dominate them.

This confirmation works both at an individual level as well as at the community level, since we direct our message to both. Thus, the broad category of deliverance applies to both healing and exorcism. We shall take up these topics in the next two chapters.

The purpose of this chapter is to lay a foundation for the discussions of both these gifts. In this introductory discussion, our aim is to describe certain aspects they both share in common.

GENERAL INTRODUCTORY INFORMATION

Christian deliverance means God rescuing someone from bondage, oppression, hardship, or domination by evil. God brings deliverance. *"Deliver us from the evil one," (Mat 6:12-13).*

When we work to deliver other people from works of Satan the deliverance ministry takes the form of exorcism. When we seek the Holy

Spirit to release people from infirmity, disease, etc., that form of deliverance ministry is called healing. With deliverance, God delivers; our part is as a facilitator.

The gifts of exorcism and healing are two of our most important tools to *expand the Kingdom of God since they demonstrate that wholeness is how God intended for His kingdom to function.*

This over-arching purpose of all apostolic ministry utilizes these supernatural gifts to demonstrate the reality, viability, and relevance of the kingdom of God. The gifts I use, ultimately, cause His kingdom to flourish and expand. Could any motive more clearly prove that the use of these gifts serves the purpose for which Jehovah-Rophi calls apostles?

Why is the need for the exercise of our deliverance gifts so great? It is because Satan enjoys such extensive and penetrating control over so many; including those who line the aisles in our Crusade meetings deserves closer inspection. Permit me to share some of the human gateways by which the Evil One gains entrance into human spirits, souls, and bodies.

To appreciate this, consider this story. It is typical of many we have heard in Africa.

Jonathan Mbrema is a true believer converted to Christ from Islam shared this testimony of God's miraculous working.

On a weekend, he and his family were enjoying a special breakfast. On such occasions, after the children were finished with their meal, the parents would let them play in the front yard. To make the kids comfortable, the parents would place a small woven mat on the grass for them to sit on.

On a particular morning, the man had not finished his tea when he felt the Holy Spirit urging him to leave the table and inspect the front yard. He ignored this prompting. After a second divine urging, he decided to inspect.

When he saw nothing out of order he thought, "Every Saturday these kids sweep this front lawn. Today I will do this for them as a surprise." He then felt that still small voice telling him to begin in the area around that mat. As he bent to move the mat, he spied a very poisonous snake under it.

With his family's help, he was able to kill it, no doubt saving the life of one or more of his children. Imagine what would have happened had he not responded to the miraculous prompting of the Holy Spirit. How wonderful our blessed God is; His mercy and miracles continue without ceasing.

PART 1 GATEWAYS SATAN EXPLOITS

Make no mistake God is sovereign over all. Therefore, Satan must operate *within* the boundaries that God has established. He cannot venture outside of these boundaries to wield power or enforce his will. For this reason, the Devil uses deception, deceit, etc. to entice people to move into the realm where he does have authority. Once he tricks a person into his domain, trouble is guaranteed to result. Let us look at four of his most prominent strategies to latch onto and drag them to where he can control them.

Deception

Deception is deliberately misleading someone in order for them to believe something that is not true. There are three primary sources of deception: Satanic Deception through fallen angels, and Satan himself; Self Deception through ourselves; and, Deception through other people.

Like clever magic tricks, deception occurs right under our noses without us catching on. Media specializes in this, and as a result the Devil has a powerful ally to entice us subtly under his spell.

To appreciate how satanic deception works; consider the example of Saul of Tarsus. Prior to his conversion, Satan deceived him into thinking that what he was doing (persecuting Christians) was right in the eyes of God. However, when God opened his eyes the Lord used him to inflict exponentially much more damage to Satan's kingdom than what Satan had used him to inflict on the Body of Christ.

Ignorance

Ignorance, i.e., lack of knowledge is a gateway he uses to great advantage. If what you don't know can hurt you (and it can), then what you don't know and don't know that you do not know can be dangerous.

Think of how many true believers rejoice in their salvation, and then assume that to darken the door of a church only occasionally is sufficient. This ignorance has robbed the Body of Christ of many talented and gifted people, and robbed them of the joy and significance from spiritual ministry. Hosea was right. Through his prophetic pen the Lord said, *"My people are destroyed from lack of knowledge,"* (Hosea 4.6).

Sin

The commission of sin leads to guilt, that results in our withdrawal from Him, and in that vacuum the guilty one is a "sitting duck" for Satan to move in on. One of the first things we notice when we begin a new ministry in a nation that God directs us to serve with our apostolic gifts is how extensively the citizens and institutions are controlled by the Devil.

Crisis

Through bad decisions, or unintended consequences, calamity descends into all of us at times. These storms of life are so unpleasant. A roaring, out-of-control situation can so distract us that we revert to survival mode. Often, in this state, we abandon our values and virtues, and Satan wastes no time taking advantage of this situation.

Deception; Ignorance; Sin; and Crisis—these four gateways provide the Devil with a wide array of opportunities to intrude into people's lives and convert them into relationship wreckers, and destiny destroyers.

To block Satan's malevolent influence, our Savior has provided deliverance, which includes healing and exorcism.

Storms of Life

Storms of life are unpleasant experiences that befall us out of no fault of our own. They are the Joseph experiences. God allows them to happen but does not plot them against us. He only does not stop them. Depending on how we handle such matters storms of life can be our stepping-stones to our promotion (like with Joseph) or they can be our downfall. They can be assets the Holy Spirit can use to our good or they can be assets Satan can use to block us from moving forward.

For example, Joni Erickson Tada, on her way as a teenager to an Olympic medal as a Springboard Diver, suffered a sever injury that left her unable to use her hands and legs. Such an experience might as well have been the end of her beautiful life, but Heaven said no.

There is not enough space here to chronicle all that God has accomplished through her ministry's global outreach. Her life mirrors one aspect of young Joseph's at the hands of his brothers: What the devil intended to use for evil, God has used to change countless lives (Gen. 50:20).

Whatever storms of life you may have faced or may be facing—spiritually, socially, materially or physically, please realize that God did not intend them to become destiny-killers, or obstacles, even though the devil wants them to be. As a result, they cannot stop God from fulfilling all that he purposes to accomplish through each of us. God is able to transform the experiences to work to our good if our focus is on him rather than our limitations.

Now that we have examined the triggers to satanic control, what are the essential steps in experiencing any type of deliverance? Permit me to share these essential steps of faith.

PART 2: STEPS TOWARD DELIVERANCE

Deliverance is as simple as applying the following steps of faith. First, one must repent and pray for God to take control on one's life. Second, one must cease from all known association and practices with those things that brought on the bondage. Third, you must become familiar with and applying those principles that relate to deliverance. Finally, you must build a close walk with the Lord via prayer and meditation, seeking His protection from temptation, His deliverance when attacked, and His wisdom to walk circumspectly.

God responds to obedience, not to levels of need. If his response was based only on need He would have come long ago because human needs continue to get more desperate every succeeding period. Human needs are worse off now than ever before in spite of technological advances. Rest assured that the Lord desires to respond to your obedience.

Deliverance ensures the end of interference from Satan. It ends his access gained through ignorance, deception, and sinful disobedience.

To receive deliverance, you need only to embrace and act on the truth that the Holy Spirit reveals to us regarding an area where sin rules. This is the truth that will set you free (John 8:31-32). Nothing beats trusting and obeying a revealed Biblical truth to drive away the Evil One's harassment.

Once we trust and act upon what we have been shown, we can expect liberty from the Evil One's harassment, and two things to occur. First, the pummeling ceases, and Satan beats a hasty retreat. Second, the Holy Spirit moves alongside us to defend us against the enemy's return. That door through which the Devil had gained access to us is shut; and when he attempts re-entry, the Savior stands there, guarding us from further attack.

The question next arises, if this is all it takes to get free of the iron grasp of the Evil One, then why do not more people not experience deliverance in one form (healing) or the other (exorcism)? Hindrances—the truth is, there are many.

To appreciate this, permit me to share three of the most common hindrances.

PART 3: HINDRANCES TO DELIVERANCE

Three failures create the conditions that hinder deliverance. Let us sketch them briefly for you.

Lack of True Repentance

Before we can experience His deliverance from the evil one, or ask Him (as the Lord's Prayer invites us to do), we must repent to Him for having violated His will. The reasons may vary. Altogether, they include ignorance, deception, disobedience, and refusing responsibly to face the storms of life.

Peter, confronting his Jewish neighbors, explained that although they had, out of ignorance, caused Jesus' crucifixion, they nevertheless, needed to repent, even though, on the cross, Jesus had forgiven them (Luke 23:34). So Peter admonishes:

> "Now, brothers, I know that you acted in ignorance, as did your leaders. But this is how God fulfilled what he had foretold through all the prophets, saying that his Christ would suffer. Repent, then, and turn to God, so that your sins may be wiped out, that times of refreshing may come from the Lord," (Acts 3:17-19).

Since we shall deal with this in a future chapter, we will spend no more time on this subject.

Failure to cease associating with Sin

Repentance also requires ceasing to associate with the sin. This includes throwing away any books, literature or multimedia that embrace non-biblical matters such as the erroneous spiritual warfare and deliverance.

It was customary in the Old Testament to destroy all that was detestable in God's sight.

This did not change in the New Testament. Jesus, in a manner bordering on violence, cleansed the temple of traders who where using God's house for wrong purposes. We are temples of God's Spirit (1 Corinthians 3: 16-17). He has no comfort living with objects that do not please God.

Christian converts in Ephesus who formerly practiced sorcery and divination publicly destroyed the materials used. "When they calculated the value of the scrolls, the total came to fifty thousand drachmas. In this way the word of the Lord spread widely and grew in power," Acts 19:19-20.

We must deal with sorcery or divination because it involves invoking or arousing evil spirits to satisfy our demands in a way that scripture forbids. Our interaction with them in the spirit-world gives them access to our lives, which they exploit.

Blind Faith

Blind faith is not useful. It provides no help when one is dealing with ignorance, deception, sin or storms of life. If blind faith were a weapon against ignorance or deception, then all Christians would have almost no problems in this area. They would need only to believe that somehow God would drop the answers to their obstacles into their heads. This is not the case.

I think back to counseling couples with financial problems. I found them trusting God to bless them materially without feeling they that they needed to apply and count on Him miraculously to overcome their financial obstacles without the necessity of applying biblical principles leading to financial freedom. Having faith in God does not enable one to circumvent His laws regarding seedtime and harvest-time. Having faith in Him, obeying His Word, and fulfilling all our required areas of responsibility that pleases him. A believer who acts with this kind of faith is not acting blindly.

PART 4: WHAT TRUE DELIVERANCE REQUIRES

As mentioned, deliverance closely aligns with healing. In His commission of the Twelve, Jesus "…called unto Him His twelve disciples, and gave them authority over unclean spirits, to cast them out, and *to heal all manner of disease and all manner of sickness."* (Matt 10:1).

Therefore, we see the gift in action by Peter; he responds to the crippled man's request for help at the Beautiful Gate:

> "Silver and gold have I none; but what I have, that give I thee. In the name of Jesus Christ of Nazareth, walk." (Acts 3:6)

As mentioned, the authority to heal is inherent in the apostolic gift. However, the provision for healing is bound in Christ's atonement. The authority to heal derives from the Scriptures. To understand this, permit me to draw your attention to the words of Jesus:

> "Has it not been written in your Law, 'I said, you are gods'? If He called them gods, to whom the Word of God came..." (John 10:34)

God called men "gods" to whom His Word came. To appreciate this, examine the context of the verse from Jesus quoted, Psalm 82:3. Notice that through the Psalmist's pen, God speaks to those whom He has given the authority to judge and to rule. As we know from Jesus' final words at His Ascension, that Divine authority extended to the Twelve, through those they anointed to ministry to this moment, and upon those whom they laid hands.

This is why, like Peter, when confronted by a person with a physical infirmity, we do not organize a prayer chain for that person, but rather say, *"Such as I have, give I unto you."*

Purpose for all Deliverance

The apostolic ministry, as we have already learned, is to expand the Kingdom, one individual, and one people-group at a time. The gifts of healing and casting out demons are strategic to the fulfillment of this purpose. They comprise the two primary tools we use to bring deliverance to people.

With this understanding of the relationship of deliverance to the exercise of healing and exorcism, along with their hindrances, gifts, we are ready to proceed with the specific discussions of the two gifts we associate with it: healing and exorcism.

Chapter 3

Healing

Part of the Deliverance Toolkit

After surgery to remove a cancerous tumor on his right shoulder, a man grew accustomed to compensating. The Surgeon had removed so much muscle-mass that when the man worshipped he could not raise his right arm.

In a Deliverance Crusades, he volunteered to be a prayer-warrior. On one night, the preacher spoke on the miracle Jesus performed after a woman, with an issue of blood, touched His garment. This miracle, recorded by Luke describes the situation:

> "And a woman was there who had been subject to bleeding for twelve years, but no one could heal her. She came up behind him and touched the edge of his cloak, and immediately her bleeding stopped. 'Who touched me?' Jesus asked. When they all denied it, Peter said, 'Master, the people are crowding and pressing against you.' But Jesus said, 'Someone touched me; I know that power has gone out from me.' Then the woman, seeing that she could not go unnoticed, came trembling and fell at his feet. In the presence of all the people, she told why she had touched him and how she had been instantly healed. Then he said to her, 'Daughter, your faith has healed you. Go in peace.'" (Luke 8:43-48)

His sermon completed, the preacher invited each to reach out and touch Jesus by faith for healing, as that woman had.

Her act of faith was courageous for several reasons: the crowd was enormous, and by the Pharisee standards, she was unclean, therefore, violating many social protocols to press through these people to touch His garment. Her determination was motivated by her desperate condition.

In this, she mirrors the many who line the aisles seeking wholeness from our meetings.

Before I relate the man's experience, permit me to share two things with you from this incident recorded in Luke. It will help you appreciate what strengthened the man in this meeting to increase sufficiently his faith to reach out to God for healing.

First, observe Jesus, the man she sought to touch. At first glance, He resembled any 35-year-old man, although slightly taller. His split beard rendered Him indistinguishable from any other man of his generation. But, look closer. As John points out, this Jesus was none other than the incarnate Logos, Jehovah. She was touching Jehovah-Rophi! Permit me to explain whose garment she touched.

In the Old Testament, Jehovah revealed Himself through the ways in which He connects with those whom He shares a covenant relationship. He introduces Himself as Jehovah-Rophi at a critical moment when Israel had run out of water in the desert wilderness, a life-and-death situation.

When they found water, it was too bitter for human consumption. God then advised Moses to throw a nearby dead tree into the water, whereupon it became sweet to the taste.

God then explained that, in this way, He was acting as Jehovah-Rophi. It means. "YHWH who heals" (literally, "makes bitter things sweet". (Ex. 15:22-26). He makes life that is unbearable to be enjoyable by drawing us to Himself and extending to us His mercy and grace so that we can experience wholeness.

Therefore, Jesus, the incarnate Jehovah-Rophi, healed this woman by making the blood killing her to become life sustaining, as He had done with the waters at Mara.

Why then did this woman touch the hem of Jesus' garment? Moses dictated its design:

> Throughout the generations to come you are to make tassels on the corners of your garments, with a blue cord on each tassel. You will have these tassels to look at and so you will remember all the commands of the LORD... (Numbers 15:38-39)

Ironically, the number of tassels—39—has two vital connections to healing. First, Peter says, "By His stripes we are healed (I Peter 2:24), and they were a total of 39 at the hands of the Roman soldiers just before His crucifixion. Therefore, the garment provided her a point of contact with the Messiah's healing ministry. Today, science confirms this to be true, since research has shown that *all types of illness can be traced to thirty-nine root-sources.*

Therefore, before she touched the tassels of His prayer shawl, this woman acted with the kind of faith that sees God as Jehovah-Rophi. She exercised healing faith. Therefore, the instant her hand contacted His garment's hem, her blood was as transformed as the waters of Mara had been. She experienced the flow of healing power from His heart to her need.

With those insights we have related about the woman with the issue of blood fresh in his thoughts from sermon he had just heard, our Intercessory Volunteers began to pray for those who responding to the Preacher's invitation to come forward for healing. As was his custom, he extended his left arm as he prayed, although he was unable to lift his right. Suddenly, it dawned on him to seek his own healing.

He reported that at that instant, he felt a gentle wind twirling about his right arm. He thought *"Could Jesus have touched my arm?"* and before he could finish the thought, his tingling right hand shot up, as fully extended as his left arm.

PART 1: PURPOSE FOR APOSTOLIC HEALING

The apostolic ministry, as we have already learned, is to expand the Kingdom, one individual, and one people-group at a time. The gifts of healing and casting out demons are strategic to the fulfillment of this purpose. Permit me to share two verses that confirm this.

First, regarding healing let us return to that tree we discussed in connection with Marah (meaning "bitter"). Recall that the "tree" thrown into these undrinkable waters to render it delicious, *xulon*, was the same word for the "Tree" (Cross) upon which Jesus was crucified to provide Living Water, i.e., salvation. If you trace this concept to the end of the New Testament, you find this "Tree" standing in the center of the New Heaven and New Earth providing healing (through its leaves) for the nations (Rev. 22.2).

Notice the connection between healing and kingdom ministry: we introduce people to a life under the dominion of the King of Kings. Within His realm, people enjoy access to wholeness, as well as safety from those controlled by the Evil One.

Second, regarding the casting out of demons, Jesus' critics accused Him that the supernatural power He used to perform miracles (including healing, and exorcism) came from Satan. In His reply, the Savior pointed out that if they were right, by casting out demons, Satan was actually working against his own interests (hardly!). Then Jesus made this powerful point:

> "But if it is by the Spirit of God that I drive out the demons, then the kingdom of God has come upon you".

The use of these gifts, *casting out of demons, as well as healing sickness, disease, and infirmity, one motive drives us: to expand the Kingdom of God by demonstrating that wholeness is how God intended for His kingdom to function.*

All of this has, as one of its over-arching purposes to demonstrate the reality, viability, and relevance of the kingdom of God. The gifts I use, ultimately, cause His kingdom to flourish and expand. Could any motive more clearly prove that the use of these gifts serves the purpose for which Jehovah-Rophi calls us to the apostolic ministry?

Why is that everywhere we turn, we encounter so many who desperately need our healing ministry? The broad answer is this: sin. However, the sin that moves so many to line the aisles in our Crusade meetings for healing enters into them through different paths. Permit me to show you some of the more common ways Satan gains access to people.

Gateways Satan Uses to Exploit People

Make no mistake God is sovereign over all. Therefore, Satan must operate within the boundaries that God has established. He cannot venture outside of these boundaries to wield his power, or enforce his will. This is why the Devil uses deception, deceit, etc. to entice people into the realm in which he does have authority. Once he "snookers" a person into his domain, trouble will result. Let us look at four of his most prominently used methods to latch onto and control people.

Lies and Trickery

These deliberately mislead someone into believing something that is not true. There are three primary sources:
- Satanic Deception (fallen angels, and Satan himself)
- Self Deception through ourselves (self-deception)

- Deception through other people

Like clever magic tricks, this kind of deception occurs right under our noses, without us catching on. Media specializes in this, and as a result the Devil has a powerful ally to entice us into his spell.

To appreciate how Satan works in this regard, consider the example of Saul of Tarsus. Prior to his conversion, Satan deceived him into thinking that what he was doing (persecuting Christians) was right in the eyes of God. However, when God opened his eyes the Lord used him to inflict exponentially much more damage to Satan's kingdom than what Satan had used him to inflict on the Body of Christ.

Lack of Knowledge

Lack of knowledge, i.e., ignorance is a gateway he uses to great advantage. If what you do not know can hurt you (and it can), then what you do not know and do not know that you do not know can be dangerously harmful.

Think of how many true believers rejoice in their salvation, and then assume that to darken the door of a church is sufficient. This ignorance has robbed the Body of Christ of many talented and gifted people, and robbed them of the joy and significance from spiritual ministry. Hosea was right. Through his prophetic pen, the Lord said, "*My people* are destroyed from lack of knowledge," (Hosea 4.6).

Trespass and Sin

The commission of sin leads to guilt, that results in our withdrawal from Him, and in that vacuum the guilty one is a "sitting duck" for Satan to move in on. One of the first things we notice when we begin a new ministry in a nation that God directs us to serve with our apostolic gifts is how extensively the citizens and institutions are controlled by the Devil.

Unforeseen Crisis

Through bad decisions, or unintended consequences, calamity descends into all of us at times. These storms of life are so unpleasant. A roaring, out-of-control situation can so distract us that we revert to survival mode. Often, in this state, we abandon our values and virtues, and Satan wastes no time taking advantage of this situation.

These four gateways provide the Devil with a wide array of opportunities to intrude into people's lives and convert them into relationship wreckers, and destiny destroyers.

To block Satan's malevolent influence, our Savior has provided deliverance, which includes healing. To help you appreciate why both are needful, permit me to use this simple illustration.

A Canine Analogy

Imagine that you and the next-door neighbor beside own dogs. Permit me to give them dumb names: 'christen' yours "Ignorant", and your neighbor's can answer to "Trouble".

Trouble is a total nuisance because he incessantly gets into your yard, and abuses your dog. However, Trouble contributes to the problem. He loves to dig holes in the hedge fence separating the two properties. Life becomes unbearable for Ignorant; he constantly nurses wounds inflicted by Trouble.

Recognizing how miserable he is, you block the holes in the fence so that Trouble can no longer harass your poor pooch. From that moment on, Ignorant has no more worry from Trouble's attacks—well, until he digs another hole in the hedge. No more bites, or worries about when they will next happen. In this safety, Ignorant can romp, play and start living a dog's life.

However, Ignorant still has one problem; the wounds that Trouble inflicted upon him. He needs healing from all of the problems caused by Trouble's access.

Here, permit me to end this analogy, to draw attention to the point of the story. Like Trouble, we need deliverance from Satan's abusive access through one of those gateways. We also need healing from all of the problems resulting from his malevolence.

With this snapshot of the difference between healing and deliverance in mind, let us explore how the distinction in detail.

Understanding Deliverance

Deliverance ensures further interference from Satan that he enjoyed because of access gained through ignorance, deception, sinful disobedience, and crises resulting from bad decisions and unintended consequences that results in the turmoil accompanying it.

To receive deliverance, one needs only to embrace and act on the truth that the Holy Spirit reveals to us regarding an area where sin rules. This is the truth that will set you free (John 8:31-32). Nothing beats trusting and obeying a revealed Biblical truth to drive away the Evil One's harassment.

Once we trust and act upon what we have been shown, we can expect liberty from the Evil One's harassment. Once we apply the Biblical principle shown to us by the Holy Spirit's illumination two things occur. First, the pummeling ceases, and Satan beats a hasty retreat. Second, the Holy Spirit moves alongside us to defend us against the enemy's return. That door through which the Devil had gained access to us shuts; and when he attempts re-entry, the Savior stands there, guarding us from further attack. There are things one can do to thwart this process; we shall deal with the three most common ones. However, first, as we have helped you understand deliverance, now, permit us to provide you with the same knowledge, but in regard to healing.

Understanding Healing

As our analogy of the canine pets revealed, deliverance rescues us from the clutches of satanic influence. Healing solves the problems that resulted from the consequences of his involvement and influence. However, one should not confuse a situation requiring healing with a bruise or scratch. Rather, think of it as a gnawing problem, ulcerated and oozing puss.

The purpose of healing is to restore the harmful effects, ranging from spiritual, social, physical, or material consequences, inflicted by the Evil One. In our meetings, we encounter problems that are scary to behold. Nevertheless, people turn to the Savior for healing, and after decades, we bear witness that He is so faithful and merciful, not only removing the consequences of evil, but also restoring the individual to wholeness.

The healing and restoration may come in different ways than we may expect. It's not a return of the same matters that were lost, even though God may work it that way for some. It may include a calling to serve Him. It may impact social relationships either in the home, or church. It may produce a career or financial breakthrough. Most often it involves physical healing from an illness.

Timing

Timing is another aspect to consider. We live in an age that wants everything yesterday. However, the Holy Spirit has His own timetable. Generally, healing occurs instantaneous; but the process may take longer.

> "Will not God bring about justice for his chosen ones, who cry out to him day and night? Will he keep putting them off? I tell you, he will see that they get justice, and quickly," Luke 18:7-8.

God will also give you the grace in doing your part to facilitate the healing process.

The following are some examples of healing processes in different areas – spiritually, socially, materially and physically.

1. Spiritual Healing

If healing occurs in a spiritual area, God will give you the grace in doing your part to facilitate healing process. For example, if it includes a wounded spirit resulting from a relationship that went sour, the healing will involve confession and executing accountability measures imposed by the Holy Spirit.

Sometimes, the combination of prayer and fasting proves to be an aid to the healing process.

If it involves freeing one from demonic influence, it is both instant, and ongoing, since the spirit set free needs to be covered from any future attempt by demons to return.

2. Social Healing

If healing is in the social area, i.e., family, interpersonal, business, God will also give you the grace in doing your part to facilitate the healing process.

If you are the problem, he will enable you to fix issues that cause problems. Do not expect Him to gift you with a new personality but a change the way the old one managed the weaknesses that caused the problems.

3. Material Healing

In the area of finances, God will enable you to cultivate a generous heart. He will also enable you to let go of expenses you can live without. These expenses not only hinder repaying of debts (if you have any) they also hinder you from giving, an avenue that God uses to release his material blessings.

4. Physical Healing

If it is in the area of physical health God will enable you to know and apply physical health principles that are in your sphere of responsibility. These are natural health principles.

Where it is in God's sphere of responsibility or power he will bring healing supernaturally. Perhaps a story relevant to our own healing ministry will add clarity.

Over the years, we have witnessed God healing countless people who flooded the aisles of our meetings seeking His relief. Jonathan's story is typical of the miraculous healing that Jesus Christ performs in lives.

He had been an alcoholic since his teen years. Now, in his mid thirties, when his hangovers were horrible and he had suffered a serious bout of sickness, he would attend a healing service. He had memorized a sinner's prayer, which he would passionately recite. As a result, he felt he was a newly born-again Christian, but he was unable to shake the control of alcohol.

He confided to a Counselor that he feared he was drinking himself to death. The Counselor then encouraged him to ask God to heal him—take all desire for drink from him.

The man cried out to God. He expressed his conviction to the Lord that He should not leave a shred of compulsion behind; the Holy Spirit must remove all of it.

After the service closed for the night, the man returned to his lodging feeling as if nothing had changed. However, the next morning, he went to work and about three hours into his day, he realized that he had experienced no desire for alcohol.

It was then that he realized that God had healed his alcoholism. Twenty-five years later, he continues to testify of how the Lord Jesus delivered him from the bottle. He tells everyone how he never again felt the urge to drink because whom the Son sets free, he is free indeed!

Hindrances to Healing

To some extent, they mirror those hindrances we shared in this topic in the chapter discussing Deliverance. Therefore, here, we shall add only new ideas.

Failure to Repent

Why the dog Ignorant dug the first hole in the hedge to allow Trouble to barrel into his life touches on the edge of why we allow sin entrance into our lives. However, before we can experience His deliverance from the evil one, or ask Him (as the Lord's Prayer invites us to do), we must repent to Him for having violated His will. The reasons may vary but they include one of these: ignorance, deception, disobedience, or refusing to face the storms of life in a self-serving way that ducks responsibility to do the right thing.

Peter, confronting his Jewish neighbors, explained that although they had, out of ignorance, caused Jesus' crucifixion, nevertheless, needed to repent, even though, on the cross, Jesus had forgiven them (Luke 23:34). So Peter admonishes:

> "Now, brothers, I know that you acted in ignorance, as did your leaders. But this is how God fulfilled what he had foretold through all the prophets, saying that his Christ would suffer. Repent, then, and turn to God, so that your sins may be wiped out, that times of refreshing may come from the Lord," Acts 3:17-19

What other aspects hinder a person's access to God's healing power?

Unwillingness to Stop a Sinning Process

Repentance also requires ceasing to associate with the sin. This includes throwing away any books, literature or multimedia that embrace non-biblical matters such as the erroneous spiritual warfare and deliverance. It was customary in the Old Testament to destroy all that was detestable in God's sight.

This did not change in the New Testament. Jesus violently cleansed the temple of traders who where using God's house for wrong purposes. We are temples of God's Spirit (1 Corinthians 3: 16-17). He has no comfort living with objects that do not please God.

Christian converts in Ephesus who had practiced sorcery and divination were asked to destroy the materials they used. They destroyed them publicly. "A number who had practiced sorcery brought their scrolls together and burned them publicly. When they calculated the value of the scrolls, the total came to fifty thousand drachmas. In this way the word of the Lord spread widely and grew in power," Acts 19:19-20.

The unscriptural spiritual warfare and deliverance may not fall in the core definition of sorcery or divination. However, it is still in this category since it deals with the spirit world outside scriptural order. The practice invokes or arouses evil spirits to answer to our demands in a way that scripture forbids. Our interaction with them in the spirit world only opens doors for them to interfere with our lives.

This is not to say sincere believers who advocated this type of spiritual warfare willfully misled people into forbidden activities. The deception flood of the erroneous spiritual warfare and deliverance teachings got so high that many of us easily found scripture to back up our resolve for direct confrontation. Believers were so zealous in their resolve to confront demonic spirits directly that they take biblical instruction scripture out of context without realizing it. Some are still zealous in such false teachings.

Mindless Faith

Blind faith is not a spiritual weapon against ignorance, deception, sin or storms of life. Only the truth is and applying it. If blind faith were a weapon against ignorance or deception, all Christians would have almost no problems. All we would need is to believe God that somehow he would drop the answers to our various obstacles. I

For instance, many believers are trusting God to bless them materially and to miraculously overcome their financial obstacles. However, few aggressively apply God's biblical principles to financial freedom. Having faith in God does not enable him to make short cuts to his laws of seed-time and harvest-time. Having faith in him and obeying his ways is what pleases him. It is fulfilling all our required areas of responsibility that pleases him.

A believer who is not sure making needed sacrifices would later solve financial problems would be less willing to make sacrifices. Such a believer assumes making sacrifices is as good as playing the lottery, gambling her scarce resources and counting on some strange statistical luck.

Few would want to make sacrifices of scarce resources on matters that have little or no guarantee of having any reward. Therefore, a believer who obeys God's word in applying his biblical principles to financial freedom has faith in God to fulfill what he is promised in his word. Faith leads to application of God's principles. It should not lead to mere belief in God to solving whatever obstacles. Such is blind faith.

Many sincere believers are facing avoidable afflictions. "My people are destroyed from lack of knowledge," Hosea 4.6. God's people, not those whose father is the devil (John 8:44) are destroyed from lack of knowledge. God's people are not destroyed because Satan is strong and furious. It happens because they lack knowledge in areas Satan has gained access.

Neither are they destroyed because they have no faith in God. It is because they are missing the knowledge that faith requires to work. May this never be the case over any one of us who have determined that we will not to live by blind faith.

CONCLUSION

As we close, permit me to share this personal account of a bonafide healing.

After a serious collision, while on a motorcycle, with a train, a robust young man suffered severe brain injury, serious damage to his eyesight, and the loss of his limbs. Although he was a true believer in Jesus Christ, the extent of this quadriplegic's handicap radically changed his life. He continued his education confined to a wheelchair.

Then he began to drift away from the Lord. In a few years, living in poverty at a friend's house, he contemplated suicide. It was then that he realized his need to rededicate his life to the Savior. His heart became so filled with the Holy Spirit's presence that he could barely contain himself. He began to serve the Lord and enjoy Him in a sustained way.

A few months later, the Lord impressed him that he should attend a Healing Service like ours. It was hundreds of miles from his home. Yet, as he expressed the urgency to respond to this call from the Lord with his pastor, the congregation provided him the funds to make the trip. When the man pulled up to the parking lot where the Healing Meeting was to take place, he called the office asking if someone could direct him to a rest room where he could freshen up for the evening's service. He was informed that he had called the Prayer Line and the voice on the other end asked if she could pray for him. He accepted her offer. In a flash, a burning sensation came over his feet and he knew that the Lord was working.

He then shared with his prayer partner that he knew God was going to heal him and asked her to make a note of it. He then declared to her and God that he was ready to receive His full blessing through healing. He gave her his phone number and asked her later to verify if all this turned out as he described by faith. He also thanked her for agreeing with him for his healing.

As the service closed, the Apostle asked all those seeking healing to step into the aisle. The man joined many. As he sat there in his wheelchair, he felt the Lord beginning to work through his body. One of the ushers asked him if he was trying to get out of his chair. Suddenly, the Spirit declared to him, "You will jump out of this chair in thirty seconds!"

Sure enough, within that time he stood for the first time in over fifteen years.

An usher then asked if he could walk. He took a few steps. He then walked up the steps to the platform beside the pulpit.

However, the healing did not stop. When he returned to his home church, the Pastor prayed for God to restore his eyesight. Again, he experienced God's power surging through his optic nerve. In a moment, he removed his eye patch; he could see because all nerve damage was gone.

The Pastor then asked him to share his testimony. He did so giving all glory and praise to God. As he spoke, the Holy Spirit visited that audience with a special anointing. That display of supernatural power resulted in many being delivered and healed.

Chapter 4

Exorcism

Part of the Deliverance Toolkit

Missionary Don Richardson asked a Sawi chief (New Guinea) why his tribe devoted all of its religious energy to appeasing evil spirits. His explanation: since the 'good spirits" pose no problem; they focused only on those they feared.

People are not blind; they perceive that the problems controlling them often stem from spiritual roots. Therefore, as we minister, I observe that same longing in the eyes of our attendees that Commodore Perry encountered, rowing toward the Tokyo shoreline. The common question: can the stranger relieve our bondage? In our services, when people discover that God is at work, enabling many to escape demonic control they line the aisles, seeking relief.

Our apostolic gift of exorcism is a most treasured and strategically important tool. As the healing gift offers the promise of freedom from disease and disability, this gift promises escape from malevolent invisible spiritual forces seeking to impose sinister wills.

PART 1: SPIRITUAL WARFARE AND EXORCISM

The term "spiritual warfare" can be misleading. The New Age movement uses it to describe a process of self-empowerment. The term does not appear in the Bible, but make no mistake, the concept of an interminable conflict between the forces of good angels led by the King of Kings and the Evil One and his legions of fallen angels is one of the recurring themes throughout the Scriptures. The final book, The Revelation of Jesus Christ, devotes most of its content to describing the final series of battles that culminate in the destruction of Satan and his minions from this planet, ushering in a universal existence free from sin, death, and evil.

To appreciate the proper exercise of this gift, it is important that you know where it fits into this conflict. To that end, permit me to share this overview of the three areas of spiritual conflict that Paul encountered. One of them is relevant to our gift:
1. Territorial Level: At this level, the Holy Spirit used Paul in a collaborative aspect; Paul wrestled with rulers, principalities and authorities in high places (i.e., territorial spirits). Ex: The Queen of Heaven, Artemis, (Dianna), headquartered in Ephesus, was a territorial spirit that had a strangle hold on Asia ((Acts 19:23-41).
2. Fallen Angel Level: Paul encountered the realm of satanic powers (Acts 19:17-20).
3. Demonic Level: hand-to-hand spiritual warfare with demon-possessed people (Acts 19.11-16). Even today, demons control people through possession, depression, and oppression.

So, how does our ministry deal with the Evil One in light of these three levels?

Although Christ gave His apostles authority over unclean spirits (i.e. evil spirits, demons), when we exercise His authority, we must honor the fact that unlike God, who exercises unlimited authority we do not. In this, our limitations are not unlike those of fallen angels. They must also operate within the boundaries established by the sovereign God. For either group to venture into areas they are not authorized brings danger and disaster. So which of the above areas does the Apostle operate (and not intrude into)?

As we shared with you earlier in our presentation of how the apostle collaborates with the King of kings in fulfilling his ministry, in two of the above territorial levels, our participation is indirect, either through the exercise of our unique gifts (preaching, healing, and exorcism), or through intercessory prayer supported by fasting, is indirect.

We do not fight evil spirits directly. God reserves this task for His angels to accomplish. To understand this, consider the example of the arch-apostle, Jesus. When Satan sought to sift Peter and finish him off Jesus prayed to God that Peter's faith would not fail and when he'd turned back from the attack he'd strengthen his fellow disciples (Luke 22:31-32).

He addressed God not Satan. His prayer was answered; Peter role to be pivotal in the foundation of the early church.

However, at the third level of demonic activity, the apostle, then and now, is authorized directly to confront spirit-beings. What accounts for this exception? When evil spirits occupy or 'possess' human beings, they have left their assigned realm, and entered one for which Christ died to redeem—the human spirit. Ironically, good angels do not have access to this realm (the human spirit). The Bible does record rare exceptions, where angels assumed human bodies on earth, i.e., as Gabriel, and Michael. The jurisdiction assigned to angels is the unseen spiritual realm, i.e. which we cannot see.

Why do demons seek to inhabit human bodies? I think it has to do with their origin.

PART 2: ORIGIN OF DEMONS

As the Old Testament unfolds, we learn the origin of demons. The sixth chapter of Genesis describes them as the union between the sons of God (Job. 1:6; 2:1) (Gen. 6:2, 4). In the destruction of the Flood, their bodies died, but because of their unique natures, (either angelic or human), could qualify for either heaven or hell, so their disembodied spirits remained on this earth. The Bible named them demons.

Jude, describes these events in detail:

> "But now the giants who are born from the [union of] the spirits and the flesh shall be called evil spirits upon the earth, because their dwelling shall be upon the earth and inside the earth. Evil spirits have come out of their bodies. Because from the day that they were created from the sons of God they became Watchers: their first origin is the spiritual foundation. They will become evil upon the earth and shall be called evil spirits. The dwelling of the spiritual beings of heaven is heaven; but the dwelling of the spirits of the earth, which are born upon the earth, is in the earth (vs. 14, 15)

He was quoting from a non-canonical book (I Enoch 15:8-10).

The passage reveals that while fallen angels operate in the heavenly realms, demons dwell on earth. For this reason, Paul distinguishes between demons/evil spirits ("powers of this dark world") and fallen angels ("spiritual forces of evil in the heavenly realms") in Ephesians 6:12.

The Nephilim were on the earth before and after the Flood (Gen 6:4). For them to survive the Flood, they would have to exist as non-material beings—demons. Demons, like their fathers, crave sex; therefore, gravitate toward sexual sins. For example, the seven demons that possessed Mary Magdalene gained entrance through her prostitution. They love to control, hence are often associated with problems related to compulsive behavior. For this reason, demons function as seducing spirits.

Understanding their origin, can you appreciate why so much of Satan's control begins through sexual immorality? A problem with an uncontrollable appetite may not be the fault, alone, of the current victim, but can be traced to ancestors who initiated the involvement. This is why the Bible says, *"The sins of the fathers shall be visited upon the sons."* Involvement in sins of the flesh pushed them into the realm of the demonic.

It also helps us understand another of Satan's foremost ways to influence people—casting fear through seducing words. Words are the best vehicle to carry ideas to ideas to our mind. There, our thoughts use the idea to stimulate emotions, which, in turn, stimulate us to act. Satan knows the key to controlling us is by sowing words into our minds. His favorite types of messages include: lying words, intimidating words, and seducing words. Consider these examples:

- Satan threatens Hezekiah (king), using the threat of Jerusalem being invaded by Sennacherib king of Assyria. Scripture tells us that the purpose of their threats was so that they could capture the Israelites' city [2 Chronicles 32:18]. Satan's goal: to use lying threats to steal what God had given Hezekiah (2 Chron. 32:19).
- Peter sank into the water when Satan's intimidating word caused him to focus not on Jesus but on the wind, and become fearful (Matthew 14:30)

It is axiomatic; all fear (except the fear of the Lord) originates in an idea implanted by Satan. His goal is to create panic that drives the person to seek his solution (which may, initially, be helpful, but in the end, has one objective: to control their thought-life.

The cultures that apostles are sent to minister to are places overwhelmed with needs. Therefore, unsaved people have been thoroughly intimidated. Hence, we encounter many who are possessed, or oppressed by his demons.

This makes the apostolic tool of exorcism to be vitally important!

The authority or influence assigned to the Body of Christ belonged to all humankind from the beginning of creation. God told Adam and Eve, *"Fill the earth and subdue it. Rule over the fish of the sea and the birds of the air and over every living creature that moves on the ground,"* Genesis 1:28.

The earth was ours to rule over while God retained authority in the heavens. *"The highest heavens belong to the Lord, but the earth he has given to man,"* Psalm 115:16.

However, through sin that came by Satan's deception on Adam and Eve we lost this authority on earth. What Jesus did on the cross was to restore the authority humanity lost by giving it to his church.

On the one hand, unbelievers live under the influence and authority of Satan who stole our birthright of ruling the earth. Satan does attempt to influence us, but he has no authority to rule over us. This veto power abides in the Holy Spirit who indwells us.

This deliverance ministry mirrors that of the Old Testament priest, except we now have a higher purpose. Our goal is to populate God's kingdom, and to redeem people to become members of the church that will rule the kingdom over which He returns to earth to rule.

Interestingly, the Bible never uses the term "demon possessed". Rather, it uses the word *diamonizomai*, which simply means, "demonized" or "influenced by demons". While a true believer's spirit can never make a home for demons, they can influence the soul and body. In dealing with matters of the flesh, the Bible exhorts the true believer to either deny it, or remove the source, i.e., the demonic influence, by casting it out.

The Bible authorizes no evil spirit ever to occupy a human body. Even Satan, in order to intrude into Job's life, had to gain permission from God. By intruding into a realm that they are unauthorized to enter, Jesus said that we—not angels—are authorized to confront them in order to liberate fellow human beings from being owned or possessed by demons. In this, we exercise the authority that Jesus had, and granted to His Twelve—to confront directly demons that take up residence in people, and evict them. Notice that commanding them to come out of an individual is not the same as making proclamations over evil spirits in realms we are not authorized to penetrate.

I respect the fact that today, a theological debate wages between those who feel that such a deliverance ministry has no scriptural justification today, as the apostles in the New Testament exercised this 'Tool'.

To such critics I say, "Praise His name". After being part of the Holy Spirit's ministry of casting out demons for decades, I can say that it is relevant, but must be conducted in a manner as prescribed in the Scripture.

Our authority to perform this eviction is the power released by invoking the mighty Name of the risen Lord and King of Kings—Jesus.

We have no power apart from His anointing and action. He responds because He has promised in His Word to do so, and in response to our faith that has its full confidence in His ability to respond. The apostolic gift authorizing us to invoke His Name (i.e., His power) is most crucial because the evil spirits that we deal with are more powerful than we are.

Of course, this ministry also works in conjunction with us preaching of the Gospel. Deliverance goes hand in hand with evangelism because by accepting Jesus as one's Savior and Lord, the Holy Spirit takes up residence in that human spirit, making demonic occupation impossible—but not demonic oppression. Praise God for the work of Jesus on the cross that liberated us from Satan's ownership and control.

By casting the evil spirits out of a person, we are simply announcing the illegal hold of the evil spirit(s) and proclaiming the liberty of the person. In and through the name of Jesus their authority over the person is removed. Christ is now the legal owner of the individual.

In addition, deliverance does not excuse a delivered individual from walking the walk that the Bible describes. He must do his part to maintain his freedom, since sin can make possible the return of those evil spirits just ousted.

PART 3: COUNSELING THOSE NEEDING DELIVERANCE

Since the word, devil, means 'Accuser', one should not be surprised to learn that one of his main tasks is to accuse the brethren (Rev. 12:10). Other schemes of his (temptation, mockery, and intimidation) are offshoots of this one. Sometimes he mixes truths about us (accuses of many things, including some things we have done).

I have observed, over many decades, that the devil's accusatory schemes usually follow along the lines of the following stages:
- He accuses you of being a failure. First, he brings up some area of your past in which you experienced some level of failure.
- Next, uses this information to make a broad, sweeping, accusation: you are (universally) a failure; in fact, he drives home the

idea that you are worthless; he is good at hammering your sense of significance into gravel.
- Building on this, he next predicts you will remain a failure forever, throwing in the insinuation that even God is made at you for your laziness and incompetence to prepare for your responsibilities, and your failure was divinely induced to teach you a lesson.

At this point the mind is spiraling dangerously away from a rational center.

Yet, I can relate to this, since he has worked my mind and heart over with these same accusations. Therefore, when people approach me for counsel in how to deal with this mental beating, I have learned to offer these seven suggestions:

1. Remember, the Holy Spirit will never accuse you so note such thoughts' source.
2. Evaluate Satan's real motivation: to prevent you from going deeper in God.
3. You do not overcome Satan by knowing more about him, so focus on Biblical verses that emphasize who God is, and what you mean to Him.
4. Acknowledge that you have an advocate
5. Guard your mind from entertaining self-accusing thoughts.
6. Praise God for what He has done, don't fret and worry about what you cannot do.
7. If a false accusation has crushed your spirit, do not react. Rather, go to the Lord in prayer, let the Lord rebuke the devil for you.

You can extricate yourself from the Devil's accusations; the key is to focus your mind on the above action steps.

As I close this section, permit me to share this story as an example of how God has used our ministry to bring deliverance to many people from the demons and unclean spirits.

Listen to this testimony of a man delivered from demonic control. He lived a supremely ungodly life. His language was a constant stream of the most blasphemous curses. His temper caused him to throw insults constantly. Everyone despised and hated him. In response, he began to show hatred at every opportunity as well as use his enormous strength to punish those who challenged him.

Soon anger, cursing, and fighting dominated his life. He sought power hoping that through intimidation people would respect him. He became obsessed with seeking vengeance against the slightest insult or perceived injury. His hatred caused everyone to despise and shun him.

He also engaged in daily bouts of sexual fantasizing that inevitably led to masturbation, as a way to deal with the turmoil after a day of spewing hatred and dishing out mayhem. It seemed to be the only thing capable of bringing him a moment of calm.

In one of these sessions, he began to blaspheme the Lord, spewing out the worst verbal evil words to assault directly the character of the Savior.

Everyone hated him, including his parents, and the extent of his hatred began to drive him insane; this is how the torment began.

Dear reader, I will now permit the young man to tell his story of deliverance in his own words.

"You see, while my desire for revenge fueled my hatred and anger to flow through me and power me to get my revenge accomplished, within my soul I was aching with loneliness for someone to understand and help me."

"Then I realized that what was driving my anger, fantasizing, and blasphemy was a demon. He revealed his name to me—'Vengeance'. He explained that it meant he who seeks power of revenge. He taught me how to deceive, pit one person against another, and use others for my own benefit."

"In no time 'Vengeance' became my closest companion, since I felt he truly understood me. When I got into fist-fights, I felt that he infused me with greater power."

"Occasionally, I would invite him to possess me. In those moments, my mind and soul became so dark and frightening. He would speak through me using my voice, only with more resonance. In these sessions, he would speak curses. If I had just experienced something bad, he would assure me that it happened because God hated me—that only he cared about me and was intent to help me become successful."

"Once, after one of his pieces of advice did not work as he promised, I confronted him that he did not know what he was doing. He then laughed at me. I felt foolish. In this situation, I then prayed. I actually poured out my heart to God, although I did so in ignorance and without faith. However, I saw that Vengeance was terrified at my attempt at praying, even apologized for giving me bad advice. I thought, "Wow, the leader of a legion is terrified of a prayer?"

"But as soon as my life returned to a normal routine he began to accuse me, insult me, and call me a coward. It was then that I realized that he was no longer my friend. Loneliness consumed me. I felt that I would never have a life like other people, so began to contemplate suicide. What kept me from committing this fatal act was my fear of hell, and of standing face to face with the true and living God."

"One night I attended a Deliverance meeting. I heard that I could be delivered from such satanic bondage. Later that night, I cried myself to sleep, even though the demon chided me as weak for spilling tears. I then prayed. Then I got the idea to type in a brief cry for help on an Internet search engine. Suddenly a blog popped up. It spoke about how to overcome sin and set us free from demonic bondage. Peace began to touch my soul."

"I felt like God was my only hope, and I told Him what I felt, while crying. Then I heard a comforting voice, and He told me "I hear you. Tell him (the demon) to go in My name, and he shall go." Then, I immediately got out of bed and went to the bathroom, and said, "Go away in the name of Jesus Christ!" and then felt something spew out along with the sounds of cursing. The demon then let out a scream. I actually felt it exiting my body. That was the last time I felt its presence or accusations."

"As I crawled back into bed, I began to sense God's presence. The impression I felt was that Jesus had taken hold of my hand. He then guided me to a crowd of unclean spirits. I screamed at them for what they had said and done to me. In this, Jesus was turning my hatred for people into a genuine hatred for evil, sin, and wickedness."

"The next morning I noticed that I no longer used curse words. Next, I noticed I had no desire to masturbate. I then searched out another service to share my testimony and praise the name of the Lord Jesus for delivering me from such demonic bondage.

"That was years ago, and today, my life is filled with joy, praise, and gratitude for my deliverance from demonic bondage."

Dear reader, I shared this story with you as an example of the countless similar experiences spanning our ministry over many decades using this vital apostolic tool of exorcism.

CONCLUSION

What a privilege to use this apostolic tool, exorcism! Yet, at every step along the way to exercising this apostolic tool, we must act in faith and under authority of the Savior who called us. We dare not go beyond the scope of our legitimate sphere of ministry.

The use of this gift in our ministry is ours only as we act under His authority, looking to Him to supply the power needed to deliver a soul from Satan's grasp. We are not like those seven sons of Sceva.

Luke, in Acts 19, describes an incident when a man and his seven sons attempted to acquire the gift of casting out demons from the Apostle Paul. Their goal was personal fame and fortune. They claimed that a demon-casting enterprise fit them since they were sons of a High Priest.

After watching Paul and Barnabas cast out demons, they approached a demon-possessed individual, and attempted to invoke the name of Jesus (as Paul had). One of these imitators said, "I adjure you by the Jesus whom Paul proclaims."

However, his results were far different than Paul had experienced. First, the demon scoffed, "Jesus I know, and Paul I know; but who are you?" Then, calling their bluff, the demon leaped on these workers of magic, overpowers, and proceeded to give all seven the beating of their lives. It then stripped each naked, and sent them stumbling away wounded and humiliated.

What an example for us all that we must not stray from the realm in which we are authorized to work. Without heaven's backing, we would approach this dangerous work without a prayer of a chance of succeeding.

Through our various deliverance events, people are set free from their bondage to Satan, spiritually, socially, physically and materially. It is deliverance ministry in its totality from Satan's kingdom into God's kingdom. Each one of us in the body of Christ has a form of deliverance ministry we've been commissioned to fulfill.

The cultures that apostles are sent to transform are places invariably so overwhelmed by human needs, that we encounter many unsaved people either so intimidated by demonic activity that they are reluctant to discuss their experiences, or are themselves oppressed by the spirit world.

For these reasons and a host of others, we thank God for anointing us with this apostolic tool. Over the years, it has enabled the Lord to influence cultures with His presence, leading many to deliverance.

As we close, permit me to share one more story

In our ministry in our travels to Africa, we have witnessed so many damaged souls from witchcraft; it is so widespread.

This testimony is typical of those who have stepped into the aisles seeking God's true relief from this evil bondage.

A man held a good position as a field supervisor in a large manufacturing facility in an African country. This required him to drive several locations, some nearly 150 km from his office.

One day he had to go to a remote site as quickly as possible. He jumped into a company truck to drive himself. What he did not know is that the regular driver of this truck, in an effort to protect himself from losing his job as driver, had consulted a witch who made sacrifices in that vehicle.

As he started the truck, the man prayed for God's protection. About ten km into his trip, he felt a strange force trying to force him into oncoming traffic. He thought maybe the problem was mechanical, but, after stopping, he learned that every system was working perfectly.

Nevertheless, once he was back on the road that same veering force took over. However, he then prayed to God for the protection of the Lord Jesus.

I felt a strange push that kept me veering to the right. I was almost crushing into vehicles heading into the opposite direction. At first, I thought it was unbalanced tire pressure causing this. So I had all pressure measured accordingly. Back on the road, again I was experiencing the same veering force! I prayed to God and asked for the protection of Jesus Christ. As I was about to reach the field station, I heard a sound in the bonnet but I just continued driving as it was already dark. When I reached the station, I realized God had given me special protection because the battery broke out of its position as I was driving. As I rested in my room at night, I wondered why all these things had happened to me. I did not know that I was battling powerful demonic forces planted in the vehicle. I prayed feverishly and I slept. While sleeping, God never revealed to me anything in a dream or scripture.

In the morning, a question from a co-worker who did not even know Jesus personally surprised me. She asked me, "Mhakura, are you okay?" I told her I was fine, and then inquired why she was asking.

She told me that at night she had a strange dream about me: I saw our two drivers Duzagi and Nolfaga seated on a cliff near a road looking at that vehicle you drove yesterday. In this dream, they had put a big snake across the front tires and another big snake across the rear tires. They were saying, "Let us see how he will drive that vehicle now!"

She continued: "But in this dream I saw you had killed the snake at the front. You had beaten the one at the back but it did not die and was still alive."

I always take dreams seriously because God has used them to speak to me. Therefore, I went back to my room and thanked God for revealing my enemies and for showing me the secrets of the spirit realm. What I later regretted was that I did not go into deep prayer that morning. Yet, from the dream, I had been told, "one of the snakes was still alive." Sure enough, as I was driving that morning in that same vehicle towards another city, one of the tire springs broke. This was a new old vehicle with very strong springs so I realized that I was dealing with very powerful wicked spiritual forces who wanted me to die. I then pulled out my pocket Bible and turned to Proverbs 26:27: *"If a man digs a pit, he will fall into it; if a man rolls a stone, it will roll back on him" Proverbs.*

This prayer formed on my lips: *"In four days, the very same thing my enemies wanted to happen to me will happen to them because it is written in this Bible.* It was my way of telling the two passengers Fred and Mary that as they had seen the power of Satan, now it was time for them to witness the power of God. Little did I know how seriously God had taken my words and the promise expressed in that verse.

That night as I was sleeping, God showed me a strange vision. I saw a big snake running out the vehicle I was driving and quickly entered the vehicle of my two enemies.

The following day as these two men were driving their car, it was involved in an accident and almost killed them.

That was four days after I had quoted the scripture in the Bible. Fred and Mary saw the broken car of the two employees and remembered my words four days ago. They said, as Pharaoh did: "Surely God is God and most powerful!"

Now that we have completed this category, we are ready to investigate the third category of tools we use in our apostolic ministry.

Category 3: Public Ministry Tools

CHAPTER 5

Repentance as a Tool

INTRODUCTION

A FEW YEARS AGO, a creative inventor, Dean Kamen, revealed the gyroscopic Segway scooter. The Press touted it as the next breakthrough means of urban transportation. It would change the way mail-carriers delivered mail in metropolitan areas. It would resolve traffic jams by enabling people to commute on this device. It would transform the way people work inside major warehouses, finding goods for shipping and stacking inventory.

Talk shows considered ways in which the Segue would require modification of entire cities.

Not a week went by without word from a television newscast heralding some new way this device was going to transform life.

Yet, today, the chatter is silent; nobody speaks about this breakthrough technology because it proved to be a colossal 'flop'.

Conversely, twenty centuries ago, if the Lord Jesus had been required to report to the Father in heaven the sum total of people He had trained and organized to change the world.

At His response, "Eleven", some attending angels might have pondered, "Did He mean eleven million? No. Perhaps we heard wrong; did He, perchance, mean "Eleven Thousand?"

After four and a half years, the team that Jesus built to complete the plan that prompted the Godhead to create man, and the galaxies included the eleven apostles He had handpicked, minus Judas.

Yet, in retrospect, those Apostles and the band they formed in the Upper Room transformed the world. Imagine what would have been Pilate's response to the man he was about to crucify would have been if he had known that within two hundred years, this Jesus dripping buckets of blood before him would be handed the keys to Caesar's Palace in Rome.

Today, the religion launched by the Nazarene carpenter, is, in this day, the fastest growing 'religion' in the world. Recently, one of the leading spokesperson for the radical Muslim movement lamented on mideast television that on average, six million Muslims annually convert to Christianity.

What makes Christianity work is the way in which God partners with man to totally transform his life (regeneration), and then provide the resources, expertise, and hands on guidance (sanctification) to ensure that he enters into God's presence (glorification)?

Certainly, no component of this process is more important than that which man must do at the outset to prepare for the Holy Spirit's work. The conviction of sin remains the work of the Holy Spirit, using the Word, and anointed preaching. Nevertheless, that man does have a role to play: he makes a true repentance.

Because salvation is so vital to all that we do on both the individual and societal levels, repentance is a strategically important tool.

To appreciate this, let us guide your thinking. Our learning journey will include an understanding of the nature of true repentance that will enable you to distinguish counterfeits.

PART 1: UNDERSTANDING THE MEANING AND SENSE OF "REPENTANCE"

"The time is fulfilled; the kingdom of God is at hand; repent and believe in the gospel" (Mark 1:15).

In His preaching, Jesus made repentance central to the Gospel message (as the above verse shows). He announced that He possessed the authority to save sinners. He made repentance crucial to gaining access to His saving work (grace and faith). He also implied that a day would arrive when the Father would withdraw this gracious offer of forgiveness, nullifying the need for repentance.

His final words, spoken at His Ascension, affirmed that repentance of one's sins for the forgiveness would be central to the message of the Gospel that the Apostles were to preach. This is why this tool is so important to our apostolic ministry; it was to theirs!

Repentance is the key to the Holy Spirit's transformation of a sinner by grace. It sets in motion a divine process that enables the repentant sinner to replace all God-dishonoring, Christ-belittling perceptions and dispositions and purposes with those that treasure God, and exalt Jesus, i.e., be born again.

Surely, nothing we do in ministering is more important than preaching the Gospel and conducting the seminars that offer insights that can transform a nation. What will move hearts to embrace our individual message of salvation as well as act on the principles and Laws of our transforming message? Nothing will occur at the deep spiritual level until the Holy Spirit acts in power; and only one thing prompts Him to action—repentance.

What is In a Word

The English word, "repent", translates the Greek word (*metanoeo*). This compound word has two components: *meta* and noeo. This second component, *noeo* refers to the mind, i.e., its thoughts, perceptions, dispositions, and purposes. The first component, meta, a prefix, means movement or change. When combined they describe this act: to experience a change your mind's perceptions, dispositions and purposes.

Why would the Gospel demand such a response from us? It's because we go where our mind goes. Hence, repentance involves not only a change of mind, but also a change of direction. The wordings Paul uses in Hebrews 6:1 makes it abundantly clear that the process involves turning from something dead to something alive by God's standards.

What is the nature of this change in perception? The Bible provides two insights.

Two things show us that repentance is an internal change of mind and heart rather than mere sorrow for sin or mere improvement of behavior.

Repentance as a Tool

The transformation takes place at the very core of one's self, but the proof of it become evident to all as fruit. Recall the words of Jesus: *"...bear fruit in keeping with repentance" (Luke 3:8)*.

The analogy of "fruit" is illuminating. While fruit is produced internally, the results become externally evident. Only one thing could produce such fruit—inward transformation. This, He urges, only happens by repenting. We repent; then the Holy Spirit takes over, and proceeds to transform us. Thus, repentance is not the new deeds, but the inward change that bears the fruit of new deeds. Jesus is demanding that we experience this inward change. This is why repentance is almost synonymous with becoming born again.

Also, notice how the above gentle command serves as a tacit appeal by Jesus for us to allow Him to transform us. That is the first insight He intends for us

Although repentance is an act mainly carried out by the Holy Spirit, nevertheless, it begins with an attitude. It perceives the true nature and damage caused by one's sin. This perception leads to godly sorrow for having committed it, and a complete renunciation of its place in our life. This leads to a change in behavior. Notice how, in His parable of the Prodigal Son, Jesus reveals this process of moving to an attitude where sin is okay, to where it is rejected as truly evil.

Permit me to point the three verses that help us understand this young man's path through repentance. To that end, notice the relationship between these two verses:

> "He squandered his property in reckless living . . . (and) devoured [it] with prostitutes"

> "Father, I have sinned against heaven and before you. I am no longer worthy to be called your son." (Luke 15:15, 30)

By connecting these two ideas, we learn that in Jesus' view of sin: the young man's throwing away his life away on reckless living and prostitutes was not just humanly hurtful; it was also an offense against heaven (God).

Elsewhere, Jesus provides us another clue as to His conception of sin. In His prayer Jesus taught the Twelve to prayer, this phrase provides us a second insight into how He viewed sin:

"...forgive us our sins as we ourselves forgive everyone who is indebted to us" (Luke 11:4)

Notice that Jesus labels sins as "debts".

Now we are ready to construct Jesus' view of sin: It that which dishonors God and puts us in debt to restore the divine honor ruined by our sin. Elsewhere, we learn that this debt is so large that no human can pay it. This is why He paid it in full on the Cross. It is ours by His complete and perfect work of salvation by grace through faith, which begins with genuine repentance, like that described by the Prodigal Son.

With this information in hand, let us notice a statement made earlier: repentance is almost synonymous with, "be born again" (John 3:7). I say this because only the Holy Spirit can reveal to the human heart this proper view of sin that leads to repentance; and only He can transform the soul so that one's behavior becomes God-centered, and Christ-exalting.

To appreciate our part, vs. His, consider these words of Jesus to the crippled man lying at the Pool of Bethsaida. Recall that He asked the man to describe his need. The man shared that when the water was troubled, he had no one to help him into it (for he mistakenly considered it to have healing power). Notice that Jesus responded by commanding the man to "Get up". What happened? In this process, we see something analogous to that occurring in true repentance.

Deep in the recesses of the man's mind, he decided to obey this command. Remember, just a second ago his legs were incapable of holding his weight; standing was impossible. Nevertheless, after Christ's command this crippled man changed his attitude: "I will get up". In the next nanosecond, supernatural power flowed into his limbs, transforming them into the legs capable of standing, but joyfully jumping up and down.

In this miracle, we see the man's decision to repent of his attitude toward his legs as analogous to the decision occurring deep within the human heart when the Holy Spirit does two things. First, He provides that person with a clear picture of what sin is (as Jesus viewed it). Second, He accepts our heartfelt acknowledgement of our guilty because of our sins.

Because of these two things, the Holy Spirit transforms our inner man so that the spirit (formerly dead or useless) can now influence our lives. It is a miracle, as surely as changing the water at that wedding in

Cana (John 2) into wine. It is not only strategic to the new birth, but also to maintaining fellowship throughout our life in Him.

PART 2: REPENTANCE AS A WAY OF LIFE

History makes much of Martin Luther's world changing "Ninety-Five Theses" he nailed on the Wittenberg Cathedral's front door. While the event is widely known, the contents are not. The first one is relevant to our subject. It read: "Our Lord and Master Jesus Christ…willed the entire life of believers to be one of repentance." Was he describing a morose life consumed with dealing with sin? No, an important liberating Biblical truth lay beneath the surface of his statement.

Luther's point: the Gospel transforms repentance, rendering it as the strategy by which the true believer grows in Christ. On-going repentance marks him as maturing; conforming to Christ's character. Repentance is integral to spiritual transformation, a source of pleasure, rather than pain.

Of all the vital aspects of our apostolic ministry, no activity trumps the importance of preaching. We seek to transform the soul of the nation we are sent by Christ to serve; and that means transforming individual hearts. So, our preaching mirrors that of the arch-apostle, Jesus: "repent and believe…" (Mark 1:14, 15).

The people we address carry in their heads a concept of repentance much different from that to which Luther alluded. This is why we spend the time in our sermons to explain the distinctions. How does Christian repentance differ from "religious repentance"?

Religious Repentance vs. Christian Repentance

In understanding the distinction between true and counterfeit repentance, Romans 8:1 is helpful:

> "there is therefore now, no condemnation in Christ Jesus".

The implication of this statement is that the true believer enjoys a relationship within Christ that makes his relationship to sin different. This is because He transfers the penalty of our sin to Him; therefore, we bear no consequences; face no condemnation.

By contrast, in religion, repentance is self-centered; its goal is to keep God happy so He will bless and answer prayers. The Gospel renders it

God-centered, giving it an entirely different purpose, i.e., to bring every sin to Him in order to weaken our need to do those things that displease Him. As such it is not something we dread; rather, we view it as a way to tap into the joy of our union with Him.

Not so, religious repentance, it considers repentance something to dread and sin as a mark of failure, and inevitably to be punished.

Other Distinctions

In religion, people are primarily sorry for the consequences of sin. The true believer also experiences sorrow over sin; but it is focused on the sin itself—the pain it caused the Savior to atone for it.

Religious uses different forms of self-flagellation to convince God (and themselves) that by self-inducing misery and remorse, they earn forgiven. In contrast, the true believer believes the Scriptures which tell us that self-inflicted suffering cannot merit forgiveness; we can only receive what Jesus, on the Cross, earned (I John 1:8, 9). Notice the phrase, "He is just." This is the basis for our forgiveness. The implications of this are staggering: it would be unjust for Him ever to deny us forgiveness, because His crucifixion accomplished perfect atonement. No, rather than earning forgiveness with our repentance, we receive it as a benefit of the salvation He attained for us at Calvary.

In religion, a person's hope lies in living a life he perceives to be adequate for God to bless them. As a result, he views every instance of sin and repentance so traumatic that repenting is a last resort. This is because this person feels that repentance is admittance that his level of moral goodness is sub-par. How different, biblical repentance: the true believer, realizing that he will not be cast off, and that his hope is in Christ's righteousness (not his) experiences a freedom to confess every flaw.

The religious person tends to let sin go unconfessed because he views repenting as an admission of failure. In contrast, the true believer, because he feels accepted and loved, freely confesses his sin and puts it behind him. He views this process as a testimony to the majesty of God's grace, and his sin and repentance as a means to his spiritual growth.

In this, his attitude resembles that of the 18th century evangelist, George Whitefield. He developed a nightly regimen for dealing with sin. It included these questions:

- Have I violated one of your commandments?

- Have I avoided people or tasks that I know I should face?
- Have I been anxious and worried?
- Have I failed to be circumspect or have I been rash and impulsive?
- Have I spoken or thought unkindly of anyone? Am I justifying myself by caricaturing (in my mind) someone else?
- Have I been impatient and irritable?
- Have I been self-absorbed and indifferent and inattentive to people?
- Have I looked down on anyone?
- Have I been too stung by criticism? Have I felt snubbed and ignored?
- Am I doing what I am doing for God's glory and the good of others or am I being driven by fears, need for approval, love of comfort and ease, need for control, hunger for acclaim and power, or the "fear of man"?
- Am I looking at anyone with envy?
- Am I giving in to any of even the first motions of lust or gluttony?
- Am I spending my time on urgent things rather than important things because of these inordinate desires?

Whitefield wrote to a friend, "God give me a deep humility and a burning love, a well-guided zeal and a single eye, and then let men and devils do their worst! Make me happy enough in you to avoid sin and wise enough in you to avoid danger, that I may always do what is right in your sight, in your name I pray, Amen."

Therefore, as we preach true repentance and the Gospel of true salvation, the Holy Spirit uses these insights to draw people to Himself. It is, as mentioned, crucial to our public ministry.

PART 3: CAIN AND COUNTERFEIT REPENTANCE

The true believers, to whom Apostle John writes in his first Epistle, worried that their repentance had not produced their salvation. Therefore, to provide them with assurance of salvation, he describes five tests by which they can know they are genuinely born again. One of them is this: you know that God has forgiven your sins. Since the key to experiencing this transformational experience of having your sins removed, he offers this analogy to help them understand the difference between Abel's genuine forgiveness, and Cain's counterfeit repentance.

The value of this analogy is the way it pinpoints out the difference between the kind of repentance that leads to forgiveness and heaven, and that, which leads to "feel-good" religiosity. To this end, let us now zero in on counterfeit repentance.

To appreciate Cain's problem, we begin with Genesis 3:17. His response to worship violated certain aspects of the curse laid down on man by YHWH. First, He pronounced a curse upon the ground, therefore rendering it incapable of producing anything acceptable as an offering for sin. Then, afterward, God established the acceptable means to covering one's nakedness (and sin)—skin of Lamb secured by sacrificing its life.

Well aware of these facts, the two brothers prepare a sacrifice to God. Both brothers brought the fruit of their honest labor (one farmed, one raised livestock). So why did God reject Cain's offering?

Cain brought things unacceptable to God since He had declared them cursed. On the other hand, Abel obeyed God, presenting Him a blood of a sacrificed Lamb. Cain came by his good works; Abel's sacrifice was a shadow of the reality that John the Baptist introduced to the Apostle John, "Behold the Lamb of God that takes away the sins of the world!" [John 1:29] The prophetic Lamb of God is Jesus, the Messiah.

Back to Cain: what created his problem? He offered something God declared to be unacceptable. What can we learn from his mistake regarding repentance? Counterfeit repentance stems from false belief.

You see a similar scenario in the Upper Room. Judas was a genuine unbeliever because he willfully refused God's offer of salvation, in spite of having witnessed the miracles and ministry of Jesus. Therefore, as a result, when Jesus handed him the "sop" it carried the sense of a final demand to make his choice. In this confrontation, Judas, instead of inviting Jesus to be his Lord and Savior, chose to invite Satan to enter his heart, and betrayal and self-destruction ensued.

Now to the congregation at Ephesus that John addresses in this first epistle, and to the reason why those that had just recently left the church (in an ugly 'split'). John points out that the problem lay in their counterfeit salvation based on a false view of Jesus' nature, which, in turn, forced them to make counterfeit repentance.

Since one's salvation hinges on the nature of its repentance, Let us examine the difference between the genuine kinds vs. its counterfeit, by describing the main characteristics of each.

Marks of True Repentance

In Christ, these true believers had discovered that the purpose of repentance is to repeatedly tap into the joy of one's union with Christ in order to weaken one's need to do anything contrary to God's heart. Also, they understand that sin can't ultimately bring us into condemnation (Rom 8:1.) Its heinousness is therefore what it does to God: it displeases and dishonors him.

They know that repentance is God-centered. Jesus suffered and paid the full penalty for all our sins; so we are not required to suffer to merit forgiveness, only receive that earned by Jesus (I John 1:8). In fact, it would be unjust of God to deny forgiveness to us. Also, they know that their hope is in the Savior's finished work, therefore, confessing their sins is not traumatic.

Most importantly, their sorrow is not primarily directed to the consequences of their sins, but for sin itself—what it does to the Savior.

They know that because of Christ's acceptance, they were free to admit all flaws (because He has already suffered our condemnation.

They repent often; they see it as inherent in their relationship with Him. Of course the process has bittersweet aspects, but it always leads to the same sweet end—joy.

If you clearly understand these two different ways to go about repentance, then (and only then!) you can profit greatly from a regular and exacting discipline of self-examination and repentance. If this revelation is available to all, what causes others to embrace a counterfeit repentance?

Cain-like Repentance

Permit me to return for a moment to a topic we considered earlier, Cain vs. Abel. I do so because we are now in a position to appreciate what motivated Cain's decision. Specifically, I wish to focus on the four most important contributors to his spiritual failure.

1. Pride: As mentioned, with Cain it was pride, "Hey, I work hard; I try to do right; and I made an effort at religion—isn't that enough?"

2. **Substituting Remorse:** To a degree this person bends his will, but he never surrenders control. Sometimes this problem arises because he feels remorse and thinks it is repentance. Because he feels deep remorse for his wrong-doing, he thinks he has met God's standard for repentance. His failure: he makes no real change in his life-direction. He has confused remorse with repentance.

   True, repentance contains remorse; however, repentance is not contingent upon feelings of remorse. Ask Esau. After trading his birthright for a single meal, he deeply regretted his mistake, but not all the remorse in the world could change what he had already done, as Hebrews 12:17 points out:

   "Afterward, as you know, when he wanted to inherit this blessing, he was rejected. He could bring about no change of mind, though he sought the blessing with tears."

3. **Willfulness:** Paul instructs us that God's kindness of God causes true repentance to take place (Rom. 2:4). This suggests that He is not kind to those who refuse to repent, as the next verse points out: *"But because of your stubbornness and your unrepentant heart, you are storing up wrath against yourself for the day of God's wrath…"*

   Why then is stubbornness fatal to true repentance? It stems from a heart unwilling to change—repentance is a choice, and the individual must want to change. It is true that God leads us to repentance, but we have to decide whether or not we want to change—repentance is a choice.

4. **Ignorance:** As Hosea wrote, "My people are destroyed for lack of knowledge." If I do not understand what true repentance is, then I am not likely to repent in the divinely prescribed manner. Another area of ignorance should be pointed out: people who experience true forgiveness soon learn that it must be repeated for one to maintain an abiding relationship. It does not end with salvation; it is the key to fellowship with Him throughout one's earthly existence.

As a result, these people, motivated by self-interests, see repentance as key to keeping God happy so He will continue to answer prayer.

Their sorrow for sin stems from a fear of its consequences or from embarrassment over having been caught committing it.

They view repentance as earned by self-infliction. They love to beat themselves up; they only feel forgiveness is justified when they have determined they have sufficiently suffered.

They equate repentance with admitting one is a bad person, so are reluctant to confess, therefore do so under duress. This theological craziness stems from equating salvation with moral goodness (even though the Bible says there is no one good enough to earn salvation apart from grace through faith.)

As you can imagine, pointing out the nature of genuine repentance, as well as spotlighting those ideas that lead to the kind of repentance that cannot regenerate one's heart occupies a major portion of our teaching ministry.

CONCLUSION

Repentance is the first and foremost response the Gospel of the Kingdom demands from an individual.

Our goal is to bring true repentance to the people we are called to minister unto. In this our ministry mirrors that which occurred among the Thessalonians. In the process, he summarizes true repentance: "… you turned to God from idols to serve the living and true God." (1 Thess. 1:9).

For this, we must make repentance one of our most important apostolic tools. It has changed the world for two thousand years since the Savior, on the first rung of the step in His Ascension, turned to the apostles gathered about His farewell and said, preach the Gospel, and in doing so emphasize the importance of true repentance. His mandate remains relevant for His Apostles in this 21st century.

Chapter 6

Kingdom Preaching as a Tool

Communicating Truth to a Contrary Culture

> Life, death, hell, and worlds unknown, hang on the preaching and the hearing of a sermon."
>
> —Charles Hadden Spurgeon

PREACHING IS AS VITAL to our apostolic ministry as a tank of oxygen to a scuba diver.

Although, similarities exist between kingdom preaching and the pastoral pulpit, some distinctions are significant. The pastor seeks to convert individual souls, while the apostle uses the microphone to transform the soul of a culture.

Post-moderns consider preaching as a tool publicly to promote a belief system. They love to consign it to that place where dinosaurs are interred and its practitioners as relevant as a typewriter repairman.

In an age where we are more aware of alternate viewpoints and globalized perspectives, should we write off preaching that seeks to proclaim persuasively truth that can redeem the soul of both an individual and a society? Hardly, I consider it as strategic to my ministry as a paddle to a canoe.

The reason is simple, the One who sends me on apostolic missions modeled the strategy; Jesus made kingdom preaching the centerpiece of His ministry strategy.

PART 1: PREACHING

To determine the nature of kingdom preaching, let us first consider what preaching is.

Haddon Robinson defines expository preaching as "the communication of a biblical concept, derived from and transmitted through a historical, grammatical, literary study of a passage in its context, which the Holy Spirit first applies to the personality and experience of the preacher, then through him to his hearers." (Robinson 21).

His definition presupposes the authority of Scripture and the need to understand, interpret, and present the truth revealed in the Bible. Surely, this aligns with Paul's idea, written to Timothy (2 Timothy 3, and 4). Following the apostle's lead, we, too, preach the Book.

Sidney Greidanus supports this view: "Bible-centered preaching," he says, "is handling the text in such a way that its real and essential meaning as it existed in the mind of the particular Biblical writer and as it exists in the light of the over-all context of Scripture is made plain and applied to the present-day needs of hearers (Greidanus p.11)."

In this manner, the apostle operates much like Commodore Perry: he presents the message he was sent to deliver; and its source is derived from the Sender's own words.

We are not traveling Bible teachers. The priority of transforming trumps the importance of informing. Nevertheless, our priority is that God, through His Holy Spirit, will speak to hearts through the Biblical text of our message.

Kingdom preaching works because it flows from a heart that knows that its message is true. It also works because it delivers two 'take-aways' to the audience. First, people leave with the sense that they have heard from the Almighty. Second, they sense that "God cares for me".

To achieve this second 'value-add' the preacher must persuade them of four things. First, they must believe that God loves them enough to tell them the truth about themselves; and, second, that absolute truth does exist. In addition, they must also believe that to be accountable for this truth is beneficial. Finally, they must believe that the One inviting them to trust Him does not look upon their needs and withhold help that only He can supernaturally supply, i.e., physical wholeness, and freedom from spiritual bondage.

The apostolic preacher operates under four convictions. First, he believes that God is still speaking through his Word by the Spirit's anointing through that preacher faithful to the Word.

Second, he knows by the nature of his calling that people still need to hear from God; that apart from grace, their lives (and existence as a culture) are now and forever in genuine peril.

Third, he knows by experience that salvation is accessible to anyone who calls upon the name of the Lord.

Finally, he knows that nobody finds life eternal if someone does not tell them how.

In the course of several decades of apostolic preaching, we have so consistently observed this truth that it has become a "given" (settled truth): God is in the business of making Himself known and heard, and for some mysterious reason, He chooses to accomplish it through the foolishness of preaching.

Now that we have a general understanding of preaching, let us explore its use as an apostolic tool.

PART 2: DEFINING APOSTOLIC PREACHING

Apostolic preaching is uniquely kingdom oriented because it is "nouthetic". To appreciate this tool in our arsenal, you need to understand this word.

The word "nouthetic" derives from a Greek word found in Col.1:28. It occurs in both the noun (*nouthesis*) and verb (*noutheteo*) forms. It is not easy to define. The most widely accepted sense of the word's meaning is confrontational. However, Bible scholars have translated it with a variety of meanings: "to admonish," "warn," "teach", "put sense into", and "to counsel". So, permit me to construct a meaning by highlighting the Greek word's central meaning components. Then the uniqueness of kingdom preaching can be understood.

With this introduction, let us focus on the following characteristics that distinguish apostolic preaching.

Components of Nouthetic Preaching

Christocentric

Nouthetic preaching is Christ-centered; it relates everything to Him. Since His Word conveys His will, it is biblical.

Biblical

Nouthetic type preaching accords quite fully with what Paul says elsewhere about the purpose and use of Scripture: "All Scripture is given by inspiration of God and is useful for teaching, for reproving, for correcting, for training in righteousness." (II Tim. 3:16). As Paul's counsel to Timothy shows, the entire Bible is nouthetically oriented, i.e., for teaching, reproving, correcting and training.

Confrontational

The apostle Paul preached nouthetically. In Colossians 1:28, for instance, Paul declared: *"We proclaim him confronting every man nouthetically, and teaching every man with all wisdom in order that we may present every man complete in Christ."*

To appreciate his approach, consider this description of his farewell message to the Ephesians elders in Acts 20. The scene is very dramatic; Paul would never see them again. In his remarks, Paul reviewed his three-year ministry at Ephesus, recalling the past, looking into the future, and describing the present. He warned about problems likely to arise. He then described his primary work in their midst: *"Be on the alert [i.e., as I was], remembering that night and day for a period of three years I did not cease to confront each one nouthetically with tears."(Acts 20:31)*

Problem-solving

Nouthetic confrontation implies a problem; it presumes that an obstacle exists that must be overcome. Therefore, nouthetic preaching is narrative preaching; we explain the Biblical text as if telling a story.

Persuasive

Nouthetic preaching tackles a problem, seeks to remove it, but by use of influence based on a compelling argument. This is why one of the above terms used to translate it is *didasko*, useful information is used to persuade (vs. threaten).

It begins with this assumption: those being confronted have a need, and its goal is to help bring about behavioral change. It then uses verbal admonition to explain consequences. In this regard, one recalls Nathan confronting David after his sin with Uriah and Bathsheba. It also brings to mind God's admonition to Eli through Samuel: *"You tell him that I will execute justice over his family forever, because he knew that his sons were bringing a curse upon themselves, and he failed to discipline them"* (I Sam. 2:22).

Eli failed to nouthetically confront his sons; to speak with sufficient strictness and seriousness, as well as soon enough to move their behavior to change. The tragedy of their fates is that if he had compared their behavior to God's standards, the outcome would probably been different. Nouthetic preaching seeks to answer the "what" rather than the "why" question, because people already know that answer; they possess a sinful nature. It focuses on these two questions: "What have you been doing?" and "What does God say can be done about it?"

Nurturing

Apostolic preaching has one over-arching, nurturing motivation: to nurture, i.e. bring benefit to the hearer. In this regard, we can learn from Paul: "I did not write these things to shame you but to confront you nouthetically as my beloved children." (I Cor. 4:14). In this his sentiments resemble that of a loving parent dealing with his child. Nevertheless, the goal must be to meet obstacles head on and overcome them verbally, not in order to punish but to help him. Therefore, the element of punishment is not dwelt upon; the message expresses a "voice" that speaks of being motivated by love and concern, in order that the hearer will draw near to Christ, and the Father glorified.

Authoritative

Apostolic preaching involves the use of authoritative instruction. In the Garden of Eden, when man disobeyed God, his conscience was awakened, and out of fear, sinful man fled, covered himself and tried to hide from God. In antithesis to running and hiding, apostolic preaching stresses turning to God in repentance, assuming responsibility and blame and admitting guilt for sin, and seeking forgiveness in Christ.

Our preaching rests upon the dynamics of redemption, and reflects this fact at every point. Therefore, its power (as well as its fearful responsibility) stems from the fact that it utilizes the full authority of God.

PART 3: GOALS OF APOSTOLIC PREACHING

What are the goals of apostolic (nouthetic) preaching? In I Timothy 1:5 Paul put it this way: *"But the goal of our (authoritatively imposed) instruction is love from a pure heart, and a good conscience, and a sincere faith."*

The purpose of apostolic preaching is to foster the love toward God and love toward one's neighbor, which God commands. Jesus summed up the keeping of the whole law as love. God's authoritative instruction through the ministry of his Word, spoken from the pulpit becomes the catalyst that Holy Spirit uses to produce loving hearts. The Bible defines love as fulfilling God's commandments. In other words, love results from taking responsibility to align oneself with His will as expressed in His Word.

Thus the goal of our preaching, as the Bible shows, is to bring men into loving conformity with God's revealed will.

Apostolic Preaching in Postmodern Age

A Christian Medical College invited Pierre, a French monk who worked among beggars in Paris after World War II, to speak during lunch period for a few minutes. He spoke through an interpreter, but so rapidly and earnestly that the interpreter gave up trying to keep up. Nevertheless, Abel's passion so captivated the students they gave him a standing ovation.

Brandt interviewed a student. How did you understand since no one here speaks French? The reply; we did not need one; we felt God's presence, and His love."

Apostolic preaching is "incarnational"; it first influences us, and then, through the encounter we have just experienced in our souls, we influence those who hear our sermon. Old Testament preachers considered the sermon they preached to be a (Hebrew word *"na'um"*), i.e., an "oracle", or "burden". The word describes the reaction they felt after having received a message from YHWH. It weighed heavily upon their hearts (cf. Numbers 23:7, Isa. 13:1, Jer. 23:33-38, Ezek. 12:10).

Apostolic preaching, especially in this postmodern age must be heart-felt; it must emerge from our personal encounters with the living

God, because this society is deluged with advertisers; to gain attention, those hawking their wares must scream. Therefore, the apostle who stands behind the pulpit must speak through his whole personality to avoid becoming another plastic voice.

Apostolic preaching is sensitive to the significance of non-logical arguments. It also employs signs and wonders. People now, as in New Testament times, respond to the message not just because of our compelling argument but because of the attendant power of God demonstrated. This completes the loop: the Holy Spirit calls us; empowers us; we experience the message given to us; we share it, accompanied by Holy Spirit anointed evidence; and it lands dead center on the spirit of the hearer.

The impact of apostolic preaching lies in the "voice" that communicates to the hearer beyond our words; it emerges from having lived the truth we communicate, thereby nestling the message in our heart.

Therefore, apostolic preaching is a real-time event. True, we do prepare; but whole-personality preaching cannot capture, in advance, the moment the Spirit seeks to bring into existence as our preaching process proceeds. I bear witness that the results resemble live theater of the highest drama, with the fate of the lonely, the lost and the listless at stake.

Apostolic preaching is about Him speaking through us, not us speaking about Him.

PART 4 MODELS OF APOSTOLIC PREACHING: JOHN THE BAPTIZER AND JESUS

Certainly, no finer servant of the living Lord ever drew breath. John the Baptizer's kingdom mindset beautifully prepared Israel to receive Jesus as King of Kings. In the process, it cost him his life. Let us examine some of the more important aspects of his the mindset for kingdom preaching.

You need not look any further than the Old Testament prophet he emulated for a first set of clues. He epitomized Elijah in speech, lifestyle, and appearance (2 Kings 1:8). Like his model, John confronted the political and moral base of Israel as well as those false prophets holding her people in a strangle old.

John's message mirrored that of Elijah: "Repent, and return to the God of Abraham; judgment is at hand". Notice how closely John's message was: "Repent, for the Kingdom of Heaven (i.e., promised to Abraham) is at hand."

Analysis of His Kingdom Message:

Our apostolic preaching performs two tasks. First, we boldly confront a languishing nation with this Good News: the anointed One, capable of transforming every life at every level has sent me to tell you that He is at hand, ready to tackle your problems.

We lift Him up because all power to transform an individual's heart or a society resides in Him. Only the Savior, working through the precious Holy Spirit can change a life, and yes, a nation. So our task is to lift Him up; make them realize that He is their solution. To do otherwise would be to attempt to share and pilfer His glory.

Second, we point people to the path that enables them to access His magnificent help.

The process begins with repentance. It perfectly prepares the way for transformation, providing a kingdom mindset—a new way of thinking.

To appreciate this word's connection to the kingdom mindset, permit me to share these insights regarding its meaning.

"Repent"

Since we have already discussed this word at length, let us focus on its relationship to a kingdom mindset. Let us focus on the unique insights we learn from John's approach to preaching repentance.

By analyzing aspects of John's water baptism, we gain insight into how God views it as the gateway to salvation. He chose a ceremony that forced one to demonstrate how dramatically his thinking had changed.

The rite that John made use of was perfect to dramatize the essence of true repentance. Let us explore his main components, beginning with the use of the Jordan River.

The Jewish culture made such a big deal out of ceremonial cleanliness that if you accidentally brushed against a person or object on the 'unclean list', then you had to go home, wash your body, and change into clean clothes before you could pursue your tasks for the day when you became ceremonially unclean through contact.

With that in mind, consider his use of the Jordan River. It was the gateway into the Promised Land. The day that the Lord parted its waters so Israel could enter into Canaan signaled the end of 40 years of wandering. As they climbed up on the bank into their new life, they circumcised all males, less than 40 years of age. Its significance stacks up with that of the first Passover; this is why they named it Gilgal (Place of Remembrance).

To emphasize the seriousness of joining him in the baptismal waters John required them to walk forty miles into a sweltering desert to be immersed in the Jordan River. This symbolism is most instructive.

Next, consider another insight into repentance that the Jordan offered. The Pharisees considered it ceremonially unclean. Therefore, by choosing it Paul was asking each participant to declare himself (and his old religion) unclean. Only the righteousness of the New Covenant would suffice.

The third thing you should know about John's rite of baptism was that it already existed. Priests commonly used a pool at the Temple to initiate Gentiles into Judaism.

Therefore, in using it, John was saying, I want you to forget everything you knew, and treasured as giving you hope. I want you to return to "square one": consider yourself as a Gentile, someone who has yet to be a true Israelite, and one who now has a new standard for spiritual cleanliness.

This apostle did not water down the Gospel message! This ceremony forced genuine repentance, and that it could only occur by supernatural prompting by the Holy Spirit.

Then, why did Jesus undergo baptism? He certainly had no sins to repent. He did it for two reasons. First, He entered Jordan to show that His kingdom ministry fully aligned with people as sinners—these are the very ones He came to save. Certainly, in John's public introduction to Him, this is clear: "Behold the LAMB of God who takes away the sin of the world".

Second, He did it because baptisms mark a life beginning a new ministry; therefore, a special enduement is required. The Bible speaks about three baptisms.

There is the baptism required for the new birth.

There is the baptism required to receive supernatural gifts, and,

There is the baptism required for the enduement (divine anointing) to embark on an important new ministry.

So Jesus, in going beneath these waters was submitting in obedience to the Father and the Holy Spirit, yielding Himself to receive their authority and enablement to begin His public ministry.

"Kingdom at Hand"

Those God calls us to serve need to know that the spiritual solutions they need are within reach. This is why the signs and wonders are so important to gaining their attention to the nearness of God in all His power. However, using signs and wonders, we are able to introduce the people to a new reality; one in which Jesus is at the center.

When the Savior preached this theme, he added two phrases: "near", and "time is fulfilled". Regarding the first, He meant to share the good news that divine help was as available ("near") as the back of one's hand; therefore, His promise was real, not being imagined. By the second, He meant, His and John's ministry signaled a true sea change.

So Jesus chose a Greek word that does not mean chronological time (*chronos*), but *kairos*, a decisive moment, which equates to "a strategic opportunity that demands a decision". It was as He preached. This is a strategic moment; the Kingdom of God is right here in your midst. Therefore, this is an opportune time; it demands action; do not let it pass you by".

"Believe"

Jesus added another component "Believe". The Greek He used, *pisteuo*, means much more than to agree with one's mind.

Many people then and now believe *in* Jesus, i.e., accept His statements as intellectually accurate. But that will not transform anyone. No the Savior's word goes further: it means not just to accept its truthfulness, but to put one's trust in it, embracing it as critical important to your life, and finding joy and comfort in resting upon its veracity.

Therefore, kingdom preaching is not about moral renewal but total spiritual transformation. Nothing less can change either a life or a culture.

Audience Reactions

How the people reacted to the kingdom preaching of John and Jesus?

Reaction to John's Ministry

John's ministry met with wonderful response. Many recognized their sinful state, genuinely repented, and put their faith in the Messiah whom he presented to them as the Lamb who takes away the sin of the world.

Nevertheless, in time, John's understanding of the Kingdom developed a flaw.

It surfaced while he was in prison, awaiting the fate of Herod for having confronted him about the sin of murdering his own brother in order to steal his wife, as described in Matt 11:1:1-3 "Are you the One, or should we seek anther?

Remember, John had no access to the wealth of information available after the Holy Spirit instituted the New Covenant in the Upper Room some 50 days after Jesus' ascension. (This is why, after extolling his virtue as the greatest of Old Testament prophets, Jesus added, "yet he was the least in the Kingdom of God").

Therefore, when he sends two of his disciples to ask Jesus this question it is understandable: "Here I am in prison, about to lose my life; if He is not the Messiah, what is the meaning of all that I have done?" Therefore, the point of his question was based on a flaw widely shared among his contemporaries.

Recall that earlier we described the Kingdom as happening in two phases: "now," and "afterward." Many people that heard Jesus were knowledgeable that the Messiah would establish His rule on earth; but failed to distinguish that from the preliminary ("now") phase. As a result, they were looking for kingdom to replace the oppressive occupation of the Romans.

John's question reveals that he, too, had misunderstood the ministry of the Messiah. He figured that if Jesus was truly the Messiah, He would perform works connected with a political deliverance of Israel - or at least the deliverance of John, who was in prison.

Jesus sends back an answer: I am the Messiah; my works prove that, conforming the description of Isaiah, but my power, at this time (now phase) will be reserved for using miraculous works to validate my message, and not to be a spectacular display intended to launch political deliverance (to come "afterward".)

However, we should not be too harsh on John, his error was a common one: many failed to distinguish between the other aspect of kingdom: Seeing the "now" aspect in full swing, he simply jumped to the conclusion that it was a prelude to the second phase as well.

Response to Jesus' Preaching

To appreciate the response of the people to the early public ministry of Jesus, we need look no further than His first sermon in the Nazareth synagogue. Several things stood out. Listen to their own words: "amazed… that he spoke with such authority."

A brief analysis of this word authority will help you appreciate their response. It Greek counterpart is the word, *ekousia*. It means this: the audience is totally convinced of its truthfulness (therefore, does not need further confirmation from a quoted expert source), and is completely "sold" on this idea: that speak really believes in what he says, and for a very good reason.

What we learn about a Kingdom Preaching from John and Jesus

1. They sought an urban focus and/or an audience with those who were not religiously powerful.
2. As we have just learned, it teaches with authority (ekou-see-ah). Why? They had never heard anyone teach quite like this before. Why? He did not give well quoted lecture, but spoke of what He knew about to them with power. In regard to apostolic preaching, we think of authority as meaning: "I know he is right; I also know that he knows he is right".
3. It is Nouthetic, as we have already discussed.
4. Apostolic preaching is kingdom-focused as compared to church-focused (pastoral) preaching.
5. It uses supernatural works to confirm that another reality is operational. However, please understand that, in regard to our use of signs and wonders, we, like the Savior, are preachers who use the gifts of healing and exorcism. We are not miracle workers who also preach.

PART 5: PRIORITY OF PREACHING THE KINGDOM OF GOD

Recently, theologians have begun to rediscover the central thread running through both Testaments—the kingdom of God. From Genesis to Revelation, He progressively reveals the nature and reality of His kingdom. From Abraham on, the message has been: I plan to build a people to share a covenant relationship and live under My rule and protection;

David's rule, forever (2 Sam.7:16). Incidentally, surveys taken reveal that the kingdom is the Bible's most important idea.

From the outset, Jesus made this preaching the dominant focus of His preaching. He is the Messiah, and therefore, the kingdom is at hand; therefore, repent. (Matt.4:19). His post-resurrection "Commission" is a royal commission to establish His kingdom. He promised that in His return, He would completely establish the kingdom. Some feel that by giving an altar call they are preaching the kingdom, while others feel that their expository sermons are proof they preach the kingdom.

While many pastoral pulpits avoid the subject, the apostolic pulpit focuses on this theme as its primary message.

It is paradoxical that surveys affirm the kingdom of God to be the Bible's most centrally important idea, yet few pulpits make it their primary, dominant theme. Many mistakenly feel that by preaching Biblical messages or calling for decisions that they are preaching this theme.

In His early ministry, Jesus did not do this. His constant focus was to reveal the nature and reality of His kingdom. He taught that the kingdom of God had come in and through Him; that He was the promised Messiah, the "anointed rule" sent to rescue His people and occupy David's throne.

At the cross, King Jesus atoned for the sins of His people. Through His resurrection, Jesus demonstrated His power over death and the beauty and wonder of a life alive before God. The remainder of the New Testament reveals how the church exists as a present day sign of the kingdom and how God's kingdom will be completely established at the second coming of Jesus Christ.

Apostolic preaching must focus on preaching the kingdom of God as a central theme.

CONCLUSION

As events in Nazi Germany pushed Europe toward the start of WWII, one British Lieutenant, Frank Whittle was busy designing a tool to aid Britain against the certain air attack by Hitler.

He devoted every waking moment to his project; he cobbled parts from every person and pile of debris he or his friends could scourer. In addition to a decided lack of funds, tools, and parts, he faced another obstacle: many who out-ranked him considered his idea unfeasible. Frank

Whittle had conceived a simple design for the jet engine, which he hoped would give England air superiority should war commence.

Nevertheless, the day dawned that he had set aside to test his new design. Many influential people assembled, including a few skeptics. That soon ended however.

After assembling his small prototype of a jet engine bolted to a massive wooden bench, Whittle fired up the engine. Its power was so extraordinary that it propelled the massive wooden bench through the window of the large airplane hanger some fifty feet away.

The British government immediately put up the money and manpower to get it into production as soon as possible.

Apostolic preaching has a similar force. It brings the authority of the Scriptures; it enlightens concerning the Kingdom of God to a "virgin" audience. It affirms the truth of its message by using signs and wonders. It confronts a nation as a unity.

It employs the best features of evangelistic preaching by speaking to individual hearts in such a way that they can understand spiritual truth with no theological background and experience transformation.

Like the prophetic pulpit, it speaks to the issues that confront the culture he stands before in such a way as to enlighten them with the laws and principles needed to bring about wholeness.

One characteristic sums up apostolic preaching: it tears down in order to build up. To appreciate how the apostle goes about this, we need look no further than to Jesus. In His last week, with his eye clearly on preparing the way for a new foundation for the Temple, of which He would be the cornerstone, he attacks the existing structure in many ways, two of which are significant to "tearing down".

First, he ousted the graft, fraud, and corruption in the existing Temple by driving the moneychangers out. Second, to show what He was about to do with the existing religious leadership, He likened them to a fig tree and cursed it so that its leaves withered immediately.

After Jesus' resurrection, and ascension, the Holy Spirit rushed into the Upper Room to begin the construction of the eternal Temple, comprised of "living stones".

Now, two thousand years later, He continues to tear down and build up using the apostolic pulpit and the special preaching gift He has anointed us with.

SUMMARY TO BOOK FOUR

Someone has facetiously written that we can reduce all of life's mechanical problems to those involving something that is stuck and needs loosening, or has come loose and requires refastening.

As a result, only two tools are required to solve all problems, Duct Tape and WD40. The first can fasten anything that has come loose, and the latter can loosen anything stuck.

While we enjoy the humor in this observation, we realize that in this age of specialization, each problem requires a matching tool. That axiom certainly applies to our ministry. The Savior's gifting of those supernatural abilities integral to the apostleship confirms our calling.

It has been our privilege to explain each to you, as well as the outcomes we use them to achieve, as well as the mindset required for this ministry as opposed to a pastoral ministry.

Thank you for journeying with us to gain a better understanding of the ministry of today's first-century apostle.

God's richest blessings,
Bertril Baird
2010

Entry Notes

As you can tell, the material presented in this first volume is based on extensive research. We consulted articles published on the Internet, as well as Commentaries and Reference Works published by variously published.

To ensure that we did not encroach upon the original author's verbiage we rewrote each article, summarizing relevant ideas in our own words.

The following is a partial list of the articles consulted.

Bertril Baird

1. Articles Consulted

Attention: Calling All Apostles: Will You Please Stand Up?!!
Spiritual Fathering: This Happened to Me! (by Randy Muse)
Apostolic Ministry: Questions & Answers / Randall A. Muse
Implementing the Apostolic: Hindrances, & Misunderstandings
The Modern Apostle and a Biblical Perspective toward Money
Understanding Spiritual Resistance to the Apostolic Movement
Anointing Flows from Head Apostle Jesus to Fathers & Sons :
Anthology of Apostolic Ministry & Doctrine / Randall A. Muse
Apostolic Idols | Apostles in Training | Seeking Covering (R. Muse)
The Spirit of the Father & Spiritual Fathering in Apostles (R. Muse)
The New Revival and Apostolic are Currents in the Same River
The Sign of Slain in the Spirit: How it is Displayed in the Bible
"The Calling of the [Modern] Apostles" authored by Pam Clark
Traits of Apostles: Recognizing the Genuine & the Counterfeit
Apologetics: ......Present Day Gifts and Modern Day Apostles
The Modern Apostle versus Missionaries by Steve Atkerson
The Apostolic Church: What It Is & What It Isn't, by J.Wies

Entry Notes

Where Are the Apostles Today? from Ministries Today Magazine
Return to Anitoch : Ten Ramifications by Jim Goll
The Interdependency of Purpose and Process by Douglas Fortune
Present-Day Ministry of the Apostles by John Noble
The Activation of Apostolic Destiny, by Timothy and Theresa Early
Apostles & Church Unity by Dr. Michael Scantlebury
Gifts from the Ascended Christ: Restoring the Place of 5-fold Ministry, by Dwayne Stone
Apostolic Purity by Dr. Michael Scantlebury
Five Pillars of The Apostolic by Dr.Michael Scantlebury
Identifying and Defeating the Jezebel Spirit by Dr. Michael Scantlebury
Christ's Love-Gift to the Church: Apostles Today by Barney Coombs
First Apostles and Last Apostles by Peter Lyne
Pandora's Pulpit by Dr. Roger Sapp
The Apostolic Church by John Eckhardt
50 Truths Concerning Apostolic Ministry by John Eckhardt
The Ministry Anointing of the Apostle by John Eckhardt
Moving in the Apostolic by John Eckhardt
Thirty Books About Apostolic Ministry by Dr. Milton Roman
Apostles of the City by C. Peter Wagner
The Last Apostles on Earth by Dr. Roger Sapp
The Gift of Apostle by Dr. David Cannistraci
Prophetic Destiny & the Apostolic Reformation by Dr. Bill Hamon
Apostles, Prophets, & the Coming Moves of God by Dr. Bill Hamon
Apostolic & Prophetic Foundations by Donald Rumble
The House of His Choosing...Is the House HE is Building, by Gabriel Heter
A Solid Foundation for the 21st Century Church by Jim Wies
The Distinguishing Marks of the Apostolic Church by Steve Schultz
Mentoring and Fathering / Steve Schultz & Chris Gaborit
His Rule in His Church by Carlton Kenney
The Present Reformation of the Church by Noel Woodroffe
Gather My Apostles by Cary Goodwin,
Intuitive Ethics: How Innately Prepared Intuitions Generate Culturally Variable Virtues, Haidt & Joseph
Apostolic Foundation, by Arthur Katz
The Ministry of Angels, by Marilyn Hickey
Worldviews, by Samuel Weaver
What is a Nation? by Ronald Grigor,
Worldview, Anthropology, and Gender: A Call to Broaden the Parameters of the Discussion, by Bruce Ashford
Transforming Culture: Christian Truth Confronts Post-Christian America, by Albert Moehler
Transforming Culture with a Messiah Complex by Michael Horton,
Apostolic Essay, by Joel Garcia
Worldview and Long View by Charles Kraft
What is the Apostleship? Christianity Today, by William Beasely and Skye Jethani
The Kingdom Is Not the Church, by Robert T. Woodworth
Kingdom Mentality in Eastern Europe, by Robert Duevunix
Church Mentality vs. Kingdom Mentality, by Grace Chennowith-Trevil

Mistaken Identity: The Church is Not the Kingdom, A Historical Premillennial Response by George E. Ladd
Following the Apostolic Mission Model by Timothy Kiho Park, Ph.D., Fuller Theological Seminary
Apostolic Leadership Archetype of Moses by Matthew Kutz
Fifteen People Who Changed The World by Trevor Butterworth
The Nature of the Apostolic Ministry By Jim Buchan
The Nature of the Apostolic Ministry, By Jay Rogers
Twice-Told Proverbs by Daniel C. Snell, Eisenbrauns, Winona Lake
Noetic Sin, Neutrality, and Contextualization: How Culture Receives the Gospel, by Mark A. Snoeberger, Detroit Theological Seminary, 2004

2. Books, Commentaries and Reference Works Consulted

A Critical and Exegetical Commentary, Ezra P. Gould, Editor, T & T Clark, Ediburgh
A Survey of the theology of the Kingdom of God by Ronald L. Klaus
Biblical Commentary of the Old Testament, C ,F, Keil, and F. Delitzsch, Wm. B Eerdmans,
Breaking the Missional Code by Ed Stetzer (B&H Academic, 2006)
Christ's Love-Gift to the Church, Apostles Today, by Barney Coombs
Church Unique: How Missional Leaders Cast Vision, Capture Culture, and Create Movement by Will Mancini (Jossey-Bass, 2008)
Compelled by Love: The Most Excellent Way to Missional Living, Ed Stetzer and Philip Nation
Contours of Christian Theology Series, Gerald Bray, General Editor, Volume: The Church, by Edmund P. Clowney, Intervarsity Press, Downers Grove, Illinois
Donald G. Bloesch, Jesus Christ, Volume four of Christian Foundations Series, Intervarsity Press
Donald Guthrie, New Testament Theology, Intervarsity Press, Downers Grove, Illinois
Expostiors's Bible Commentary, vol. 1 - 12, J. R. Douglas, edit. Zondervan, Grand Rapids
Holman New Testament Commentary, Max Anders, Gen. Ed., Holman Reference, Nashville
Introduction to the Old Testament, by R. K. Harrison, Wm. B. Eerdmans, Grand Rapids
John Calvin, The Institutes of the Christian Religion, Hendrickson Publishers, Peabody, MA
John Garfield, The Kingdom of God and Marketplace Ministry
John Gill, Body of Doctrinal and Practical Divinity, Westminster Press, Philadelphia, PA
Kingdom Come Why does it matter? By Philip Greenslade, A Passion for God's Story
Knowing God, J.I Packer, Intervarsity Press, Downers Grove, Illinois
Missional Church: Vision for Sending of Church in North America edited by Darrell Guder
Pulpit Commentary, H. D. M Spense & Joseph S. Exell, Editors, Wm Eerdmans, Grand Rapids
ReJesus: A Wild Messiah for a Missional Church by Alan Hirsch and Michael Frost Robert G. Clouse, ed., The Meaning of the Millennium (IV Press, 1977)
Robert Jamieson, A.R. Fausset & David Brown, A Commentary Critical and Explanatory on the on the Bible, George H. Doran Company, New York City.

Entry Notes

Strong's New Exhaustive Concordance of the Bible, James Strong, ed., World, pub., Iowa City

Synonyms of the New Testament, Richard C. Trench, editor, Wm. B. Eerdmans, Grand Rapids

The Analytical Hebrew and Chaldee Lexicon, Benjamin Davidson, ed., Zondervan

The Bible Speaks Today, John R. W. Stott, Series Editor, Inter-Varsity Press, Leicester, England

The Book of Proverbs Chapters 1-15. NICOT by Bruce Waltke, Eerdmans, Grand Rapids

The Complete Word Study of the Old Testament, Spiros Zodhiates, World, Pub., Iowa Falls

The Englishman's Greek Concordance of the New Testament, Samuel Bauster and Sons, London

The Expositors Bible Commentary, Frank E, Gabelein, General Editor, Zondervan

The Fear of God, by J. Gresham Machen

The Forgotten Ways: Reactivating the Missional Church by Alan Hirsch (Brazos, 2007)

The Gospel of the Kingdom. George Eldon Ladd. Wm. B. Eerdmans Pub. Co. Grand Rapid.

The Great Giveaway: Reclaiming the Mission of the Church from Big Business, Parachurch Organizations, Psychotherapy, Consumer Capitalism, and Other Modern Maladies by David Fitch

The Hebrew-Greek Key Study Bible, Spiros Zodhiates, ed., World Bible, Publisher, Iowa City

The Life and Times of Jesus the Messiah, by Alfred Edersheim, T. Clark, London

The MacArthur New Testament Commentary, Moody Press

The Ministry of the Missional Church: A Community Led by the Spirit by Craig Van Gelder

The New American Commentary, E, Ray Clendenen, Gen. Ed, Broadman & Holman, Nashville

The New International Commentary on the Old Testament, Book of Proverbs, Bruce K, Waltke, Wm. B. Eerdmans, Cambridge, UK

The New International Dictionary of the New Testament, Colin Brown, ed., Zondervan

The NIV Application Commentary, Terry Muck, Gen. Editor, Zondervan, Grand Rapids

The Open Secret: An Introduction to the Theology of Mission by Lesslie Newbigin

The Pictorial Encyclopedia of the Bible, Merrill C. Tenney, ed., Zondervan, Grand Rapids

The Pillar New Testament Commentary, Eerdmans, Grand Rapids

The Radical Reformission: Reaching Out without Selling Out by Mark Driscoll, Zondervan

The Septuagint Version of the Old Testament & Apocrypha with English Translation, Zondervan

The Shape of Practical Theology, Ray S. Anderson, Intervarsity Press, Downers Grove, Illinois

The Shaping of Things to Come: Innovation and Mission for the 21st Century Church by Alan Hirsch and Michael Frost (Hendrickson, 2003)

Theological Dictionary of the New Testament, by G. Johaannes Botterweck and Elmer Ringgren, Theological Dictionary of the New Testament, Gerhard Kittel, Ed., Wm. B. Eerdmans,

Theological Dictionary of the Old Testament,

Theological Wordbook of the Old Testament, Vol. 1 and 2, R. Laird Harris, ed., Moody Press,
Thomas Watson, Body of Practical Divinity, Westminster Press, Philadelphia, PA
Tyndale New Testament Commentaries, R. P. Martin, Editor, EErdmans, Pub., Grand Rapids
Vine's Complete Expository Dictionary of the Old & New Test., W. E. Vine, Thomas Nelson,
Word Biblical Commentary, Bruce M. Metzger, General Editor, Thomas Nelson, Nashville
Works of Flavius Josephus, Wm. Whiston, Transl., Baker Book House, Grand Rapids
Wuest's Word Studies From the Greek New Testament, Wm. B. Eerdmans, Grand Rapids

www.ingramcontent.com/pod-product-compliance
Lightning Source LLC
Chambersburg PA
CBHW062015220426
43662CB00010B/1335